ART OF THE WORLD

NON-EUROPEAN CULTURES:

THE HISTORICAL, SOCIOLOGICAL

AND RELIGIOUS BACKGROUNDS

THE ART OF
BURMA, KOREA, TIBET

BY

ALEXANDER B. GRISWOLD

CHEWON KIM

PETER H. POTT

CROWN PUBLISHERS, INC., NEW YORK

Frontispiece: *Gilt bronze unicorn, 18th century. In Lamaist art the unicorn sometimes replaced the deer or gazelle. It always appears as one of a pair of animals, enclosing on both sides a wheel—the symbol which in Buddhist doctrine serves as a reminder of the place where Buddha first preached, i.e., the Gazelle Park at Benares. Gilt figures of this type also occur as altar decorations and on the roof-ridges of temples. In the latter case they are usually larger and made of less precious metal.*
Rietberg Museum, Zürich

1964
PRINTED IN HOLLAND
LIBRARY OF CONGRESS CATALOG CARD NUMBER: 63-20855

LIST OF PLATES

LIST OF FIGURES

BURMA

ABBREVIATIONS USED FOR WORKS CITED ABOVE:

De Beylié   *L. de Beylié*, Prome et Samara, Paris, 1907.
PG   *U Lu Pe Win*, Pictorial Guide to Pagán, Rangoon, 1955.
Brown   *P. Brown*, Indian Architecture, Bombay, 1956.
Yule   *Captain H. Yule*, Narrative of the Mission sent by the Governor-General of India to the Court of Ava in 1855, London, 1858.
JBRS   *Journal* of the Burma Research Society, 50th Anniversary No., Rangoon, 1960.

KOREA

ACKNOWLEDGMENTS

The following museums and individual collectors kindly allowed reproduction of the objects shown in the plates on the pages below:

Rietberg Museum, Zurich 3
National Museum of Korea, Seoul 75, 83, 86, 102, 103, 113, 117, 129, 133, 138
Tŏksu Palace Museum of Fine Arts, Seoul 87, 90, 119, 125, 136 below, 141, 149
Chun Hyung-pil Collection 115, 116, 118, 139, 143, 147
Sohn Jai Hyung Collection 136 above
Yi Hong-kun Collection 145

G. Tucci, *Tibetan Painted Scrolls* 164, 205, 209
British Museum, J. C. French Collection 173
Rijksmuseum voor Volkenkunde, Leyden 167, 177, 179, 183, 187, 195, 197, 199, 201, 203, 207, 211, 215, 217, 219, 221, 223, 225, 227, 229, 231, 234-235
Musée Guimet, Paris 191, 213
Museum van Aziatische Kunst, Amsterdam 237, 240

The plates on the following pages were kindly supplied by:

W. Bruggmann, Winterthur 3
J. A. Lavaud, Paris 23, 37, 41, 44, 48, 51, 54, 55, 75, 83, 86, 87, 90, 103, 113, 115, 116, 117, 118, 119, 125, 133, 136, 139, 141, 143, 145, 147, 149, 191, 213
R. L. Mellema, Amsterdam 57
J. Skeel, Pluckley 173

Figures 1, 3, 4, 6–13, 18, 21d, 24, 25 and 29 in the section on Burma were drawn by H. Prüstel, and Figures 26 and 27 by U Ba Nyan.

CONTENTS

TIBET

BURMA
A. B. GRISWOLD

Whenever a son was born to the ruler of Suvannabhūmi, it is said, a terrible she-demon sprang up from the sea and devoured the child. It happened that two monks, sent from India by the Emperor Aśoka to convert the people to Buddhism, arrived just at the moment when she was leaping out of the waters to get her gruesome meal. She was guarded by an army of imps, each in the form of a lion with two bodies joined to a single head. The monks quickly put her to flight by creating twice as many imps of similar aspect; then they pronounced one of the Buddha's Discourses, the *Brahmājāla*. Much relieved at so happy an outcome, the king was converted to the Doctrine, and a large number of his people followed him.[1]

Now Suvannabhūmi, the 'Golden Land', is supposed to be equivalent to Rāmaññadesa, the country of the Mòn people of Lower Burma. It seems to me quite possible that one of its seaports received the Doctrine as early as the third century B.C. when Aśoka was reigning in India. But further progress must have been painfully slow. The land was covered with swamp and forest, travel was difficult, and the people were scarcely ready to grasp the refinements of the Doctrine. Routing the demon won the day; the *Brahmājāla*, a masterpiece of close-knit argument against every sort of superstition, was added for good measure. We may wonder how many of the listeners understood Pali, or could have followed the argument if they did.

The doctrine of rationalism, indeed, has always been in danger of contamination from the beliefs of its neighbours, no less in India than in South-east Asia, for a huge population of sprites and demons have haunted the whole region since immemorial times. *Theravāda* Buddhism, the 'Doctrine of the Senior Monkhood', is alert to the danger; but instead of trying to obliterate the sprites from men's minds it puts them to use as figures of speech. So a happy system of metaphor has come about, which allows rationalists and pious believers to interpret the Doctrine in accord with their different points of view.

Theravāda Buddhism

To the rationalists it is a positivist philosophy, and at the same time a moral code based on self-restraint, kindness, and enlightenment. Man's goal should be to eradicate evil and delusion from his nature, and so achieve the serenity of *nibbāna* (Sanskrit: *nirvāna*). The Buddha was a human teacher, not a god; having attained Enlightenment, *bodhi*, which is *nibbāna*, he spent the rest of his life trying to teach others how to do the same. He proposed to abolish suffering, not by reference to any deity but by purely human means: he showed that the gods, if there are such beings, are no less subject to the law of impermanence than men and animals. There is nothing like a soul that can be reborn, though the consequences of every deed that is done go on for ever; what is usually called rebirth or transmigration is nothing but the continuing energy of past action. At his death, technically called *parinibbāna* ('final nirvāna'), the Buddha was Totally Extinguished, so there is no possible use in praying to him. The monks aim to set an example of virtue and rational behaviour, perfecting their own minds and educating others. Some specialize in studying the Pali texts and preaching the Doctrine. Some devote themselves to intense meditation, *samādhi* and *jhāna*: the exercise begins with breath control; then it goes on to mental concentration, with or without the aid of fixing the gaze on a device *(kaṣina)*, such as a patch of colour, a spot of earth, a cup of water, the air in an empty bowl, or the flame of a lamp; then by progressive stages it proceeds to abstraction and trance.

Pious believers, on the other hand, cannot help feeling that the Buddha is a kind of super-god who will listen to their prayers. They take transmigration as a literal reality: at death every creature is reborn as some other creature, whether god or demon, man or beast. The only definitive escape from the round of rebirth, in which delights are brief and misery long, is to eradicate all evil in oneself, to gain Enlightenment, and so, at death, to be entitled to Total Extinction. But *nibbāna* is an utterly remote contingency; meanwhile there are the relative pleasures of this world and the possibilities of temporary sojourns in heaven; so prudent people take care to perform good actions, laying up a store of acts of merit that will entitle them to rewards in future lives.

In addition to the Theravāda the Indians brought Brahminism and Mahāyāna Buddhism to South-east Asia. Indian monarchs traditionally regarded themselves as the protectors of all religions, and the South-east Asian kings followed their example. The different systems lived peaceably enough together; and though there was some sharp rivalry there was little or no religious persecution. Indian Brahmins had honoured positions as advisers in secular matters to Buddhist rulers, and in all matters to rulers who professed the Hindu religions.

While there are no tangible relics of Suvannabhūmi that go back to the time of Aśoka or anywhere near it, the Mòn of a later period have left a great many. These 'polite and jovial people', as an old Chinese writer terms them, were highly skilled in the arts, drawing their plastic tradition mainly from the Indian late Gupta. In Siam, under the hegemony of the kingdom of Dvāravatī (6th–10th century A.D.) the eastern Mòn produced splendid monuments and a profusion of beautiful sculpture, nearly all dedicated to the Theravāda. The known remains left by the western Mòn of the same period, though less numerous, attest no less talent, and are fairly balanced between Buddhist and Brahmanical. It is hard to say whether their cults were similarly balanced, or whether the fortunes of discovery have hit chiefly upon the temples of royal Brahmins in a predominantly Buddhist land.

Pyu Another people, the Pyu, were settled in Central and Upper Burma in the Irrawaddy valley. They were doubtless kinsmen of the Burmese who arrived later; at least their language, unlike Mòn, belonged to the Tibeto-Burman group. At Śrīksetra (old Prome) they have left extensive remains of monumental brick architecture, as well as sculpture and minor arts of a high order. Their FIG. 1 characteristic stupa form was a massive cylinder surmounted by a cone. Their FIG. 2 temples, making bold use of the radiating vault, display a diversity of plans, which may roughly be summed up under two sorts which later reappear at Pagán: the 'central pillar' type, and the 'hollow square'. The Theravāda predominated, but Brahminism and the Mahāyāna are also attested. Around the 8th century, it seems, the centre of Pyu power shifted to the north, probably to Halin in the Shwébo district. The Chinese, in the T'ang History, give us a vivid account of a Pyu city around 800 A.D.:

> The compass of the city-wall is faced with glazed bricks: it is 160 *li* in circumference. The banks of the moat too are faced with brick. Within the walls there are over a hundred Buddhist monasteries with courts and rooms all decked with gold and silver, coated with cinnabar and bright colours, smeared with kino and covered with embroidered rugs [the *New T'ang History* adds 'the king's residence is also like this']. It is their custom to love life and hate killing. When they come to the age of seven,

FIG. 1 – *Bobo-gyi stūpa, Śrīksetra*

both boys and girls cut their hair and go to live in a monastery. On reaching the age of twenty, if they have not awakened to the principles of the Buddha, they let their hair grow again and become ordinary townsfolk. They do not wear silk because, they say, it comes from silkworms and involves injury to life. There are twelve gates with pagodas at the four corners: the people all live within. They are acquainted with astronomy and delight in Buddha's Law. They wear gold-flowered hats and caps of kingfisher feathers strung with various jewels. The king's palace has two bells, one of silver and one of gold: when enemies are at hand they burn incense and strike these bells, thus obtaining omens concerning their fate in the coming battle.[2]

Upper Burma lived under the shadow of Nan-chao, a powerful kingdom in Yünnan. Scholars at one time believed the rulers of Nan-chao were Tai,

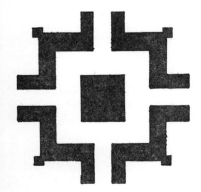
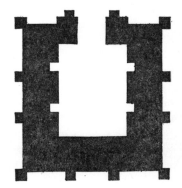

FIG. 2 – *Plans of Lemyethna and Bèbè temples, Śrīksetra*

members of the same race as the Siamese and Shan; but it is becoming increasingly clear that they were a Tibeto-Burman people, perhaps the ancestors of the Lolo. In 832 they attacked the Pyu in their northern capital and carried off the population as slaves; and they made raids into the Mòn country as well.

Burmese Meanwhile another Tibeto-Burman people, the Burmese *(Mranmā)*, were migrating from their old homeland on the borders of Tibet and China, entering Upper Burma from the north-east and east. Around the 9th century they gained control of three important areas: Minbu and Kyauksè with their abundant rice, and Pagán, strategically located at the junction of the main trade-routes. They were not yet Buddhists. They worshipped the Nats, a heterogeneous pantheon of tree and river sprites, serpents, ancestors, and the spirits of celebrities who had met with a violent or tragic death. The most powerful were the two Mahāgiri Nats, tree sprites whose images were installed in a shrine on Mount Popa thirty miles south-east of Pagán. This extinct volcano, with slopes covered with flowering trees, was known to the Burmese as the 'flowery mountain', the 'golden mountain', or the 'great mountain', *Mahāgiri*. Here the Nats were worshipped at an annual festival, a drunken orgy where spirit-mediums danced ecstatically.

Nat-worship remained deeply ingrained; but the Burmese in their new home were in close touch with the Mòn and the Pyu, by whom it seems they began to be converted to Buddhism. There is some evidence that around the year 1000 a Burmese ruler of Pagán built an ordination hall, an operation which always marked the triumph or revival of orthodox Theravāda Buddhism in a Burma community.[3]

*   *

*

PAGÁN PERIOD It is only in the last few decades that the history of Burma in the Pagán period and earlier has begun to be properly reconstructed. The chief credit for progress on this huge task is due to Messrs G. H. Luce and Pe Maung Tin, the learned editors of the *Inscriptions of Burma*, and to their associates on the Burma Historical Commission. The definitive history has yet to be published; but meanwhile they have given us a series of valuable articles and bulletins, based on a study of the donative inscriptions and of references in Chinese histories. The inscriptions, of which several hundred attributable to the Pagán period are known, have the inestimable advantage of providing contemporary source material. So have some Chinese accounts. The outline that emerges from these studies proves to be very different from the accounts given in the Burmese chronicles.[4]

The earliest extant Burmese chronicle [remarks Mr Luce] is dated 1520, little more than two hundred years after the fall of Pagán. It has only a page about the Pagán period, and this is mostly legendary or wrong. Two centuries later U Kalā's Chronicle, and three centuries later the Glass Palace Chronicle (1829), have nearly 200 pages on Pagán. Whence this spate of new information? — Well, the kings had ordered histories: and kings have to be obeyed. The authors did their best with the materials easily available: a very few inscriptions or copies of inscriptions, dim local memories, legends and folklore. They eked it out with fiction, stories borrowed from Jātakas or other Indian books, with miracles, portents and other moral and diverting stories. As men, one can but sympathize with them. As wise and witty authors, one admires them. As historians, however, one is bound to note their limitations.[5]

* *
*

King Aniruddha (Anorathā), who reigned at Pagán from 1044 to 1077, enlarged the Burmese domain from a small principality to a strong kingdom comprising the greater part of Burma. In a lightning campaign he swooped down on the old Mòn city of Thaton, the rich centre of an ancient culture; and having captured it he carried off its royal family to Pagán, together with most of the Theravāda monkhood and a number of skilled artisans. After that the other Mòn and Pyu cities, as well as a number of the tribes, made their submission. *Aniruddha*

The arrival of the Mòn captives at Pagán had far-reaching consequences. It greatly strengthened the Theravāda. Mòn pandits and administrators in due course were given positions of influence; Mòn architects and craftsmen, working in collaboration with the Burmese and Pyu artisans who were already there, began to create a new city. The Mòn royal family, installed at Pagán, seem to have been treated with respect though their liberty was restricted.

It appears that Aniruddha, while doubtless a generous patron of all the religions represented in his kingdom, personally professed the Mahāyāna.[6] The monuments attributed to him are few but imposing.

With the reign of his second successor, Kyanzittha (1084–1112), the pace of temple-building quickens. Instead of using force to hold his kingdom together, Kyanzittha sought to unite it by persuasion. While he reserved the most lavish honours for the Theravāda, he was broad-minded in religious matters, considering himself to be not only a Bodhisattva but also an *avatāra* of the god Visnu. He sent a mission to India to restore the Mahābodhi temple at Bodhgayā, the most venerated monument in the world to all sects and divisions of Buddhists. One of his queens was a devotee of the Mahāyāna. And of course he patronized the Brahmins, and used them as advisers. *Kyanzittha*

It was doubtless to ensure the loyalty of his Mòn subjects that he gave his daughter in marriage to a Mòn prince and made their son, Alaung Sithu, heir to the throne of Burma. In any case Kyanzittha had a special affection for everything Mòn. All his inscriptions are in the Mòn language, and his temples in the Mòn style.

In the reign of Alaung Sithu (1113–c. 1155), though the Mòn style of temple still predominated, a more specifically Burmese style began to develop. In the reign of Narapati Sithu (1174–1211) the Burmese style triumphed; at the same time close relations were established with Ceylon, fountain-head of the Theravāda; and a new sect, the 'Sinhalese', sprang up at Pagán, professing the same doctrine as the 'Former Order', as the Mòn brotherhood came to be known, but differing from it in matters of monastic discipline. Tantric Buddhism remained popular, but was not a serious rival to the Theravāda.[7]

The last sovereign ruler of Pagán was Narasīhapati (1256–87). Burma was invaded by the Mongols, who were masters of China and an empire stretching from the Yellow Sea to Poland. Narasīhapati fled; and in 1287 the Mongols took Pagán.

*   *
*

Pagán
PLATE P. 23

The ruins of the old city lie in a broad arc ten or twelve miles long on the left bank of the Irrawaddy, which glistens like a band of pale satin between green fringes. This is the 'Dry Country', the *Tattadesa* of 11th- and 12th-century inscriptions. Part of it is duneland, torn by ravines and swept into queer forms by the hot wind; part is sandy plain, with a scattering of bean-fields and sugar-palm plantations; most of it lies uncultivated, with goats browsing among stunted bushes and giant euphorbia. In the villages which straggle along the river-bank and the stream-beds the light drifts down through a leafy filter of tall shade-trees — the pippala with quivering foliage, the acacia with mottled yellow bark, and the tamarind gnarled and pitted by a thousand years of slow growth.

The walled city occupied only a small part of the huge area demarcated by the ruins, doubtless because at the time of its greatness it expanded far beyond the original defenses and its security was felt to be so unquestionable that no new walls were needed: Pagán in those days was majestically entitled *Arimaddanapura*, 'the city that tramples down its foes'.

FIG. 3   The Sarabhā Gate which gave access to the walled town still stands, with its pair of massive shrines like sentry-boxes containing images of the Mahāgiri Nats. It is almost the only old piece of secular architecture that remains. The ordinary houses, which were perhaps not very different from those of the

FIG. 3 – *Sarabhā Gate, Pagán*

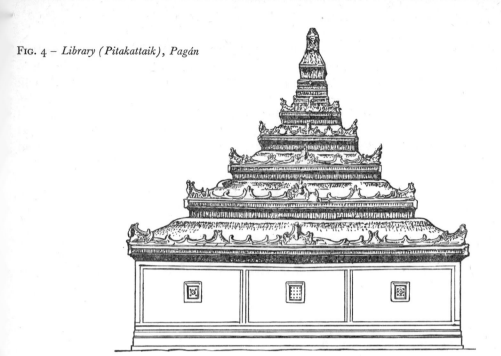

Fig. 4 – *Library (Pitakattaik), Pagán*

villagers today — made of bamboo strips woven into elegant patterns of brown and citron — disappeared long ago; and so did the palaces, which were of wood. But the monuments dedicated to religion, made of brick and stucco, survive on a vast scale and in bewildering quantity.

They have suffered much from warfare, from looting, from neglect, and worse still from restorations made by persons of greater piety than judgment; yet the dry climate has preserved far more here than in any other complex of brick architecture in South-east Asia. With the exception of the Brahmin temple and a few structures connected with the Mahāyāna, every one of them was devoted to Theravāda Buddhism, which is still the religion of the Burmese today.

*   *
*

We know from donative inscriptions that princes and princesses — following an example set by Indian royalty during the Buddha's lifetime — sometimes turned their own residences into monasteries and presented them to religion. Frescoes and bas-reliefs show us many such palaces, made of wood — surely teak — elaborately carved and gilded, and set about with airy pavilions hung with awnings. Nothing would be more natural than for other donors to imitate that architecture when they built anew for the monkhood; and so, just as the Chinese had noticed among the Pyu, monasteries and palaces looked much alike, which explains the paradox that the monks, though committed to a life of poverty, lived in splendid premises.

Most of the monastery buildings at Pagán were made of wood, and so are lost to us; but fortunately there are some exceptions, which were made of brick in imitation of wooden originals. An example is the library, said to have been built by Aniruddha to house the Buddhist scriptures from Thaton, and repaired in the 18th century. The ruins of the So-min-gyi monastery show one of several possible dispositions, with rows of cells around a court, a forechamber at one end and a chapel at the other. The *Upālisīma* (Upali Thein), a building of unusual type, dating for the most part from the post-Pagán period, is an elaborate ordination hall, a copy of a wooden structure having a long central nave with a ridge-roof, flanked by a pair of side-aisles with lean-to roofs. The architectural ornament bears no relation to the vaulted interior, but lucidly reveals the structure of its wooden prototype. At either end of the building are simulated pillars and cross-beams, and simulated barge-boards terminating the gable and the roofs of the side-aisles, while the doorways are crowned with smaller simulated barge-boards. Wooden buildings of the same sort were evidently the models for the forechambers of innumerable temples.

FIG. 4
FIG. 5

FIG. 6

*   *

*

Cetiyas Anything that serves to recall the Buddha and his Doctrine is a *cetiya*, a 'Reminder'. In a broad sense the term includes the scenes of the Great Events

of his career, his bodily relics and the monuments built to contain them, records of his words, pictures or images of his Person, and replicas of any of these things.[8]

Applied to architectural monuments, the term *cetiya* is more or less interchangeable with *stūpa* (Pali: *thūpa*), a mound of earth or masonry built to contain holy relics.[9] But it is convenient to call the entire monument a *cetiya*, and to reserve the word *stūpa* for its essential part, a solid structure whose form varies from a low rounded dome to a hemisphere, a bell shape, or even a bulb. It stands on a base, which may be very elaborate; and it is surmounted by a stylized honorific parasol. Sometimes, between the stupa and the parasol, there is a box-like member called the *harmikā*.

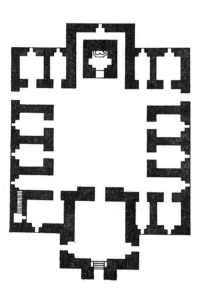

FIG. 5 – *Section and plan of So-min-gyi monastery, Myinpagán*

FIG. 6 – *Upālisīma (Upali Thein), Pagán*

There are thousands of cetiyas at Pagán, ranging in size from miniatures to huge mountains of masonry, and varying much in form. If we concentrate on the larger ones, we shall note four main types. It is tempting to attribute a certain historical significance to them, and to see in each the relationships that caused it to be introduced, though naturally the introduction of a new type did not stop people from building monuments of older types.

Four types of cetiya FIG. 7

Type I has a bulbous stupa somewhat reminiscent of the Tibetan *chorten.* The earliest example at Pagán, the Bupaya, was perhaps built by the Pyu in the 8th or 9th century.

FIG. 8, 9

Type II has a bell-shaped stupa, encircled at mid-height by shallow mouldings. Its top merges directly into the broad cone, ringed with mouldings, that represents the parasol. It seems to derive from the old Pyu cylindrical type which had a flange and terraces at the bottom, and a massive cone on top (Fig. 1).[10] I do not know when it was first introduced at Pagán, but it became Aniruddha's favourite, serving as the model for all the great monuments attributed to him. The Burmese prided themselves on being the successors of the Pyu; and Kyanzittha, in spite of his partiality for the Mòn, claims in an inscription to be the reincarnation of the founder of Śrīksetra. A monument of Type II, the Shwé Zigon (*Jeyyabhūmi*), built by Kyanzittha, is considered to be the most 'national' of Burma's monuments, a focal point of patriotism.

The stupas of Type II have octagonal bases of one or more storeys, furnishing terraces that are sometimes wide enough for circumambulation, the rite of honouring the stupa by moving around it in the direction of the sun (clockwise). The Lokananda, built by Aniruddha, has two usable octagonal terraces, and three atrophied ones above, all with crenellated parapets. Often the whole complex of stupa and octagonal base is superimposed on a great pyramid with lesser stupas at the corners, and a circumambulatory terrace with a crenellated

FIG. 8

FIG. 7 – *Bupaya, Pagán*

FIG. 9 parapet at each storey. The pyramid of the Shwé Zigon has three storeys. That of the Shwé Sandaw, another of Aniruddha's foundations, has five. The huge Mangalacetiya (late 13th century) is a free copy of the Shwé Zigon. The Dhammarājika (late 12th) has a pyramid of unusual design, as it is pentagonal in plan.

Type III also has a bell-shaped stupa encircled at mid-height by mouldings. But the round or octagonal base provides no usable terraces; the mouldings at mid-height are bolder than in Type II; there is a *harmikā*, with re-entrant angles, between the stupa and the parasol; and the parasol in made up of separate disks.[11] The Seinnyet Nyima, built in the 12th century, is a good FIG. 10 example; it is ornamented with delightful figure-work in stucco, and stands on a pyramid of three storeys.

A variant of Type III, pot-shaped instead of bell-shaped, represents the Vase of Plenty *(punnaghata)*. One of the lesser stupas at the corners of the Seinnyet Nyima takes this form (see Fig. 10, at the left, on the second terrace).

Type IV has a bell-shaped stupa standing on a round base of several atrophied storeys without usable terraces. But it has no mouldings around the bell at mid-height; it has a heavy square *harmikā*; and the parasol is a slightly concave cone ringed with mouldings. The outstanding example is the Chapata. This type, FIG. 11 copied from a model often seen in Ceylon, was introduced in the last years of the 12th century by the Sinhalese sect, doubtless as the reaction of strict orthodoxy against the extravagances of the pyramid cetiyas.

* *
*

PLATES 1, 2 – Above: Part of the ruins of Pagán, with Ananda temple in background. *Cf. pp. 18, 31*
Below: Myinkaba Ku-byauk-ngè, built in about 1211. *Cf. pp. 33, 36*

FIG. 8 – *Lokananda cetiya, Myinpagán*

FIG. 9 – *Shwé Sandaw cetiya, Pagán*

Design of a cetiya The design of a cetiya, whether it is a simple mound or an elaborate monument, is not functional in the sense of helping us to see how it is constructed; an inert mass of brick invites no such question. It is functional in an entirely different sense, for all its parts are intended to make the religious mechanism work more perfectly.

The elaborations are not mere decoration designed to please the eye; yet the builders aimed, at least incidentally, to create something beautiful and arresting. The aesthetic sense was no less lively for being subordinated to a deeper purpose. The monument was an offering to religion, to be as handsomely presented as the donor could afford. Some motifs, though not the most important ones, may have had no more significance than the decoration of a silver dish in which a kneeling princess offers fruit to a monk. Some, such as the stucco garlands on the body of the stupa, recall real offerings placed there by worshippers. Some are lucky tokens. Some are probably magical and astrological paraphernalia whose exact use escapes us.

To the most serious Buddhists, magic and divination, though not necessarily ineffective, are an inferior kind of science that distract the mind from the business of real Enlightenment. The cetiya's proper function is to 'Remind'. This it sometimes does by means of didactic matter ranged around its base, such as plaques illustrating the Previous Lives (Jātakas) (cf. below, p. 42). The stupa itself is a Reminder of *nibbāna:* whether or not it actually contains relics, it is thought of as a reliquary. When there is a pyramidal base, it recalls the cosmology of the Indians, who conceived of a lofty mountain, Meru, standing on a flat world; at its foot lay the continents and islands, surrounded by the vast ocean that extended to the perimeter, where it was bounded by a rocky wall. Mount Meru was encircled by six or seven concentric rings of mountains and seas; its terraced slopes were peopled with sprites and fabulous animals, and the gods dwelt on its summit.

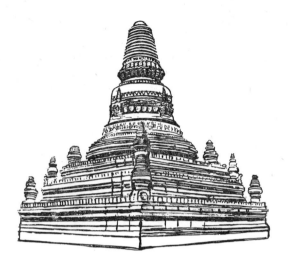

Fig. 10 – *Seinnyet Nyima cetiya, Myinpagán*

The symbolism is designed to allow a certain freedom of interpretation: the pyramid usually has three terraces, sometimes five, but over and above them are one or more partly atrophied terraces, octagonal or round. The lesser stupas at the corners may be taken for the lesser peaks of Meru and of its encircling mountain chains. Fabulous animals, sprites and godlings act as guardians, to terrify evil-doers and comfort the pious. The stairs leading to the terraces usually have balustrades in the form of a *makara* (sea-monster): like the rainbow, which is identified with the makara, they are ladders from earth to heaven. The topmost terrace is the Tāvatimsa heaven, the abode of the gods who have Indra as their king. The stupa recalls the Culāmani, the reliquary monument which is the most conspicuous feature of the Tāvatimsa heaven. The tiers of the parasol above it recall the heavens of Brahmā and even more abstract abodes of the blessed soaring far above in the atmosphere.

Every cetiya is in a sense a copy of some famous model in India, at no matter how many removes, but seldom a very exact one, either because small deviations accumulated in the process of copying and recopying, or because the design was transmitted from one place to another by the intermediary of a miniature model which would require improvisation to copy on a monumental scale. The pyramidal base is characteristically South-east Asian, though of course not exclusively so. Pre-Buddhist beliefs have helped to shape its growth. The Burmese have a strong inclination to build stupas on hill-tops, which they explain on the grounds that the value of an act of merit increases in proportion to its difficulty; but is the habit not also a relic of times when stupas were built on the sites of pre-Buddhist mountain cults in order to signify their conversion to the Doctrine? These cults, indeed, kept their hold on the minds of the Burmese long after they migrated from their earlier home and settled in the plains: Mount Popa was the spiritual centre of the old Burmese world.

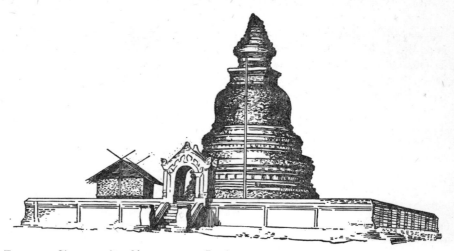

FIG. 11 – *Chapata cetiya, Nyaung-u, near Pagán*

If it was a great act of merit to build a stupa on a real hill-top, it would surely be an even greater one to erect an artificial mountain and put a stupa on its summit. Reflecting the sun's rays in its jewelled finial and flower-draped gilded surfaces, the stupa diffuses its beneficent influences; and when it is raised high on a pyramid their range is multiplied. To ordinary men it is a flowery hill and golden mountain like the memory-haunted Popa; and by causing their hearts to leap it provides the impulse towards heaven. To learned monks who are indifferent to the gods it denotes the 'fiery energy' *(teja)* that comes from meditation on the fire device.

*   *
*

Cave-temples Since immemorial times holy men have liked to live in caves. The absence of luxury, the utter quiet, the cool penumbra — all are conducive to peace of mind and deep meditation. The Buddha himself went into retreat for a time in a grotto, where he received a memorable visit from the god Indra. Monks often take up their abode, temporary or permanent, in caverns. In regions where natural caves are lacking, substitutes can be dug in hill-sides: Ajanta and the other great cave-temples of India provided rich settings for austerity.
Several hills in the Pagán area are pierced with artificial caves for the use of monks. The Thamiwhet Umin has a row of cells dug in the side of a low cliff and reinforced with brick vaults; their arched entrances, now crumbling and overgrown with vegetation, might pass for a part of the natural landscape no more than slightly modified by the hand of man. At the Myathat Umin the cell-entrances are framed in rectangles of brick, while a crenellated terrace above them recalls the lowest storey of an artificial mountain.
The 'temples' of Pagán unite the theme of the artificial mountain with the theme of the natural hill pierced with artificial caves. Strictly speaking the term

26

'temple' is a misnomer, since the Theravāda has no structures dedicated to any god; but as it is both convenient and familiar we shall use it to describe the structures which the Burmese, with greater propriety, call *kū*, 'caves' (Pali: *guhā*). The reason for the name is not poetic fancy; it is because the functional part of the temple, the interior, is a system of caverns — vaulted tunnels and chambers — built in a mountain of masonry.

The radiating arch, and its derivative the vault, are used on a grand scale, and at every opportunity. At first glance these great pointed vaults recall the Gothic; but in fact they are fundamentally different both in purpose and in composition. The cathedral-builders strove to enclose greater and greater volumes of space in the lightest possible fabric that would still be strong enough to endure; but the Burmese heaped up bigger and bigger mountains of masonry, and no matter how large the tunnels and chambers may be, they are small in proportion to the totality of solid matter. The vaulting, unlike the Gothic, does not itself leap into the air, but supports a mountain whose multiple peaks soar skyward far above it. It is made up of a succession of brick arches, each of which is laid against the face of its predecessor, and each is complete in itself — except that at certain points a long stone slab is inserted, running through several of the arches to key them together.[12]

The bricks are always fashioned with care and made to fit together with the least possible intervening space. Often the binder, made of a mixture of mud and glue, was laid on in such a thin layer that it is practically invisible.

The Kyaukku Umin stands like an illustration in an architectural text-book to show how the temple form might have evolved — although it was actually built long after the evolution had been completed. The site is a cliff-side, which plunges downward from a broad plateau to a projecting shelf 10 to 15 metres below, and then continues its plunge down the ravine to a small stream. The temple, which stands on the projecting shelf, is built into the hill-side in such a way that the little stupa crowning the hill-top rests on a two-storeyed pyramid that looks as if it were built on the roof of the temple. In reality the pyramid is autonomous; the temple walls and roof could be stripped off without disturbing it. Its bottom storey is unusually tall, consisting of a double pillar of masonry that clings to the hill-side like a buttress, around three sides of which the temple has been built almost as if it were an afterthought. The impression is confirmed by the architectural treatment of the pillar, which has all the usual mouldings of a stupa base, though by way of exception they are of carved stone instead of stucco. The pillar is pierced at either side by a tunnel, giving access to an extensive network of tunnels that run deep into the hill. It is tempting to think that the stupa and its tall base, together with the artificial caves, were there first, and the temple built on it later; but it is more likely that the whole complex is a copy, at one or more removes, of an earlier complex where something of the sort had occurred. Just as in that hypothetical model, the interior of the temple is for the most part blocked by the pillar; the usable portion is hardly more than a broad corridor running around the pillar and roofed with heavy vaulting.

Kyaukku Umin

FIG. 12

* *
*

Fig. 12 – *Kyaukku Umin, Nyaung-u, near Pagán*

More common — for the greater part of Pagán is on flat land — is a form of temple derived by a different route from the stupa and its base. This process, too, had been completed centuries before by Indians and Mòn and Pyu; but though the Burmese architects had only to copy the final product, it is easy to visualize the evolution, for several temples at Pagán bear obvious traces of it.

Whenever there is a festival hundreds of temporary shelters spring up, consisting of awnings of cloth or matting attached to a wall or supported by posts. FIG. 13 We can imagine a stupa standing on a tall square base, in the middle of a rectangular precinct which is bounded by a brick wall having the usual applied pilasters and crenellated coping; we can image a festival day when awnings are hung from the top of the stupa-base on all four sides, stretching outward and downward to the coping of the boundary wall; we can imagine that so convenient an arrangement would eventually be translated into permanent materials. In this sort of temple (Fig. 14) the stupa that appears to stand on the roof really stands on a massive pillar that blocks most of the interior; the undulating slope of the roofs recalls awnings; and the exterior is still conceived as a precinct wall with pilasters and crenellations.

FIG. 14 The stupas of the Abèyadana and the Patothamya, built in Kyanzittha's reign, are of Type III. Several temples of Burmese style, built in the latter half of the 12th century and the 13th, have stupas of Type II, the 'national' model. FIG. 15 One of these is the 'tally temple'. For every ten thousand bricks that went FIG. 16 into the construction of the gigantic Sabbaññū temple, one brick was set aside to keep the count; and when the work was finished, these 'tally bricks' were used to erect this little temple nearby. It must have taken some ingenuity to use up the precise number of bricks and at the same time achieve a satisfactory design. The composition is wonderfully suggestive of a Burmese mountain strewn with cliffs and pitted with grottoes; and at the same time it evokes, in miniature, a section of the huge Himalayan landscape where saints and hermits meditate in caverns, while the radiance of their fiery energy bursts out in tongues of flame and illuminates the quivering leafage above.[13]

28

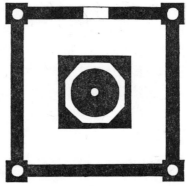

FIG. 13 – *Left: hypothetical evolution from cetiya with temporary awnings (left half-section) to temple (right half-section). Right: plan*

Instead of a large stupa, the crowning feature of most temples at Pagán is a large *śikhara* with a small stupa on top of it. The śikhara is a sort of bulging obelisk, square in plan, with two or three shallow re-entrant angles. Each face, seen in elevation, is a curvilinear trapezoid broken into numerous horizontal shelves, interrupted by the projection of either one or two similar but progressively narrower trapezoids, and finally a smooth lancet in the centre. In the Mòn style the shelves are crisply delineated, and the lancet has several arched openings. Later on, in the Burmese style, the shelves increase in number and tend to grow vague; while the lancet is liable to have its openings reduced to a mere sketch in stucco, or to lose them altogether.

FIG. 19

FIG. 20

The stupa on top of the śikhara is nearly always of Type II. In the Mòn style the transition between śikhara and stupa-base is masked by four or eight large wedges; in the Burmese style the wedges, if present at all, are less conspicuous.

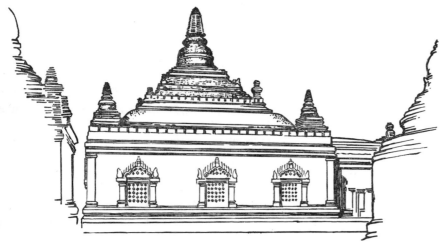

FIG. 14 – *Abèyadana (Piyaratna) temple; Myinpagán*

FIG. 15 – *Tally temple near Sabbaññū, Pagán*

FIG. 17 The śikhara is clearly related to the same feature in Indian architecture, for instance in Orissa. There the basic unit of the Brahmanical temple is a stone sanctuary-tower, a square cella with a tall superstructure consisting of a succession of small false storeys. The cella has no central pillar; it is an un-obstructed chamber, small in relation to the exterior dimensions, as the walls have to be thick enough to support the heavy stone corbelling that holds the superstructure. On top is a large ribbed disk, the *āmalaka* fruit.

FIG. 18 If we now look at a temple like the Nagayôn, built by Kyanzittha, the first thing we shall notice is that while the Indian tower stands exposed to the eye, Kyanzittha's is hidden, up to two-thirds of its height, by a square en-closing structure, whose sloping roofs suggest an origin in temporary awnings pinned from the tower to a precinct wall, in much the same way as we have suggested for the central pillar type. Mòn or Pyu building habits, perhaps in imitation of an older Indian tradition, have replaced stone and cloth with brick, and corbelling with vaults. Apart from these things the two temples are sufficiently alike for us to take the Nagayôn for a copy of a small portable replica of the other, or of some similar Indian temple. We have the same horizontal shelves of the false storeys; we have a similar lancet, but with the false dormers of the original now interpreted as arched openings; we have the amalaka changed into a stupa, but supported by wedges that recall the double-bodied lions of the model.

FIG. 16 Some temples at Pagán are built on the 'hollow square' plan (as in Fig. 2b): the original Brahmanical plan of the small square cella is respected. But more often, even though they have the śikhara, they have the central pillar inside, and the method of construction is the same as in the stupa-crowned temples. Rather surprisingly, the central pillar was used even in the Nat-hlaung-kyaung, the royal Visnu temple built in the 11th century.

The main unit of most of the temples is square in plan, often with re-entrants and projecting bays. Usually a forechamber is attached to one face, and some-

FIG. 16A – *Plan of Sabbaññū temple*

30

times to all four. Huge temples like the Ananda and the Sabbaññū are ingenious growths, achieved by enlargement and reduplication of the same elements possessed by the smaller shrines.

The Ananda (built c. 1105) is Kyanzittha's masterpiece and the triumph of the Mòn style (Fig. 19; also Plate p. 23, the large white temple with gilt śikhara, at the top of the picture). The Glass Palace Chronicle tells a curious story of its origin, which is informative, even if not historically true.[14] One day eight Indian monks stood for alms outside Kyanzittha's palace; and after they had received food they told him, in answer to his inquiry, that they had formerly lived in the Nandamūla grotto on Mount Gandhamādana. The king listened eagerly as they described the place, and invited them to return every day during the rainy season so that he could feed them and learn more about its wonders. Now Mount Gandhamādana and its grotto are imaginary places in the Himalayan fairyland, but there is no reason to suspect the monks of falsehood: their abode in India had doubtless been a copy of that mythical landscape.[15] When they illustrated their description by conjuring up a magical apparition of the grotto by the power of their meditation, the king determined to copy it on a vast scale in masonry. The architectural prototype was perhaps the Ananta cave-temple in the Udayagiri hills of Orissa. Kyanzittha's building, indeed, is a hundred times more splendid. No doubt the vision was too; and it may have been partly shaped by recollections of Paharpur or some other temple in Bengal, or perhaps the partially homonymous Ananta Vāsudeva at Bhuvaneśvara in Orissa, which was then approaching completion. 'Copying' allowed so large a measure of freedom that we cannot be sure. A less prosaic answer is more to the point: the real model of the Ananda, with its gilded śikhara and its gleaming white walls and lesser spires, is indeed the sun-bathed snowy Himalayan fairyland as the Indian monks had seen it in their meditation.

The proportions of the Ananda are majestic: the height to the top of the pinnacle is approximately 52 metres, the overall length over 88 metres. The roofs, which bristle with a profusion of small stupas, śikharas and guardian figures, are sloping, as usual in the Mòn style. Below the crenellations of the parapets are long rows of glazed plaques representing the Previous Lives (cf. p. 45).

Ananda

FIGS. 19, 19A, 19B

PLATE P. 23

PLATE P. 37

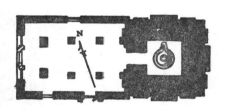

FIG. 17 – *Parasurāmeśvara temple, Bhuvaneśvara, Orissa, India*

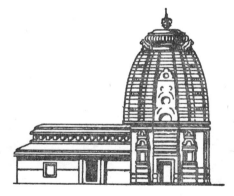

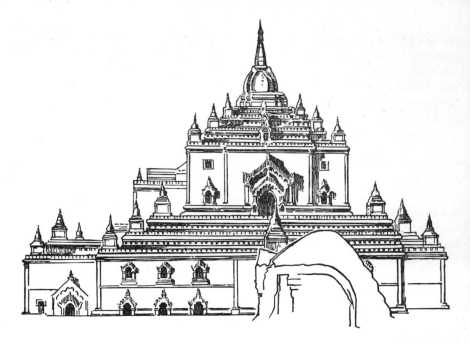

Fig. 16 – *Sabbaññū temple (Burmese: Thatbyinnyu), Pagán. Above: façade. Below: section*

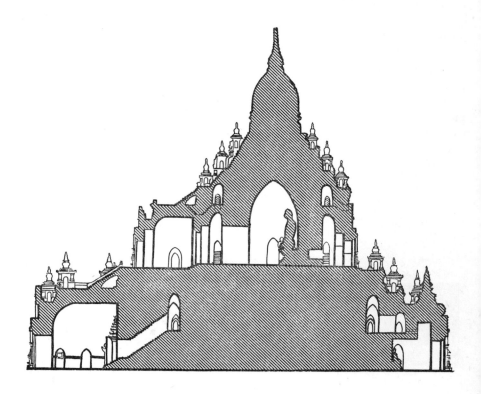

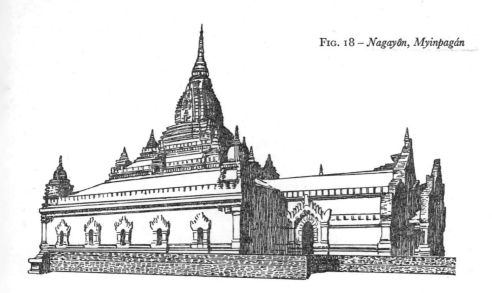

Fig. 18 – *Nagayôn, Myinpagán*

The biggest temple at Pagán is the Dhammayangyi. Though built around 1160, when the transition to the Burmese style was already under way, it is distinctly of Mòn style, and follows the plan of the Ananda. Its sloping roofs are especially conspicuous, in contrast to the flat terraces favoured by the Burmese style.

Unlike the temples of pure Mòn style, which hardly ever have more than one storey in the interior, the Burmese style sometimes has two. The change begins with the Sabbaññū (Pali: 'omniscient', pronounced Thatbyinnyu in Burmese), built in the mid-12th century and transitional between the two styles. Structurally it is a huge temple of the hollow square type, standing on top of a massive base which is in effect a temple of the central pillar type. The roofs are flat, and provide no less than seven usable exterior terraces, four at the lower storey and three on the upper. FIG. 16

Several of the greatest temples of the Burmese style follow much the same scheme, including the Culāmani, the Tilominlo and the Gawdawpalin. FIG. 20

Smaller one-storeyed temples of Burmese style are legion. A good example is the Myinkaba Ku-byauk-ngè, built in the early 13th century. The lower roofs provide a succession of flat terraces; but the upper ones are sloping. PLATE P. 23

In about half a dozen temples the curvilinear śikhara is replaced by an obelisk with straight sides that converge towards the top. The most renowned example is the Mahābodhi (13th century?), a passable imitation of the great temple at Bodhgayā which Kyanzittha had sent a mission to repair. Others might seem to be inspired by the same source, but the resemblance is altogether too vague to be convincing: for example, the Wet-kyi-in Ku-byauk-kyi (early 13th century). The horizontal shelves of the tower are alternately broad and narrow, the broad ones containing *tondi* with figures of Śrī, the goddess of good luck. The lancet contains niches with seated images of the Buddha. PLATE P. 41

*   *

*

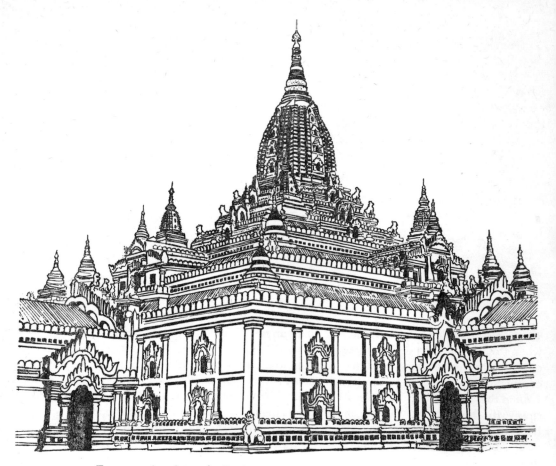

Fig. 19 – *Ananda temple, Pagán*

The temples, like the cetiyas, are magic mountains with stupas on top. The śikhara, rising above the mass of the temple, is the highest peak of a vast mountain system. Usually we can take it for granted that it is Meru; but sometimes it might be some other magic mountain. The fact could easily pass unnoticed, for those peaks too are microcosms.

Ornamentation   The ornamentation of a temple is no more 'functional' in the ordinary sense than that of a stupa. Heavily-vaulted structures are made to look far lighter than they really are; the undulating roof of a corridor suggests an awning; brick and stucco often masquerade as wood. Though the exterior ornament is perfectly logical in the relation of its own parts to one another, the discrepancy between it and the interior has been a source of consternation to some western architects: they see it as a deliberate, almost shameful falsehood.

No criticism could be less to the point. In the Buddhist view all architecture is 'artifice'; there is no use insisting on a structural fact that anyone can discover if he cares to; and in any case it is irrelevant to the usefulness of the building.

If ornament has any value, it is not to give the public a lesson in brick building construction, but to awaken a sense of aspiration. This can best be done by evoking the idea of heaven, by means of the magic mountain of which the abodes of earthly royalty are but imperfect copies. That explains the paradox that these huge brick structures present themselves simultaneously as mountain systems and as airy pavilions; or to be more precise, the brick mass is the mountain system, while the ornamented gables, doors and windows — originally for the most part gilded — are celestial palaces in the form of microcosms.

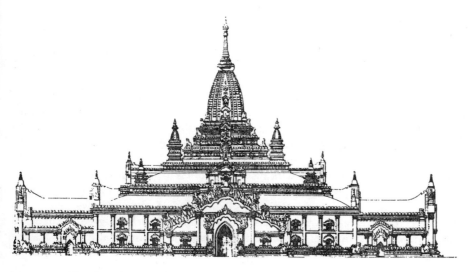

Fig. 19A – *Façade and section of Ananda temple*

35

The ornament is firm and crisp. It tells its story lucidly, though the story is a metaphor of wooden forms rather than a factual statement in brick. The decorative matter, no matter how profuse, is so managed that it will not detract from the sense of clarity. Foot-mouldings consist of several rows of sharp undecorated geometry, and two or three rows of lotus-petals. Usually enough of the pilaster is left plain so as to make its supposed function apparent; triangular floral motifs hang from the capital, and others spring up from the base towards them. Sometimes a pilaster is pervaded with leafage, the vacant spaces on either side making it stand out in sharp relief (Fig. 21A, at the centre.) Chaplets of flowers hang from the cornice, or droop from the mouths of Glory-Faces. The chaplets are more realistic than one might suppose: exactly the same thing, made of tiny fragrant blossoms threaded together, can be bought at any festival today. Yet the stucco chaplets may also be thought of as strings of costly jewels offered as an act of merit that is sure to redound to the donor's advantage. A leering goblin, crouching at the angle of a cornice, frightens away bad and stupid demons, but hints to wiser heads that he is nothing but a joke.

Gables and doors, windows and niches, are usually crowned with simulated barge-boards in the form of multifoil arches. The turned-up ends contain the heads of crocodile-dragons *(makaras)*, realistic or stylized; the two halves of the arch are their bodies, fringed with spiky horns.

An alternative treatment for windows and doors is to give them pediments made up of horizontal shelves, the roofs of celestial palaces. Often the two treatments are combined, the dragon barge-boards being put in front and lower down, thus we have the palace seen in anamorphosis, with its entrance greatly enlarged. The dragon is a symbol of flowing water, streams and canals, a precious feature in so dry a country; he is a rainbow, the ladder to heaven. But water is not his only element. He is charged with fiery energy; he spouts flames and disgorges salamanders in the form of lion or bull; and the spiky horns on his back burst into jets of fire. Often the whole arch is alive with salamanders, wild geese, and bird-women *(kinnarī)*, presided over by the goddess Śri. The solar and aquatic elements, whose abundance guarantees a prosperous husbandry, sprout into leaf and flower. The scrolls that luxuriate on the arch and cling to the pilaster are both foliage and flame: foliage because the arch marks a cave-mouth in a forest landscape, flame because the cave-mouth is illuminated by the fiery energy *(teja)* generated by the meditation of the Buddha inside the cave.[16]

All this fiery iconography was originally enhanced by gilding. Sometimes in addition the flame-tips (says Yule, who saw them in 1855 when more of them remained than now) were 'composed of pointed glazed white tiles, which

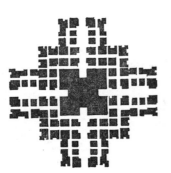

FIG. 19B – *Plan of Ananda temple*

PLATE P. 44
FIG. 21A

FIG. 21C

PLATE P. 23
FIG. 20
FIG. 21A LEFT
FIG. 21D

PLATE P. 44
FIG. 21A RIGHT
Iconography
FIGS. 21B, 21D

FIG. 21D

PLATE 3 –Vinīlakajātaka. Glazed ornamental plaque from Ananda temple. Early 12th century. *Cf. pp. 31, 45*

must once have given an extraordinary lustre and sparkling effect'.[17] On festival nights, as we know from donative inscriptions, the architecture shone with the light of thousands of lamps.

If we have insisted on the symbolism of light, of gleaming surfaces, of jets of flame springing from cave-mouths, it is because the architecture is meaningless unless these things are recognized. Fiery energy attained by meditation is, to simple-minded people, stupendous magic; to the orthodox, it is both the means and the evidence of gaining Enlightenment.

As blazing mountains, the temples of Pagán make an overwhelming impression. Yet that impression does not necessarily exclude others; the possibilities are endless. Here I shall mention but one more, to show how a sensitive Buddhist may perceive an entirely different sort of symbolism which is at first glance by no means obvious: the śikhara temple is a vase containing a lotus.

FIG. 22

FIG. 22 RIGHT

When U Lu Pe Win, the learned former Director of the Burma Archaeological Survey, first pointed out this symbolism to me, I must have seemed incredulous; so he showed me the proof — a bronze lotus with hinged petals, dug up in the ruins of Pagán. When the petals are closed, the flower is a bud; when they are open it is full-blown, with a śikhara in its centre. Below the flower is a roundel of more petals, occupying the same relative position as the terraces of a temple; below that is a system of scrolls like the twisted lotus-stems that grow under the surface of the water — and also like the floral scrolls so often seen in cornices. The base of the bronze suggests the foot-mouldings of a temple, whose alternations of concave and convex are often compared in literature to the Vase of Plenty. When the bronze flower is fully opened, the petals are seen to contain small figures with hands folded in the attitude of homage. They are surely the donors who built the temple which is here copied in miniature. When the petals are closed again, the donors are embedded in their act of merit, and enfolded in the Lotus of the Doctrine.   *   *

                                                              *

FIG. 20 – *Gawdawpalin temple, Pagán*

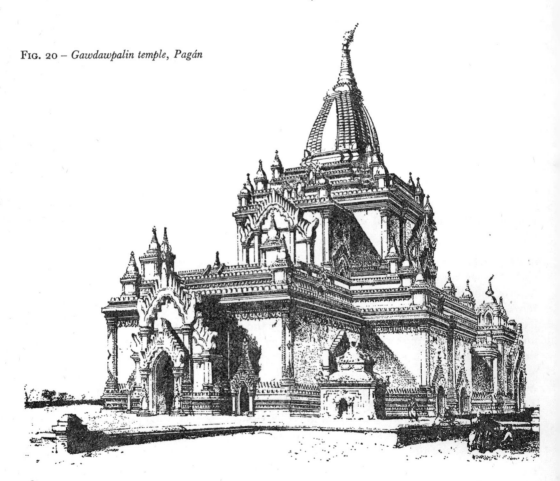

Fɪɢ. 21A – *Architectural detail of Sembyo-ku*

The conclusion reached by some writers, that all the best work at Pagán was done by Indian architects, is entirely too hasty. No one will deny the intensity of Indian influence, but we should stop for a moment to ask just how it was brought to bear. By the presence of Indian architects? By a deliberate attempt to copy Indian models? Or through a centuries-old Indianizing tradition inherited from the Pyu and the Mòn?

Indian influence

The śikhara was known in Burma in the 8th century, if not before; there are examples at Śrīksetra, and there may have been others at Thaton that have not survived. The general concept of the śikhara at Pagán, and particularly its mode of construction, unquestionably derives from one of those sources.[18] That does not exclude the possibility that certain particular ones were copied directly from Bengal or Orissa. We know that Kyanzittha sent a mission to Bihar to repair the Mahābodhi temple, and some of his śikharas look very much like those depicted on Indian bas-reliefs and votive tablets of the Pāla period.[19] We have already noted the affinities with Orissa. But the circumambulatory corridor must come from the Mòn or the Pyu, whether they evolved it themselves from temporary structures or derived it from Gupta temples of the sort found at Aihole.

As to the minor ornament — scrolls and leafage, Glory-Faces *(kīrtimukha)* and chaplets, lucky goddesses, birds, and so on — almost everything at Pagán has its counterpart in Orissa. It is often strikingly similar in detail; but its use is

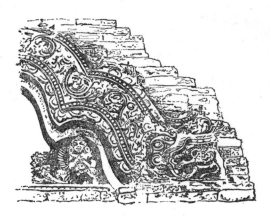

FIG. 21B – *Architectural detail of Pyathat Shwé Gu, Pagán*

FIG. 21C – *Architectural detail of Culāmani temple, Minnanthu, near Pagán*

entirely different. In Orissa the sculpture and decorative matter eat into the architecture, confusing the visual relationship of its parts, providing instead a stupendous impression of floating imagery and mystical speculation. At Pagán a shaft that is thought of as bearing weight never writhes or melts; there is not a hint of eroticism in the sculpture; and the decorative matter is confined to places where it cannot possibly obscure the simulated organic structure.

Likenesses to Sinhalese architecture can be discerned; but except for the stupas of Type IV they are less conspicuous than we might expect in view of the close religious associations with Ceylon.

The flame-tipped dragon-arch belongs to a tradition widely manifested in South-east Asia from a very early date. Pagán uses it over doorways generally without an intervening lintel; and as the same peculiarity is attested at Śrīkṣetra and in Dvāravatī bas-reliefs we can be pretty sure that Pagán got it from the Pyu or the Mòn.

Some of the inscriptions indicate that skilled artisans were imported from India, and there may have been architects among them. But the Mòn and the Pyu had long ago learned the lessons of Indian architecture and adapted them to their own inclinations through a gradual evolution; in Burma long before Aniruddha's time there was an established way of doing things. The direct Indian influence was more in the detail than the general design of the buildings. No doubt Indian bas-reliefs and miniature stupas were imported in large numbers, not to mention clay votive tablets which were the souvenir postcards of the day. No doubt the bits and pieces of temples depicted on such objects were frequently copied, but they were not put together in the same way as in India. What Indian architect would have allowed such broad surfaces of exterior walls to go unadorned?

PLATE 4 – Obelisk of Wet-kyi-in Ku-byauk-kyi. Probably early 13th century. *Cf. p. 33*

FIG. 21D – *Architectural detail of Culāmani temple, Minnanthu*

Clay plaques The introductory volume to the Buddha's biography, so to speak, consists of the 550 *Jātaka* tales dealing with his Previous Lives, anecdotes that he and his disciples told in order to settle disputes or illustrate points in the Doctrine. Many of them are very old folk-tales. To make the story applicable to the question at hand, to clinch the argument and draw the moral, the Buddha and his contemporaries are likened to different characters in the tale; or, putting it more literally than was perhaps the original intention, they are identified as having themselves been those characters in a previous incarnation: 'The Bodhisatta was born as a deer; Ananda was the King of Benares', or 'The Bodhisatta was born as a Brahmin', 'The greedy monks were the hermits', and so on.[20]

The tales are illustrated, in a kind of short-hand technique, in clay plaques designed to be readily understood by everyone, including the least instructed. Often, it might be hoped, delight in anecdote would attract simple people and lead them by easy stages to undertake a study of more serious matters. The proper place to install them was therefore on the outside of the monument, whether stupa or temple.

Three series are unglazed terracotta. The first, at Aniruddha's Shwé Sandaw, deteriorated badly from exposure to the weather. That is probably why most of the next two series were put indoors, at the two Petleiks. At the Shwé Zigon and the Ananda Kyanzittha used glazed ceramic plaques, which he could put outdoors where he wanted them. So did his successors at the Dhammarājika (1196–98) and the Mangalacetiya (13th century).

The *Mātangajātaka* tells the story of an incarnation in which the Bodhisatta was born as Mātanga the Untouchable. Soon after his marriage he renounced the world and went to live as an ascetic in the Himalayas, where he quickly gained miraculous powers. He then returned briefly to his wife and told her to tell the neighbours that her husband was the god Brahmā. The townspeople were

convinced by a few timely miracles; Mātanga returned to the Himalayas; and his wife became the object of a cult which made her immensely rich. One day their son, who had grown up believing himself to be the offspring of Brahmā, invited a huge company of Brahmins to take food at his house, when Mātanga suddenly appeared in his Untouchable's garb. The defiling presence broke up the party in confusion. The lad told his servants to beat the intruder, but before they could do so he rose miraculously into the air and sat there beyond their reach. The guardian sprites of the city, hurrying to help Mātanga, beat the lad and the Brahmins into insensibility, and gave their necks such a twisting that their heads faced backward. Mātanga's wife begged him to intervene on behalf of her son; whereupon he provided a charm that restored both the lad and the Brahmins to normal.[21]

This story is illustrated in one of the Petleik plaques. The inscription reads PLATE P. 48 '*Mātangajāt*', followed by its number in the series, 500.[22] Four different moments are presented simultaneously: the Bodhisatta miraculously sits in mid-air; underneath him his son kneels in the polite position he would assume for feeding the Brahmins; the mother, wearing a gauzy skirt, is standing in an attitude of dismay; and four Brahmins are laid out flat on the ground with their heads twisted backward.

In the *Vinīlakajātaka*, the Bodhisatta was King of Mithilā. A female crow in his city used to receive visits from the king of the golden geese, who flew down from the Himalayas to see her; and in due course she produced an offspring of dingy colour. Now her lover already had two other sons by a golden goose mother. These two geese, who lived with him in the Himalayas, deplored their father's

PLATE 5 – Detail of Myinkaba Ku-byauk-kyi. Built by Rājakumāra, c. 1113. *Cf. pp. 36, 46*

44

frequent absences and feared some harm might come to him in his visits to the city. Upon learning that his main motive was now to see their half-brother, they offered to go and fetch him so that they all might live together in safety. They flew down to the city and perched him on a stick, taking the two ends of it in their beaks, and flew off homewards again. Unfortunately their passenger, filled with pride at his conveyance, happened to look down at the city, saw the King of Mithilā driving a magnificent chariot drawn by white horses, and boasted that he was like him, while his two half-brothers were like the horses. When the king of the geese heard the story he was so disgusted that he sent the foolish bird back to town.[23]

One of a large series of green-glazed plaques on the roof of the Ananda temple PLATE P. 37 illustrates this story. The title *Vinīlakajāt* is written below the scene, together with the number 160. The purport of the plaque is so obvious that it needs no comment.

*   *
*

The temples were built for the same general purpose as the cetiya monuments, but they fulfil it rather differently. Like them they are fiery mountains on the outside; but unlike them they are penetrable: they are containers for other sorts of Reminders.

Some of the Reminders are bas-reliefs, carved in stone; some are frescoes, paintings *a secco* on the interior walls; some are statues of stone or masonry, originally covered with lacquer and gold-leaf. Monks and laymen alike, by visiting the carved scenes of the Great Events of the Buddha's career, performed the equivalent of pilgrimages to the sites themselves; whether the value of a pilgrimage is purely psychological, as some hold, or magical, as others feel, the results were no less real. The learned could read long extracts from the Canon and the Commentaries painted on the walls; everyone could examine the illustrations, in paint or bas-relief. Scenes from the Previous Lives re-appear here in fresco, where they are protected from the weather. The bas-reliefs and some of the paintings have a more formal and specific character, illustrating the Life of the Buddha, sometimes in the most minute detail. The temples, moreover, are image-houses, having as their central objects of contemplation that particular form of Reminder that portrays the Buddha's Person.

The foreign influences to be discerned in this sculpture are rather different from those in architecture. There is little of Orissa. In some of the bas-reliefs and bronze images of the Buddha there is so much of the Pāla that we may attribute them to Bengal artists; others strikingly recall Ceylon. Certain Bodhisattvas might almost be Nepalese. But the more ancient Burma tradition was not forgotten, and in due course it absorbed the foreign influences.

In the painting there is much of Bengal, something of Ceylon, Nepal and Tibet; but no direct foreign influences can fully explain this rich art, which seems to stem mainly from the same tradition as Ajanta, carried on through the centuries by Mòn and Pyu painters whose work has entirely perished.

PLATE P. 44 In temples of Mòn style the inside is dark and solemn; the windows are shaded with stone or terracotta lattices, while carefully placed light-shafts in the super-structure admit spotlights that bathe the cult images in golden radiance.

Burmese temples, on the other hand, are bright and airy, allowing the sculpture and frescoes to be plainly seen.

The interior plan of the main unit is square, with or without projecting bays. In the central pillar type, the narrowness of the corridor in relation to its great height gives a sense of aspiration, which is increased by the slope of the demi-vault springing from the outer wall and abutting against the pillar. The pillar may be partly hollowed out to form a chamber, thus approaching the hollow square type of temple; but more often it is square and solid, with a niche at each face for a cult image; or if there is only one cult image the other sides will have scenes of the Buddha's life. This is a very happy arrangement, permitting the circumambulant to honour the image and study the scenes simultaneously. In some śikhara temples there is no central pillar; like the Brahmanical cella, the interior chamber is small but unobstructed. But what might seem to western eyes so much more normal an arrangement was really less satisfactory. The only way to permit the cult image to be circumambulated would be to put it in the middle, but that seems to have been done rarely: habit required it to have a reredos, which is awkward in the centre of a chamber. More often it was placed against the back wall.

The Nanpaya, a delightful brick temple with stone trim, is associated with the captive king of Thaton.[24] Its interior is unusual. It is a hollow square, but with four stout piers supporting the superstructure, as if they were the remnants of a central pillar pierced through and through by two intersecting tunnels. Above the piers are arches, with pediments surmounted by stupas of Type III.

The piers have friezes of Glory-Faces disgorging wealth in the form of strings of pearls and flowery chaplets, and large bas-reliefs of the god Brahmā, holding lotuses in his hands — buds, half-opened and full-blown flowers (Fig. 23). He wears a rich head-dress, the 'matted hair' of Brahmin ascetics transposed into luxurious terms. He looks gentle and a trifle decadent.

Three of his four faces are visible; they have a distinctly Mòn character, and it is tempting to think they are modelled on that of the captive king. The usual

FIG. 23 – *Bas-relief in Nanpaya temple, Myinpagán*

46

FIG. 24 – *Fresco from a temple at Pagán: divinity offering garlands*

'vehicle' of Brahmā, the wild goose *(hamsa)*, is also the heraldic device of the Mòn people. He is not seated on it here, but there are some wild geese in a cornice not far away, and a whole flock of them in a dado on the outside of the temple. Contrary to the opinion expressed by some writers, the Nanpaya is a Theravāda temple. The captive king, in the guise of Brahmā, is offering flowers to some Reminder of the Buddha, perhaps a statue or a reliquary, now lost, that stood in the middle.

The inside of most temples is, or was, richly decorated. The mouldings and pilasters, whether in stucco relief or simulated in paint, have exactly the same forms as those on the outside, as if to recall the ancient evolution that created the temple. In like manner the doorway leading from the forechamber to the main unit has the same sort of pilasters and arch as an exterior doorway, and is flanked by a pair of guardian figures. The great image-niche receives similar treatment, for the Buddha is conceived as standing or sitting in the doorway or porch of a palace or monastery, or — what is architecturally the same thing! — the chamber of a cave.

Several temples have rows of iron hooks along the springing and the apex of the the demi-vaults that roof the corridors, evidently for hangings which occupied exactly the same position as the awnings I have assumed to have been a factor in the evolution of temple architecture. In many of the smaller temples such hangings are simulated in fresco instead. The designs, suggesting Persian carpets, perhaps give a clue to the nature of the real fabric.

Apart from that, there are all sorts of intricate painted designs, held together in a coherent geometric scheme of bands, medallions and squares. They may seem to be merely decorative, but they usually turn out to have some useful meaning, didactic or magical. Pious divinities, floating in the air above the cult images, or kneeling below them, offer flowery garlands. There are retrospects of the innumerable Buddhas of the Past, whose careers, save for a few formal variations, duplicate that of the historical Buddha. There are scenes of the heavens and the hells, and landscapes of the Himavanta with its fantastic bestiary. There are animals entwined in foliage that grows from their own tails, and more salamanders budding off into leaf and fire.

A few temples such as the Abèyadana (late 11th century), dedicated to the Mahāyāna, have paintings of Bodhisattvas. In addition two or three late 13th century temples have Tantric frescoes of erotic character.

PLATE P. 51

PLATE P. 51
FIG. 24
FIG. 25

FIG. 26
FIG. 27

FIG. 28

*   *
*

PLATE 6 – Mātangajātaka. Terracotta plaque at the Petleik. Latter half of 11th century. *Cf. p. 43*

The main function of a temple is to expound the Buddha's biography, and to reveal his Person in sculptured form.

Unlike the Previous Lives, which are admittedly fables, the Final Life is history expressed as legend. The reliefs and pictures that illustrate it are usually called 'Scenes from the Buddha's Life', although technically he was still a Bodhisatta until he attained Buddhahood at the age of thirty-five, and a great many scenes refer to the earlier period of his career. Whereas the Previous Lives are illustrated with humour, pathos, or whatever attitude the subject may suggest, these scenes are charged with religious solemnity, showing us not so much a succession of events as the acts of a stately ritual.

The Ananda temple contains over fourteen hundred carved stone panels illustrating the Final Life.[25] Most of them, I believe, though not all, are contemporary with the temple (early 12th century).

FIG. 25 – *Part of a fresco (from a temple at Pagán), depicting the Buddhas of the Past*

I illustrate the plaque representing the Bodhisatta's Fast. In his struggle to attain Buddhahood he has spent six years performing austerities, reaching their climax in a fast so severe — the *Nidānakathā* tells us — that he became as thin as a skeleton and would soon have died had not the gods gathered ambrosia and rubbed it into the pores of his skin. The gesture of the right hand, 'calling the Earth to witness', does not really belong to this incident, but to his ultimate triumph a little time later: it is not so much an anachronism as a prophecy.

In several temples the eight Great Events of the Final Life are illustrated in a single fresco. Similar compositions appear in miniature reliefs, which I suppose were intended for worship in a private chapel rather than a large temple. The Archaeological Survey possesses a graceful composition of this sort, carved in a piece of dolomite no more than a few centimetres high. The main event is the Enlightenment, with the Sage seated in the centre in the posture of 'calling the Earth to witness', flanked by a pair of standing gods. His throne is a lotus, supported by the pair of dragons whose duty is to guard the axis of the world. Above is the Bodhi tree, merging into a kind of garland that represents a forest

PLATE P. 54

FIG. 29

FIG. 26 – *Fresco from a temple at Pagán: fantastic beast and foliage*

FIG. 27 – *Salamanders: fresco from a temple at Pagán*

peopled with godlings, birds and monkeys. Three other scenes are grouped vertically at each side. The order is not chronological, but designed for symmetry. At the bottom, to our left, is the Nativity. Above it is the First Sermon; the Buddha holds his hands in front of his breast, in the gesture of turning the Wheel of the Doctrine; a lotiform wheel on the front of the throne identifies the scene. In the corresponding position on the right is the Grand Magical Display; the Buddha sits in the same attitude, but there is no wheel on the throne; a sorry-looking little figure at the corner is perhaps a humiliated heretic. Above the Magical Display is the Descent from Heaven; the Buddha is flanked by Indra and Brahmā, one of whom holds a parasol above him; a female disciple kneels in an attitude of homage at his feet. Below the Magical Display is the Monkey's Offering; the Buddha sits holding the bowl of honey in his lap; the monkey appears three times. Opposite the Descent from Heaven is the Taming of the Elephant; except for the Buddha, the figures are rather indistinct. At the top of the composition is the *parinibbāna*.

The Myinkaba Ku-byauk-kyi, built by Kyanzittha's son Rājakumāra (c. 1113), contains a fine series of frescoes painted in rich colours on a brown ground. One series represents the Buddha's different sermons to divinities and human beings, for example to the god Subrahmā and five hundred nymphs, and to King Ajātasattu and his court.[26]

PLATE P. 55 The progress from the glittering exteriors, with their gay celestial palaces, their visions of fiery power, and their homely anecdotes, to the more subdued scenes of worship inside the temple, with the ever-present energy disciplined and concentrated, and the solemn scenes of the Final Life, reaches its climax with the cult images. These were not only the chief objects of contemplation for worshippers but also the supreme achievement of the artists. It is sad to relate that time has not treated them gently. For in order to reinforce their magical identification with the Buddha's Person it was the practice to seal up relics

PLATE 7 – Fresco in the Wet-kyi-in Ky-byauk-kyi. Probably early 13th century. *Cf p. 47*

FIG. 28 – *Cosmic mountain with Bodhisattvas, from a fresco in Abèyadana temple*

FIG. 29 – *Dolomite relief from Pagán: the 'Great Events of the Final Life'*

inside them, enhancing the merit of the donation by adding a quantity of jewels; and as thieves were naturally aware of the practice most of the great cult statues have in the course of centuries been mutilated in order to reach the treasure. Subsequent repairs, if any, are liable to be in a debased style. The statues, no matter how badly damaged, that have been spared this last degradation are still the most impressive.

FIG. 30

* *
*

In an inscription recording the donation of a monastery in 1343, a princess says:

> This realm of Pagán is so named because it is the fairest and dearest of lands. It is also called Arimaddana because its people are warriors who vanquish their foes, and even its name is terrible. Its folk are free from pain and danger, they are skilled in every art, they possess the tools of every craft, they are wealthy, the revenues are past telling and the land is full of useful things. Truly it is a land more to be desired than the Himavanta. It is a glorious realm and its people are famed for their splendour and power. The monastery I have built stands to the east of the capital.[27]

The eulogy is a wistful retrospect, for by this time Pagán was no more than a shrunken province. A descendant of Aniruddha, ruling as a vassal of the Mongols, kept up a semblance of majesty, but he was really controlled by the Shan princes who had made themselves masters of Kyauksè. The rest of Burma had been parcelled out to other vassals, most of them Shan, though Toungoo on the Sittang river maintained a precarious independence under a Burmese dynasty.

There was no longer any reason for a large population to live at Pagán; the value of the site had been strategic, not economic; and in the changed patterns

53

PLATE 8 – The Bodhisatta's Fast. Stone relief in Ananda temple. Early 12th century. *Cf. p. 49*

PLATE 9 – Fresco with two preaching scenes. Myinkaba Ku-byauk-kyi, c. 1113. *Cf. p. 50*

Fig. 30 – *Thandawgya image, Pagán*

of power other centres had all the advantages. Pagán remained a place of pilgrimage because of the sanctity of its relics; some of the monasteries and temples continued to function; but the city gradually decayed. Its inhabited sections dwindled until at length they were no more than a handful of quiet villages, separated from one another by stretches of arid land and huge broken monuments.

After the 13th century the arts went into decline. In the 15th there was a revival at Pegu under a Mòn dynasty; in the 16th a Toungoo prince made himself king of a re-united and independent Burma; and his successors at Ava, Amarapura and Mandalay were lavish patrons of the arts. Building prospered; painting and wood-carving flourished; the production of Buddha images in stone and bronze was enormous, and some of them made as late as the 17th or 18th century are not lacking in style. The architecture of Pagán had set an enduring stamp on Burmese building habits; its monuments, especially the Shwé Zigon and the Ananda, were copied again and again, sometimes on an imposing scale. But neither architecture nor the other arts ever came near recapturing the sublime perfection of the classic period.

PLATE P. 57

56

PLATE 10 – Bronze image of the Buddha wearing the royal attire. Burmese, 17th or 18th century. Location unknown. *Cf. p. 56*

NOTES

[1] *Mahāvamsa*, XII, 42 f.; Taw Sein Ko, *The Kalyāni Inscriptions Erected by King Dhammaceti at Pegu in 1476 A.D., Text and Translation*, Rangoon, 1892. The Kalyāni inscription furnishes the detail that the imps were double-bodied lions; it also gives the most specific (and I believe the earliest) identification of Suvannabhūmi. It describes the incident in terms that evidently localize it in the area of Mount Kelāsa, thirty miles north of Thaton (now inland, because of changes in the coastline). In 1098 Kyanzittha repaired two venerable pagodas in the vicinity, which may have been intended to commemorate the incident.

[2] Condensed from Mr Luce's version (G. H. Luce, *The Ancient Pyu*, in Burma Research Society Fiftieth Anniversary Publications, No. 2, Rangoon, 1960, pp. 318–319).

[3] G. H. Luce, *Old Kyaukse and the Coming of the Burmans*, JBRS XLII/1, p. 91.

[4] For the Pagán period, the late Professor G. E. Harvey in his standard *History of Burma* (London, 1925) relies partly on the inscriptions and partly on the chronicles, so his account differs somewhat from that I give, particularly on religious matters. For the post-Pagán period, since the chronicles are more reliable, his account requires less amendment.

[5] G. H. Luce, *A Century of Progress in Burmese History and Archaeology*, JBRS XXXII/1, p. 80.

[6] The evidence is the votive tablets bearing his 'signature'. The chronicles give a very different picture.

[7] This Tantric sect is usually identified with the Ari, which may or may not be right.

[8] For an interesting discussion, see A. K. Coomaraswamy, *Elements of Buddhist Iconography*, Cambridge, 1935, pp. 4 f., and his '*The Nature of Buddhist Art*', in Rowland, *The Wall-Paintings of India, Central Asia and Ceylon*, Boston, 1938, pp. 8 f.

[9] By a singular confusion *caitya*, the Sanskrit equivalent of *cetiya*, is used by some writers as a contraction for 'caitya hall', a hollow structure containing a stupa.

[10] Note that the monument in Fig. 1 has the cone partly crumbled away. The small cetiya on top is a later addition.

[11] Something very much like Type III is attested in Dvāravatī art. It occurs also in the miniature crowning member of a pediment in the interior of the Nanpaya temple, which surely reproduces the perished glories of Thaton; see p. 47. I know of no cetiyas of Type III that can be positively attributed to Kyanzittha, but it appears as the crowning feature of several temples built in his reign (e.g. Fig. 14). Type III also appears in Pāla art (see Coomaraswamy, *History of Indian and Indonesian Art*, New York, Leipzig and London, 1928, Fig. 228). Something very similar appears in another Pāla relief combined with a Śikhara like the one on the Ananda temple (ibid., fig. 229).

[12] The lavish use of vaults at Pagán raises a question. The Indians, though long acquainted with this mode of construction, seldom used it; when a space was to be roofed over with masonry, they preferred the method of corbelling — because, it is sometimes said, the true arch 'never sleeps'. How then did the architects of Pagán, though so obviously respectful of Indian example, evade the interdiction? Some scholars say they were following a tradition of brick architecture which was once abundant in Bengal and northern India (e.g. Bhītārgaon), though most of it has disappeared; others point to Central Asian example, or to Muslim architecture. There may well be a measure of truth in their answers; but it seems likely that the Pyu, whose system of vaults Pagán inherited, had themselves derived it from an old type of Indian subterranean construction. Such vaults are not 'restless'; by inclining their component arches slightly from the vertical, they can be laid without centering; and the thrusts are negligible. Nothing about them need shock Indian sentiment if they are thought of — as indeed they must be — not as a means of roofing over a space, but as a means of reinforcing a cave.

[13] Another temple with the same type of stupa may be seen in the Plate on p. 23 near the upper left corner. The Kondaw-gyi and the Nandaminya should also be mentioned. A few examples are pentagonal instead of square, such as the Nga-myet-hna, whose interior reveals the architect's skill in dealing with vaults intersecting at unusual angles.

[14] Pe Maung Tin and G. H. Luce, *The Glass Palace Chronicle of the Kings of Burma*, London, 1923, p. 110. For an interesting discussion, see Duroiselle, *The Ananda Temple at Pagán*, Memoirs of the Archaeological Survey of India, No. 56, pp. 6f.

[15] In Pali literature the Gandhamādana is the favourite resort of Paccekabuddhas. It is sometimes described as a mountain in the Himalayas (see Malalasekera, *Dictionary of Pali Proper Names*, London, 1960, II, p. 22, s.v. Nandamūlapabbhāra), sometimes as a mountain range beyond the seven ranges that encircle Meru (ibid., I, p. 746, s.v. Gandhamādana). Nandamūla is the name of its crowning tableland, which contains three caves.

[16] The basic iconography of the cave-mouth had been established a thousand years earlier in Gandhāran art, when it depicted Indra's visit to the Buddha in his grotto. It is, as Foucher writes, 'un creux de rocher en forme de niche... Les flammes du *tejas* développé par la *samādhi* [du Bouddha] lèchent les parois de la grotte' (*Art gréco-bouddhique du Gandhâra*, Paris, 1905, p. 494). The description would apply equally well to the dragon-arches at Pagán. In another example, Foucher continues, 'tout au bord de la caverne, de bizarres chevelures tournoyant autour d'un noyau central, comme celles des soleils d'artifice, pourraient derechef faire songer à des flammes: en fait, ce sont seulement des indications de brousse' (ibid., p. 496). We may well ask whether the ambiguity between flame and foliage, which is evidently intentional at Pagán, was entirely accidental at Gandhāra. On the whole question of symbolism, see F. D. K. Bosch, *The Golden Germ*, The Hague, 1960.

[17] Henry Yule, *A Narrative of the Mission Sent by the Governor-General of India to the Court of Ava in 1855*, London, 1858, p. 49.

[18] The fact that the crowning stupa is usually of Type II might suggest a Pyu origin; but the Mòn may have had something similar too. The Nanpaya temple, presumably the most typical Mòn monument of any (cf. p. 47), has unfortunately lost its stupa.

[19] E.g. Coomaraswamy, *History of Indian and Indonesian Art*, New York, London and Leipzig, 1927, Fig. 229.

[20] In this context, of course, 'Bodhisatta' (Pali), though it is the same word as *Bodhisattva* (Sanskrit), does not refer to the mythical Bodhisattvas of the Mahāyāna; it simply means the historical founder of Buddhism in a previous incarnation.

[21] For the full story, see Cowell (ed.), *The Jātaka or Stories of the Buddha's Former Births*, London, 1957, vol. IV, pp. 235f.

[22] In the usual series it is number 497, but some of the numbers at Pagán run differently. See Luce, *The 550 Jātakas in Old Burma*, Artibus Asiae, XIX 3/4, pp. 291f.

[23] Cowell (ed.), op. cit., vol. II, pp. 26f.

[24] According to one tradition, it was built by the captive king himself as a residence and later converted into a temple. But dwellings were always made of light materials. According to another tradition, it was built by one of his descendants as a memorial to him on the site of his palace, in the late 12th or early 13th century. (For the two traditions, see the article by U Mya, in Archaeological Survey of India, *Annual Report*, 1934–35, p. 101.) The style suggests a date around 1060.

[25] See Duroiselle, *The Stone Sculptures in the Ananda Temple at Pagan*, Archaeological Survey of India, *Annual Report*, 1913–14, pp. 63f.

[26] For the stories, see Malalasekera, *Dictionary of Pali Proper Names*, London, 1960, vol. I, p. 32, vol. II, p. 1226.

[27] Tun Nyein, *Inscriptions of Pagan, Pinya, and Ava*, Rangoon, 1899, p. 134; quoted in Harvey, *History of Burma*, p. 78.

KOREA

BY

CHEWON KIM

The Korean peninsula is in the northern part of the Asiatic continent forming
a natural bridge between China and Japan, a position which has dictated the
political and cultural destiny of the Korean people for almost two thousand
years.

Korea has been greatly influenced by cultural elements from China. In return
she has served as a transmitter of Chinese culture to Japan. Because of this
Korean culture and art as such have seldom been the subject of intensive study
by the rest of the world, and this neglect has obscured the significance of Korea's
true cultural position in the Far Eastern community of nations.

In terms of population and size Korea is the smallest of the three countries.
Today the Japanese population is three times that of Korea, and both are
dwarfed by the overwhelming size of the Chinese population. As a small
country bordering on China, Korea always had to yield to great pressures from
the continent. Very few changes of power in Asia failed to affect Korea strongly.
The Mongolian invasion during the Koryŏ Dynasty and the Manchu invasion
during the Yi Dynasty are still terrible memories to her people. The warlike
Japanese invaded Korea throughout her history, sometimes as pirates, sometimes as an organized military power—as in the Hideyoshi invasion at the end
of the 16th century. Hideyoshi was a Japanese war-lord who set out to conquer
China, and to this end asked permission for passage through Korea. When
Korea refused, Hideyoshi attacked and the whole Korean peninsula became a
battle-field for six years. During that period almost all the material culture of
the country, including temples, palaces, books, paintings, and other works of art
were destroyed.

Only since the archaeological surveys of the last fifty years, which have brought
to light many important lost works, has it been possible to write a history of
Korean art. Even so we still lack sufficient material to allow us to trace the
development of styles in detail. For the present a history of Korean art is therefore inevitably more or less a description of extant works in chronological order,
in so far as such an order can be established.

One often hears it said that there is no need to write a history of Korean art
because it shows only some provincial aspects of great Chinese art. It is true, of
course, that Korean art bears much more direct influence from China than
Japanese art does. However, close observation reveals that Korean art manifests
a quite different feeling: true, it is expressed in the prevailing rhythmic style of
the Far East, yet to the eyes of the close student it is as independent of the arts of
China and Japan as the arts of England are from those of the other European
countries to which they are related by a basic classical western tradition.

When I was requested to write the Korean section of this book I was reluctant to accept the task for many reasons. Firstly, no aspect of Korean art has yet been thoroughly studied, either at home or abroad, so I feared that it was premature for a single author to write an entire art history of Korea. Secondly, a history of Korean art covering a span of two thousand years could not possibly be written in such a compact form with only a limited number of plates. Finally, I felt ill–equipped to attempt this work in a language which was not my mother tongue, trained as I am in the archaeology of Korea, rather than in general art history. But many of my foreign friends have encouraged and assisted me by making many suggestions and by putting the manuscript into readable English. Through working at the National Museum of Korea for more than a decade I have been in a good position to utilize recent archaeological finds and to obtain permission to reproduce photographs of various collections.

The travelling Exhibition of Korean Arts in Europe 1961–1962 was an excellent opportunity to assemble works of art from various private collections and a great proportion of the colour photographs were taken in Paris while the collection was housed at the Cernuschi Museum. The photographs of places in Korea and objects not included in the travelling exhibition were taken specially for this book by Mr Kyung-mo Lee.

I owe my deepest thanks to my friend Hwang Suyŏng, professor of Buddhist Art of Tongguk University, who carefully read my manuscript and made various important suggestions which were incorporated in the text. My sincere appreciation is also due to Father Richard Rutt who has put my English into a readable form. His wide knowledge and deep understanding of Korea made him a great help to me. I would also like to thank Dr Werner Speiser of the Museum für Asiatische Kunst, Cologne and Mr G. Holle of the Holle Verlag for having included Korea in the Art of the World Series and inviting me to write this section.

Chewon Kim

I. ORIGINS

The origin of the Korean people is still somewhat obscure. They are probably of Tungusic stock and may have originated somewhere in northern Asia. Their language is classified by philologists as belonging to the Ural-Altaic family, a *Language* language group quite distinct from the Chinese, though use has been made of the Chinese characters in writing Korean.

Archaeological investigation has shown that there are three different kinds of *Archaeological* Neolithic pottery. The first is a type of coarse, thick-walled undecorated pottery *evidence* with a flat base, fired at a low temperature and coloured red or brown. It has been found at inland sites, in hills as well as in valleys, usually accompanied by abundant stone implements, apparently used in agriculture. This fact reveals that these people were already sedentary. Such pottery has been found all over Korea and Manchuria.

The second type is the so-called comb-marked pottery which is said to be closely related to the pottery of the same name found in Scandinavia, by the Volga, in Finland and in Siberia. This type usually resembles a flower-pot. It has a round base decorated with parallel wavy lines, and was fired at a slightly higher temperature than the first type. Often this pottery contained quartz or mica. It is found on sites along rivers or on the sea coast alongside fishing utensils made of bone and horn, indicating that this pottery was made by people who were primarily fishermen. Korean comb-marked pottery has been found all round the peninsula, from the Tumen river along the coast of the Eastern Sea to Pusan, and from there up the coast of the Yellow Sea to the Liao-tung peninsula in Manchuria.

The last type of Neolithic pottery is a polished red thin-walled type which may be related to the so-called Chinese painted pottery of Honan and Kansu provinces.

In addition to these three types of Neolithic pottery there is a fourth kind, the proto-Silla pottery, which came into Korea from the continent, characterizing the period of transition from stone to metal. Silla pottery and the Iwaibe pottery of Japan probably originated from this proto-Silla variety.

It is difficult to say just when the Neolithic period ended. At any rate, north-western Korea, because it was closer to China, adopted metal at the end of the Warring States period in China, i.e. some time during the 3rd or 4th century B.C. The knife-shaped coins which were used in the Chinese states of Yen and FIG. I Ch'i have been found in abundance in mountainous areas not far from the Yalu river. As they never appeared in the Lo-lang tombs, they are obviously remains of a pre-Han dynastic period. Closer observation has also revealed that in this very region where the knife-shaped money was discovered there existed in those early days an ancient route connecting the Chinese mainland to Korea.

FIG. 1 – *Knife-shaped coins. Nyŏng-byŏng, North Pyŏngan province. 3rd–4th century B.C. National Museum of Korea. Length 13.7 cm*

Archaeological investigations in other parts of the country, on the other hand, have clearly shown that elsewhere the Stone Age continued until beyond the first century A.D.

One of the most interesting features of the early metal culture of Korea is that some metal artefacts were Scythian in origin. The Scythians were a nomadic people who appeared on the northern shore of the Black Sea a few centuries before Christ and had considerable contact with the Greeks and other western peoples. Having no writing system of their own, they left no documents. But over the last century many of their cultural remains have been discovered in Mongolia and various parts of China. It is therefore not surprising that some of their remains should be found in Korea also.

FIG. 2 Two bronze buckles from Yŏngch'ŏn are typical examples of Scythian ware. Two kettles found near P'yŏngyang closely resemble the so-called Hsiungnu kettles. There is much other archaeological evidence that the non-Chinese culture under Scythian influence of the pre-Han period even penetrated far south in Korea.

There is one more interesting and important relic from early Korea: the dolmen. These megalithic remains are found all over Korea except in South Hamgyŏng province. Two types of dolmens are distinguished: the northern type and the southern type. The northern type strongly resembles the dolmens of Europe and consists of four or five stone slabs of which four serve as walls, standing vertical to the terrain, with the last and largest one laid horizontally over the others, the whole forming a kind of large stone table. The imposing dolmen of Unyul in Hwanghae province has a horizontal cover stone about 8.5 metres long.

On Sŏkchon mountain, in South P'yŏngan province, 300 metres above sea-level, is a group of twelve dolmens of which the largest is about 1.5 metres high with a cover stone more than 5.5 metres long and about 3.7 metres wide.

In contrast to the northern type of dolmen the southern type resembles the Japanese *go*-table. A large flat stone is laid on the surface of the ground, and underneath it may be found any one of a wide variety of burial arrangements. The commonest is a kind of buried cairn construction, or a cist of stone slabs, but several other forms have been found. Since the cover stone nearly always lies directly on the terrain, it presents an entirely different appearance from the northern type. In the cairn or stone cist burial objects have often been found, in one instance even a complete human skeleton, showing clearly that the southern type was definitely a burial structure, whereas no similar objects have so far been uncovered from the northern type of dolmen. However, since the northern type was exposed, its contents could easily have been taken away. It is now generally accepted that Korean dolmens, judging from their artefacts, belong to the period of transition from stone to metal.

What was the earliest form of religion in Korea? No conclusive evidence in this regard has been produced so far, but it is probable that Shamanism was the predominant religious cult of early Korea. Shamanism is still practised in various parts of northern Asia, and it is still the most popular cult among farmers in the rural areas of Korea. Buddhism was introduced into Korea in the 4th century A.D., but Shamanism was so deeply rooted that even Buddhism has not been able to replace it. Many Buddhist rites have, however, been adopted by the Shamans. Even today in the outskirts of Seoul, there are several Shamanistic shrines. The most famous sanctuary of Shamanism is on the top of Tŏngmul mountain, mid-way between Kaesŏng and Seoul, where a whole community of Shamans is occupied with the cult throughout the year. Pilgrimages are made there continuously from all over the country. *Religion*

Korea of course has its legendary figures such as Tang'un, the divine forefather of the Korean people and Kija, a noble from China who is said to have come to Korea at the end of Shang China to found a dynasty himself. But all this has no historical foundation. At the end of the period of the Warring States in China, according to another Chinese historical source, a man named Wiman from the state of Yen emigrated to Korea and organized a state which he called Wiman Chosŏn. Historians usually believe that Korea's historical period begins at this time, a fact which gains plausibility since it coincides with the archaeological finds of Chinese origin mentioned above. HISTORICAL PERIOD *Legendary epoch*

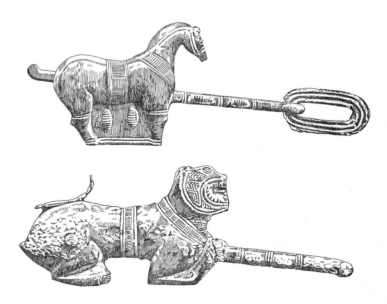

FIG. 2 – *Two bronze buckles. Yŏng-ch'ŏn, North Kyŏngsang province. 1st–3rd century B.C. National Museum of Korea. Horse: length circa 18 cm. Tiger: length circa 19 cm*

Lo-lang period Chinese influence was intensified by the conquest of Korea by Wu-ti of the Han Dynasty of China in 108 B.C. Wu-ti was determined to break the power of the Hsiungnu to the north and wished to outflank them in Korea, destroying all possibility of an alliance between the Koreans and the Hsiungnu. He established four provinces (*ch'un*) north of the Han river with administrative units similar to those in China proper. Han records indicate that they had a very large population, greater than that of the purely Chinese provinces of Shantung and Liaot-ung at the time. Resenting foreign domination, the native Koreans harassed the territory under Han control by repeated attacks, and by 75 B.C. the four original provinces were reduced to one, Lo-lang, with its capital at P'yŏngyang. Lo-lang remained prosperous and strong for four hundred years as an important outpost of China, even after the Han Dynasty itself had fallen. It was also able to establish another province called Tai-fang on the west coast of central Korea early in the 3rd century.

Lo-lang's culture was purely Chinese, transplanted to Korea from the continent. Many Lo-lang tombs, which were centered around the present city of P'yŏng-yang, were excavated early in this century. Archaeologists then brought to light many aspects of Chinese culture and art, before scientific excavation of Han remains had been carried out in China proper. The tombs of Chinese officials yielded objects of the highest standard, among them some of the most beautiful lacquer wares ever found and gold work showing a finely elaborated filigree technique.

The impact of this Chinese culture upon the surrounding native Korean tribes, still partially in the Stone Age, must have been tremendous. They organized themselves into states and from the 2nd century onwards three Korean kingdoms emerged in succession: Koguryŏ in the north, Paekche in the south-west, and Silla in the south-east. Of these three kingdoms Kogyruŏ was the strongest. It conquered Lo-lang in the 4th century and Tai-fang soon afterward, putting an end to the existence of the Han colonies in the Korean peninsula.

II. THE THREE KINGDOMS

Although the Koreans in the Chinese provinces undoubtedly received great stimuli from the Chinese and grew rich and strong, they were often resentful of Chinese power and tried to break it. It was one of the so-called Puyŏ tribes of Tungusic stock that launched the first significant attacks on the Chinese province of Hsuan-t'u. Later these Puyŏ tribes expanded into a stronger political unit called Koguryŏ, successfully conquered Hsuan-t'u and became a threat to the remaining provinces of Lo-lang and Tai-fang.

HISTORICAL ORIGINS *Koguryŏ*

According to legend Koguryŏ was founded by a man named Chumong in 37 B.C. and its first capital was situated near Yüan-jen, on the river Hun-chiang in Manchuria, until the end of the 2nd century A.D. Today almost nothing remains there except a few unimportant ruins which have not as yet been investigated by scholars. Koguryŏ moved its capital some time in the 3rd century to Chi-an, east of Yüan-jen, on the banks of the Yalu river, and then eventually to P'yŏngyang for the last period of her history, from the 5th to the middle of the 7th century. This last period corresponds to the Six Dynasties and early T'ang periods in China.

By its proximity to China Koguryŏ was ideally situated to receive cultural influences from the mainland. The incorporation of a large population, including the conquered people of Lo-lang, gave them further cultural stimulus. It was also Koguryŏ which first introduced Buddhism to Korea, in 372 A.D.

The southern half of Korea was occupied by a tribal people called the Han. They were of three main groups: Mahan in the south-west, Pyŏnhan in the centre, and Chinhan in the south-east.

The three Han

The Chinese viewed the Han tribes as having very little discipline, which meant no doubt that the Han people were culturally backward: 'They lived in huts, which looked like graves with an entrance at the top, without discrimination as to sex or age. Some houses were built of wood and looked like the jails in China. Their clothes were made of hemp, sometimes of silk decorated with jewels.'

The Han tribes made very slow political development and it was only in the middle of the 3rd century that the kingdom of Paekche emerged as a leading power in the struggle against China. The people of Paekche, like the people of Koguryŏ, seem to be descended from the Puyŏ. They had their first capital somewhere near Kwangju (not far from Seoul) but, pressed by the enormous power of Koguryŏ, moved to the present city of Kongju (in South Ch'ungch'ŏng province); and then eventually moved the capital for the second time to Puyŏ, a name written with the same Chinese characters as those for the ancient Tungusic tribe.

Paekche

FIG. 3 – *Chiang-ch'un Chung (Tomb of the General), T'ung-kou, Manchuria. Koguryŏ Dynasty, 5th century. Height 13.5 m*

Silla From one of the tribal units of Chinhan another kingdom emerged somewhat belatedly in Korean history: Silla. At the beginning of the 5th century the Korean peninsula was thus divided into three rival kingdoms — Koguryŏ, Paekche and Silla. This situation continued for about three hundred years until
Great Silla Silla unified the whole peninsula in the 7th century. We speak of Silla after the unification of the peninsula as Great Silla, to distinguish it from the state of Silla in the pre-unification period, which is known as Old Silla or Silla of the Three Kingdoms period.

ART OF KOGURYŎ On the banks of the Yalu river, which forms the frontier between Manchuria and Korea, there is a relatively large plain on the Manchurian side called
Wall-painting T'ung-kou. This is where Koguryŏ had its second capital. On hilly places surrounding the plains and by the river-side, there are thousands of tombs covering tremendous areas. All these tombs have been looted, probably many hundreds of years ago, even as early as the time of Koguryŏ's downfall in the 7th century A.D.

Two types of tomb are distinguishable: stone tombs and mounded tombs. The
FIG. 3 large pyramid-shaped tomb called Chiang-ch'un Chung (Tomb of the General) at the foot of Mt. T'u-k'ou-tzū typifies the stone tomb. Near the Chiang-ch'un Chung there are many more similar stone tombs, though none of them have retained their original shape as well as the Chiang-ch'un Chung. Half the tombs in the T'ung-kou plain are, however, mounded tombs which have an interior stone chamber. They deserve our special attention, as some of them contain murals giving us vivid pictures of these warlike people. There are scenes of everyday life, and scenes of rituals illustrative of the view of the world the people had at the time. All the mounded tombs are constructed in a square or rounded form, apparently after the dynasty moved the capital to P'yŏngyang in the early 5th century.

PLATE I – Hunting scene from 'Tomb of the Dancing Figures'. Wall-painting on plaster. T'ung-kou, Manchuria. Koguryŏ Dynasty, 5th–6th century. *Cf. below*

The wall-paintings of this period have so few parallels that it is not easy to speak of cultural affinities, but they show considerable originality. Their realism is at variance with the insistent symbolism common in Chinese works of art. For instance, the name of the Tomb of the Dancing Figures is derived from a dance scene painted on part of the wall of its main chamber.* A group of men and women are shown performing a dance accompanied by a group of people lined up below. On the left wall of the same chamber there is a hunting scene. It shows a group of hunters at full gallop, chasing a tiger, a deer and a smaller animal. A mountain range very roughly drawn divides the scene, and in the topmost part of the painting there is a cloud design such as we can also see on the ceiling of this chamber, conveying the idea of a blue sky. The painting is

Tomb of
Dancing Figures
PLATE P. 71

* Cf. W. Speiser, *China*, Plate p. 104.

spontaneous, free and powerful; animals and men are depicted in vigorous movement. The colour was hardly faded when the tomb was opened, nearly sixteen hundred years after the painting was executed. No picture shows better the warlike Koguryŏ people, who spent their whole life on horseback in the Manchurian plain and defeated even the strongest power in the East of that time. The dome-like ceiling above the vertical wall represents the celestial world, while the main walls below represent the terrestrial world. The surface of the ceiling is covered with paintings of various designs: a circular symbol of the moon containing a toad, another circular symbol of the sun containing a three-legged crow, or constellations represented by small circles joined together by three parallel lines and a large number of flying clouds. The Japanese scholar Kiyoye Nakamura considered the constellations depicted here not as mere decorations but as fairly faithful representations of the principal constellations. There are other interesting scenes: men and women flying through the air, immortals riding on cranes, mythical animals such as the white tiger, blue dragon, red phoenix, unicorn, galloping horse, etc. All these drawings were painted with such originality that, though they often lack sophistication, they nevertheless show the free imaginative genius of this remarkable people.

It is obvious that the Koguryŏ people intended their tombs to be microcosmic. This idea originated in the ancient Orient as a belief in the existence of a magical correspondence between the microcosm and the macrocosm, between the human world and the universe, between earthly beings on one hand and compass directions and constellations on the other. According to this idea all events in life, age and sex, birth and death, are connected with the greater plan of the universe and are believed to have magical connections with it. It is highly interesting to find this theory represented in the wall-paintings of the Koguryŏ tombs. No doubt it reached Koguryŏ via China, having originated in another more distant part of the Orient, for we know that the same idea also held sway in Indonesia and India, and probably in some other parts of Asia too.

The P'yŏngyang area

FIG. 4

Twin Pillars Tomb

In the vicinity of P'yŏngyang, the third capital of Koguryŏ (from 427 onwards) there are also numerous tombs, mostly mounded ones with only a few stone tombs. Some of these mounded tombs also have wall-paintings, which were studied rather earlier than those of the T'ung-kou plain. The most important of all the tombs with walls-paintings is the Twin Pillars Tomb. There is a short corridor between the main chamber and antechamber. Both main chamber and antechamber have interesting ceilings constructed with so-called triangular corbels, each layer protruding further than the one below. On each side of the corridor there is an octagonal pillar, and from these pillars the name of the tomb is derived. On the upper part and at the base of the pillars are lotus decorations; the body of the pillars is decorated with dragons. On the northern wall of the main chamber the main personalities, a man and his wife, are seated at table attended by servants. On the eastern wall a procession of ladies and children is led by a monk moving toward the seated couple. A girl holding an incense-burner on her head walks in front of the procession. In the centre of the ceiling is a lotus flower, surrounded by symbols of the moon and sun with cloud

FIG. 4 – *Twin Pillars Tomb (interior). Near P'yŏngyang. Koguryŏ Dynasty, late 5th century*

designs and other miscellaneous decorations such as lozenges and phoenixes. The decoration of the antechambers is similar to that of the main chamber. The astrological blue dragon and white tiger are drawn on the eastern and western wall respectively. The whole painting is executed with far more skill and care than any in the tombs of T'ung-kou and may be dated as late 5th century A.D.

The great tomb of Uhyŏn-ni

The great tomb (Taemyo) of Uhyŏn-ni has another excellent wall-painting. It was found in comparatively good condition, executed directly on the flat surface without plaster. On each side of the entrance at the south is painted a red bird. The blue dragon, the white tiger and the black warrior are painted on the east, west and north walls respectively, with great realism and skill. On the ceiling again, lotus, flying angels, immortals, unicorn and other animals are drawn, with a dragon as the central figure. Here also the ceiling represents the celestial region, while the lower parts represent the terrestrial world. Thus we see here again the idea of the microcosm.

Comparable to the wall-paintings of Koguryŏ are some of the pictorial tomb decorations of the later Han Dynasty which have come to light in the neighbourhood of Liao-yang, Manchuria. However, these paintings have not been sufficiently studied for us to be able to speak of their relationship to the wall-paintings of Koguryŏ. More intimately related to these wall-paintings are some of the works of early Chinese masters such as Ku K'ai-chih of the 5th century whose works, or imitations thereof, we can still see today. No doubt Koguryŏ's artist must have been influenced by general Chinese trends of painting and this must have continued for some length of time. However, since nothing like them has yet been found in China, Koguryŏ's wall-paintings represent some of the most precious artistic documents left to us in the Far East. It is to be hoped that we may some day find more missing links in the history of painting so that we can evaluate them more accurately.

Apart from wall-paintings no other worth-while works of art have survived from Koguryŏ, so complete was the destruction of all its cultural remains. Only some giant roof tiles have been found on its ancient sites, demonstrating the size and splendour of a wooden architecture which has long since disappeared.

In the Exhibition of Korean Art that toured Europe in 1961 and 1962 there was a small Buddhist statuette from Koguryŏ. This statuette is the only bronze figure of Koguryŏ the present writer has ever seen. It is dated 571 and shows characteristics common to the Three Kingdoms period. Apart from this figure, small Buddhist figures made of clay are known, which have some similarities with the bronze figure. But these few figurines cannot possibly show us the high standard which Koguryŏ's sculpture must have attained at that time.

ART OF PAEKCHE

Paekche, despite its prosperity and location in the richest part of Korea, was never militarily strong. Pressed by Koguryŏ from the north, Paekche was forced in 475 to move its capital southward from the Han river valley to the modern town of Kongju, which offered a position geographically easier to defend. Here in Kongju Paekche lasted for over sixty years, long enough to reorganize and gain new strength, so that in 538 King Sŏngwang moved the capital once more to the modern town of Puyŏ, which has a wide plain around

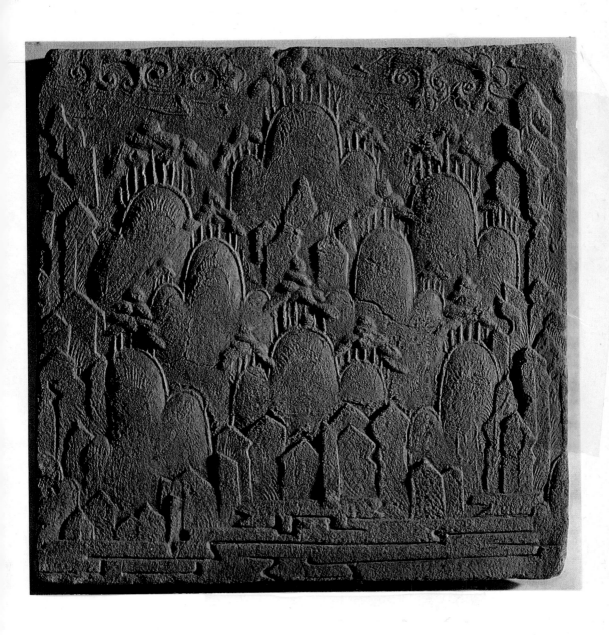

PLATE 2 – Tile in grey clay with landscape in relief. Found at Puyŏ during excavation of temple. Paekche Dynasty, 7th century. *National Museum of Korea. 29.6 × 28.8 cm. Cf. p. 76*

it offering better possibilities for development. It was this king of Paekche who encouraged Buddhism as the state religion through such famous monks as Kyŏmik, and who cemented Paekche's relations with the South Chinese dynasties and Japan. It was also during his reign that Buddhism was transmitted to Japan, thus starting a new cultural era in that country.

Remains of Paekche Unfortunately very few cultural remains have survived from Paekche. At its first capital of Kwangju near Seoul a couple of tombs were excavated, but no remarkable burial objects were found. At a fortified site not far from the Han river two fine bronze incense-burners were discovered. No wooden or stone construction on the surface has so far been discovered in this region.

Kongju Near Kongju, Paekche's second capital, we were more fortunate in finding a royal tomb built of tiles. This tomb, usually called the 'Tomb of Songsanni', has a tomb-chamber with a vaulted ceiling such as is also found in Central and South China and Indochina. The tiles also were similar in size and design to those found in South China and were laid in alternate vertical and horizontal blocks. A subterranean drain was made to keep the inside dry and small niches were made in the wall, probably to hold Buddhist images. On the tile walls of the tomb the deities of the four cardinal points—the blue dragon, white tiger, black warrior or tortoise, and red phoenix—were painted on white plaster. The uneven surface of the tomb's interior was ill-suited for such paintings, and now the pictures are hardly recognizable, but judging from older photographs they were very powerful drawings, reminiscent of some of the wall-paintings of Koguryŏ.

Puyŏ In another tomb near Puyŏ, the third capital of the dynasty, there is a stone chamber made of granite slabs. Originally the walls of the tomb were also painted, but they have now faded away, leaving only a lotus flower and flying clouds on the ceiling. All these tombs were plundered long ago and almost nothing has been found in them, so we know little of the splendour of the objects which must have accompanied the nobles after their death, but some ear-rings, a bronze ornament from a crown, sword ornaments, horse ornaments, silver buckles, comma-shaped jewels and quantities of glass beads were found in these Paekche tombs. All these objects closely resemble those found in early Silla tombs.

Buddhist images From time to time small Buddhist images have been found on some sites of ancient temples. A small Buddhist sculpture was found at a spot which was supposed to be the site of a temple at Kunsuri, in Puyŏ. The image with its archaic facial expression is similar in style to the period of the Six Dynasties in China. It has crossed scarves with saw-tooth drapery edges as well as a complex crown head-dress.

Tiles Of the few finds in and around Puyŏ the ornamental tiles are best known. There were dozens of tiles, each a foot square, with eight different designs found together in a row at the site of a temple. They were made by moulding in relief.

PLATE P. 75 The plate on page 75 shows a tile in this series. A narrow band of decoration at the bottom represents water. In the middle a building is set before conventionalized rounded mountains topped by pine-trees. At the top are cloud forms. On the right there is the figure of a priest walking towards the house in the centre. The whole tile might represent the idealized landscape where the immortals are said to dwell. The earliest landscape painting in China itself is not much older than this tile, and so Paekche's landscape art on these tiles may be regarded as a very important stage in the history of Far Eastern art.

In 1959 a rock-cut triad of the Paekche Dynasty was found near Sŏsan in a valley in South Ch'ungch'ŏng province. This beautiful group has been overlooked for more than forty years, although many scholars passed through this valley in search of Korean art treasures in the area. It undoubtedly constitutes the most important discovery of Paekche art to date. The present writer had the pleasure of giving it the first close examination. A large Buddha of more than life-size with unusually wide-open eyes is flanked by a seated Maitreya with crossed legs on the left and a standing Bodhisattva on the right. This type of grouping is rare and all three figures have archaic features, yet are executed with masterly command of sculptural technique and may be dated roughly to the end of the sixth century. It is probably the oldest rock-carving preserved in Korea. *Rock-carving of Sŏsan* PLATE P. 79

Anyone who visits Puyŏ today will find a five storeyed stone pagoda on a relatively large open space in the middle of the town. This is the only visible monument extant from Paekche days. The pagoda has been traditionally, but mistakenly, called the pagoda of the conquest of Paekche because the T'ang general Su T'ing-fang after his conquest of Paekche had the story of his victory inscribed on the first storey of the pagoda, and people for a long time believed that the pagoda itself was erected by the general for that purpose. The pagoda originally stood in front of the Golden Hall of a Buddhist temple. Whether the temple was burned down by General Su T'ing-fang is not quite clear. However, during the Koryŏ period a temple called Chŏngnimsa was here and it has therefore been suggested that the pagoda should be called 'the Chŏngnimsa pagoda'. It is generally regarded as one of the oldest and most beautiful stone pagodas in Korea with its rare simplicity and perfect proportions. To the north of the pagoda still stands the beautifully sculptured octagonal stone pedestal of a Buddhist image which was originally in the Lecture Hall of the temple. The image itself is now lost, replaced by an ugly head which the villagers call the portrait of General Su T'ing-fang. Judging from the remaining stone pedestal, it is, however, probable that the image was not from Paekche, but from the Koryŏ Dynasty. *Pagoda of Chŏngnimsa* FIG. 5

The temple plan of Chŏngnimsa is exactly the same as those of early Japan. The entrance gate, pagoda, Golden Hall and Lecture Hall were all in a line on a north–south axis in a rectangular enclosure. This temple plan, called in Japanese 'Shitennoji plan', is also to be found at the site of another temple in Kunsuri, near Puyŏ, and elsewhere.

The second architectural relic of the Paekche kingdom is the stone pagoda on the site of the Mirŭksa temple, at Iksan, North Chŏlla province. This enormous pagoda has been partially destroyed and only the eastern part is still preserved. One can see at a glance that this pagoda shows a technique based on the *Pagoda on the site of Mirŭksa* FIG. 6

FIG. 5 – *Pagoda of Chongnimsa, Puyŏ, South Ch'ungch'ŏng province. Paekche Dynasty. Height 8.35 m*

structures used in wooden architecture. According to the theory advanced by the late Ko Yu-sŏp this pagoda is earlier than the Chŏngnimsa pagoda, since the older a stone pagoda is, the more it will have retained elements of wooden architectural technique.

As we have seen in the temple plan of this period, there are many common elements between Paekche culture and Japanese culture of the same period. This is not surprising, because it was primarily Paekche which sent waves of scholars, priests and artists to Japan to lay the foundations of her early culture. In Nara, where there are many early Buddhist temples, we can still find many works of art which must have been made by Paekche craftsmen, or at least *Kudara Kannon* under their influence. The name of the famous Kudara Kannon, which is in the Horyuji, Nara, means literally 'Avalokiteśvara from Paekche', and the image is said to have been carved by a Paekche artist, or under the influence of his school. This slender noble wooden statue, more than life-size, has a unique beauty and dignity, and must be considered one of the great sculptural master-pieces of Asia in all times. Sometimes nationalist-minded Japanese scholars have regarded the Kudara Kannon as a product of the influence of South Chinese dynasties. This is reasonable, because all the arts of Paekche were directly influenced by South China and bear many South Chinese characteristics with only limited influence from the North Chinese dynasties.

PLATE 3 – Rock-carvings at Sŏsan, South Ch'ungch'ŏng province. Paekche Dynasty, close of 6th century. *Height circa 2.8 m. Cf. p. 77*

The Kuse Kannon in the Yumedono of the same Horyuji at Nara is generally also regarded as having been carved by Paekche artists. It is an irony of history that the Paekche artistic genius has bequeathed its legacy more abundantly in Japan than in its homeland. What we find on Korean soil today is only a small proportion of what was once created there.

SILLA AND ITS ART   Silla emerged last among the three kingdoms of Korea, just as Koguryŏ's power reached its peak. This means that Silla was a backward country and developed only very slowly into a political unit. The reason for this tardiness was that Silla, cut off by Koguryŏ in the north and Paekche in the south-west, had very little direct contact with continental culture.

Silla emerged out of the settlement called Saro, one of the tribal units of Han people in southern Korea mentioned earlier, and was a very small power centred around the modern town of Kyŏngju. Saro soon became a leading state, forming a federation with surrounding Han tribes, and at that time seems to have been headed by three families, Pak, Sŏk and Kim.

FIG. 6 – *Pagoda on the site of Mirŭksa, Iksan, North Chŏlla province. Paekche Dynasty. Height 14.28 m*

80

At the beginning of the 6th century the kingdom came to be referred to in Chinese characters as Silla, the Chinese title *wang* was introduced for the king, and a *nienhao*, or Chinese-style year-title, was first used. The official adoption of the name of the country and the introduction of a sinicized title for the ruler signalized the reorganization of political institutions along Chinese lines.

The Chinese system of political institutions brought with it Confucianism, but it had little success with the Silla people. The aristocratic ruling class was not attracted to Confucianism, with its closely associated examination and merit system; moreover at that time Confucianism was relatively weak in China itself.

Confucianism and Buddhism

Buddhism probably came to Silla during the reign of King Nŭlchi (417–457) by way of Koguryŏ. But it was officially accepted only under King Pŏphung (527) and then favoured strongly by the royal court, as was also the case in Koguryŏ and Paekche. It brought the prestige of Chinese culture with it; and the comparatively optimistic Mahāyāna Buddhism combined with Indian mysticism seems to have appealed to the Silla people who were still living under primitive Shamanist superstition. The spontaneous response of Silla society to Buddhism gave the artistic genius of the Silla people the necessary stimulus for creating one of the most remarkable cultures in human history.

Fortunately for students of Silla art, the dynasty left posterity far more remains than either Koguryŏ or Paekche. This happened because Silla's ancient capital never became a battle-field and when Silla fell to the succeeding Koryŏ Dynasty the country was taken over peacefully, the last king of Silla even being given a princess to marry, so becoming related to the Koryŏ court. No violence or looting occurred. The traveller will find to-day huge tombs and impressive stone structures in and around Kyŏngju which attest to the greatness of the ancient kingdom. There are still some fifty large tombs dominating the landscape. The largest is Ponghwang-dae, 21 metres high and about 85 metres in diameter, so large that until recently the villagers believed that all such tombs were natural hills. Some of these tombs were destroyed and levelled. Many of them have lost their upper part, and the villagers have often made vegetable gardens or built cottages on them. So far about fifty other large tombs have been excavated scientifically, or at least closely examined, by scholars.

Tombs

The first important tomb to be excavated was the Gold Crown Tomb. In September 1921, during the construction of a new house in Kyŏngju, the people reached the centre part of the tomb and local scholars, amazed by the richness of the finds, urgently notified the governmental authorities of the discoveries. Professors K. Hamada and S. Umehara, both of Kyoto University, rushed to the spot and carefully studied the tomb, and an excellent report was issued soon afterwards. After the Gold Crown Tomb, many more tombs were excavated: the Lucky Phoenix Tomb, the Tomb of the Ornamented Shoes, the Gold Bell Tomb and the Ho-u Tomb among others, and we are most fortunate to possess now fairly good information about the tombs of the Silla Dynasty of the Three Kingdoms period.

Gold Crown Tomb

The tombs of this period have the so-called stone-block structure. Each contains two oblong wooden coffins, an inner and an outer one. The outer coffin could be called a wooden chamber. It was covered first by stones of the size of a man's head, taken from near-by rivers, and then with earth. The coffins were so placed that the head was to the east and the feet to the west. A considerable space was left at the eastern end of the outer coffin, which was filled with such burial objects as ceramics, bronze vessels, iron kettles and horse harnesses, among other things. The coffins no longer exist, having decayed, leaving only a few fragments. All the stones have collapsed. The corpse was buried fully dressed with all personal ornaments exactly as they had been worn in life. These ornaments were usually a crown made of gilt bronze or sometimes of pure gold, gold ear-rings, rings of gold or silver, gold, silver or gilt-bronze bracelets and a gold or gilt-bronze girdle. There is almost no difference in the ornaments of men and of women; but if there is a large sword, it is likely that the tomb belonged to a male. Most of the tombs cannot in fact be identified, owing to the lack of

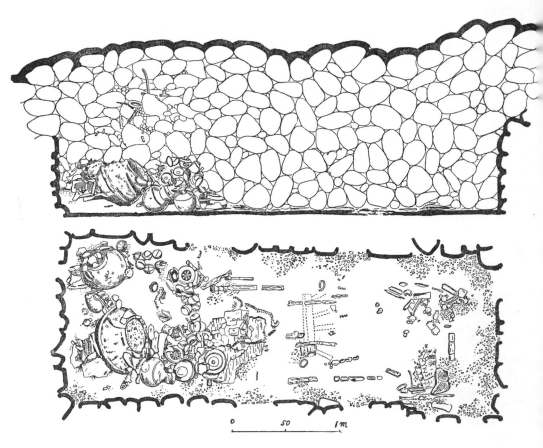

FIG. 7 – *Plan and elevation of the Ho-u Tomb, Kyŏngju. Old Silla Dynasty, 5th century*

PLATE 4 – Gold crown and two pendants from the 'Gold Crown Tomb' in Kyŏngju. Old Silla Dynasty, 5th–6th century. *National Museum of Korea. Height of crown 44 cm, diameter 18.3 cm; length of pendant 25 cm. Cf. pp. 81, 84*

reliable historical records, but the tombs in Kyŏngju itself appear to have been those of royalty, or at least of nobles of the first rank.

Let us examine some of the more remarkable finds from the Gold Crown Tomb. The name was given because the first pure gold crown was discovered in this tomb, and the name has been retained although later two further pure gold crowns were found in other tombs by scientific excavations. The crown of the

PLATE P. 83 Gold Crown Tomb is also by far the most elaborate crown so far discovered. The outer part is a circlet of cut sheet-gold decorated with a punched dotted line and saw-tooth pattern. From the front of the circlet rise one central and two flanking uprights of equal height. Each of the uprights is crossed by three trident-shaped bars which look like tree-branches. At the back of the circlet on each side stands a curved upright of greater height than those in front, each with four alternating projections. These curved uprights undoubtedly resemble reindeer antlers. The circlet and the five uprights have altogether fifty-seven comma-shaped jewels of green jade and one hundred and thirty round gold spangles, attached by twisted gold wire. These, when in motion, would create an illusion of great richness. Within the crown, as a central element, is a pointed cap of cut gold from which rise two long wing-like arms. The third element of the crown is the double pendants suspended from each side. The finial has a comma-shaped jewel of green jade with a gold cap which appears to bear an animal face.

The crown has a striking barbaric splendour and is unique in the Far East. A similar gilt-bronze crown has been found in Japan, but this can be said to show Korean influence. Interestingly enough, there seems to be some connection between this gold crown of Silla and a gold diadem found in Novocherkassk, South Russia. On this latter diadem there are whole reindeer and tree-shaped ornaments as well as an eagle. This resemblance in ornamental motifs cannot be merely coincidental. The South Russian diadem can be dated to the 3rd century A.D., Silla's crown roughly to the 5th or 6th century.

A theory has been advanced that this Silla crown has a Shamanistic character. It is implausible that the buried person was a simple shaman, for there is no doubt that the crown came from the tomb of a king or noble. But considering the possibility that Shamanism was the predominant religion of Silla during the Three Kingdoms period, the king or noble might well have used a crown with Shamanistic character. Also it is very likely that the crown was ceremonial and was given to the man only after death, like the bronze shoes which could not conceivably have been worn during his lifetime. In the Gold Crown Tomb a gold girdle with seventeen pendants was also discovered. The symbolism of all these pendants has not yet been explained. A pendant with a flat fish-shaped finial as a kind of amulet, nevertheless, strongly suggests that the girdle also had a Shamanistic character.

Equally splendid are the gold ear-rings. The prettiest of them were discovered in a tomb in Pomun-ni, Kyŏngju, and are all decorated in granule technique with groups of circles and floral designs placed within a framework of hexagons.

Pottery   The pottery of this period has a great similarity to Japanese Iwaibe-type pottery and is found in abundance in every tomb. The colour of this ware is grey with a bluish cast, ranging from lighter to darker tones. The clay is very fine, but sometimes mixed with small pieces of quartz. They were fired at a high temperature, creating a porcelain-like hardness. Glaze was never used in the first period, but very often a so-called natural glaze, produced by accidental contact between blown wood-ash and the clay of the ware during firing, is to be observed. The presence of the ash causes the silicon content of the clay to fuse at a relatively low temperature and form a primitive glaze. The major pottery types are the mounted cup with or without cover and the jar with round or flat bottom, with tall or short neck and with or without attached foot. There are also small figures in the shape of men or animals. A pair of vessels deserve special attention. The pottery figure in the form of a mounted horseman is one of PLATE P. 86 the burial objects in the Gold Bell Tomb. The horseman himself was made separately from his mount. The horse is partly hollow, with a spout in the breast and a cup-shaped funnel on the crop, which indicate that it was a kind of pouring vessel. However, it was probably never used for that purpose. The horseman, with cap and military costume, seems to be a noble, and there is another horseman representing a man of lesser rank. Many objects which were presumed to be horse trappings had previously been found in Silla tombs, but it was for a long time impossible to re-assemble them because all the leather parts had decayed, leaving only the metal pieces. From this ceramic figure it was possible not only to reconstruct the harness, but also to ascertain a great deal more about the customs of the Three Kingdoms period.

Together with this grey pottery, which is usually called Silla pottery, there is a minor group of a different type: light reddish in colour, but very soft, obviously fired at a very low temperature. The types of this group are very simple, mostly round pots or oblong smaller pots with a flat bottom. Though these second types of pottery are found together with the grey pottery in the same tomb, they comprise only a small portion of an entire find of pottery from any tomb.

Some of the most important Buddhist images from this period should be *Buddhist images* examined here. Let us take a Maitreya from the collection of the Tŏksu Palace Museum of Fine Arts and another Maitreya from the collection in the National Museum of Korea. Both figures were traditionally described as being from the Silla Dynasty of the Three Kingdoms period. In fact, however, it is not at all certain whether they really came from the Silla Dynasty or whether they should not rather be considered as products of Paekche.

The plate on page 87 shows the Maitreya of the Tŏksu Palace Museum of Fine PLATE P. 87 Arts, the largest bronze image of this deity from the period. The right elbow rests on the right knee and two fingers of the upraised hand gently touch the cheek. The folds of the drapery are in soft and natural lines, reminiscent of some Maitreya figures of the Northern Ch'i Dynasty in China. The image seems to be intended to be viewed in profile. The graceful line curves slightly over the chest and spreads out gently to reach the base. This Maitreya is also known to have an almost exact duplicate, but in wood, in the Koryuji, Kyoto, Japan. This Japanese counterpart is presumed to have been made by a Korean

PLATE 5 – Vessel in shape of a mounted horseman. Grey clay. From the 'Gold Crown Tomb'. Old Silla Dynasty, 5th–6th century. *National Museum of Korea. Height 25.8 cm, length 29 cm. Cf. p. 85*

artist, or at least under the guidance of a Korean master. The Maitreya of the National Museum is slightly smaller, but is in the same posture as the first one. While the first one is naked to the waist, this one has a scarf covering both shoulders and flaring out over the arms. The expression, with its archaic smile, suggests that the Maitreya of the National Museum could be dated a little earlier than the other one.

PLATE P. 90 There was probably a special cult of Maitreya, as there are so many beautiful Maitreya images of this period. The plate on page 90 shows another Maitreya, very simple in form, the arms almost like pipes. It has nevertheless an elegance never seen in Buddhist images of later ages and gives a vivid impression of a supernatural being.

PLATE 6 – Maitreya. Gilt bronze. Old Silla or Paekche Dynasty, early 7th century. *Tŏksu Palace Museum of Fine Arts. Height 91 cm. Cf. p. 85*

FIG. 8 – *Ch'ŏmsŏng-dae (observatory),
Kyŏngju. Old Silla Dynasty, 7th century. Height 9.29 m*

Ch'ŏmsŏng-dae

FIG. 8

On the outskirts of the modern town of Kyŏngju stands a very interesting stone
structure called Ch'ŏmsŏng-dae, which means 'star observatory'. It was constructed during the reign of the Queen Sŏndŏk (632–647) and is about 9 metres
high and 5 metres in diameter. It has a cylindrical form narrowing at the top,
with an entrance which can be reached only by a ladder reaching half-way up
one side. Two layers of rectangular stone bars are placed on the top and there
is nothing inside the structure except a filling of stone rubble reaching to the
level of the entrance. Unfortunately we have no literary source whatsoever to
show how this oldest astronomical observatory was operated, neither has any
similar object been found in the Far East to be compared with it. But
recent observation has shown that the observatory was built with 364 cut
stones. It is possible that one of the original stones was lost at some stage in the
building's long history, for this is almost exactly the number of days in the year.
This number cannot be a mere coincidence and it appears now to be reasonably
certain that this star observatory had at least some religious purpose besides
the mere observation of constellations. A close study of the observatory might
show us very interesting aspects of the thought of the period.

A second structure of the period is the pagoda of the Punhwangsa, a temple in Kyŏngju. The temple building itself has long since been destroyed, but the pagoda is still standing, though it no longer retains its original form. A record in the Tonggyŏng Chapki says: 'the nine-storeyed pagoda of Punhwangsa is one of the three treasures of Silla. During the Imjin (Hideyoshi) invasion, the enemy destroyed half of it. In later years a stupid monk wanted to rebuild the pagoda and so destroyed the remaining half.' The pagoda is constructed with thin slabs of a special kind of stone and appears to be brick-built, which is the usual form of a pagoda in China. Obviously this is an imitation of the Chinese brick pagoda. In spite of the above record, the present proportions of the pagoda do not look as if the pagoda originally had nine storeys. It now retains only three. On the four sides are doors flanked on either side by guardians in the style of the Six Dynasties of China and the four corners of the terrace on which the pagoda is standing are guarded by stone lions in the same style. The lions are a bit damaged, but they are very powerful sculptures. When the pagoda was restored very interesting objects, including comma-shaped jewels, round beads, tube-like jewels, scissors, a needle-case, and pierced metal ornaments in the style of the period of the Six Dynasties in China, were uncovered in the pagoda body between the second and third storeys.

Pagoda of Punhwangsa

PLATE 7 – Maitreya. Bronze. Three Kingdoms period, 6th century. *Tŏksu Palace Museum of Fine Arts. Height 28.5 cm. Cf. p. 86*

III. GREAT SILLA

Koguryŏ was always the strongest of three Korean kingdoms and undisputedly the most powerful neighbour of the Sui Empire which unified China after many centuries of disruption. Koguryŏ even threatened Sui China by alliance with Turkic nomads in the north Mongolian plains, so Wen-ti of Sui dispatched a great expeditionary army against Koguryŏ in 598. This expedition ended un- *Unification of* successfully, but Sui repeated its attack with even greater force in 612, again *the country* without success. The unpopular and costly expedition against Koguryŏ was the direct cause of the downfall of Sui, which was replaced by the T'ang Dynasty in 618.

Koguryŏ remained powerful, and constituted no less a danger for the new dynasty in China than it had done for the Sui Dynasty. This fact led the Emperor Ta-chung of T'ang to repeat the attack on Koguryŏ several times, but Koguryŏ was always strong enough to repulse the Chinese attacks.

In the meantime there was constant fighting between the three rival Korean kingdoms in the south, especially between Paekche and Silla. When Silla was in a difficult strategic position, she asked T'ang to co-operate against Paekche, whereupon a great Chinese army landed in Korea. Paekche eventually fell to the joint Silla-T'ang army in 660. The joint military operation continued this time against Koguryŏ from the south and, because of internal disunity, Koguryŏ surrendered soon afterwards in 668, thus ending the Three Kingdoms period in Korea.

The conquest of Paekche and Koguryŏ was achieved mainly by the T'ang army and Silla served more or less as an auxiliary force. It was also soon obvious that T'ang intended to absorb the entire Korean peninsula directly into its territory. But the rulers of Silla were clever enough to drive the T'ang forces out eventually and then succeeded in unifying the whole of Korea, starting a new epoch which is now called the Great Silla period.

The Great Silla period carried Korean culture to an unprecedented height. *Influence of* T'ang was one of the most brilliant and prosperous periods in all Chinese *T'ang culture* history and Great Silla's close relationship with T'ang was also very fruitful in the cultural field. Many Korean monks and students went to China and many Chinese priests, artists and scholars came to Korea in return; Buddhism dominated the entire society of the Great Silla period. Splendid temples were constructed throughout the country and a golden age of Korean art was opened which was never again equalled in Korean history. The capital of the Silla Dynasty, the present town of Kyŏngju, was made a duplicate of the capital of the T'ang Empire and luxurious palaces were built for the ruling houses.

But all these structures have long since vanished and we have now only two principal sources of information about the arts of the Great Silla period. One is the tombs which are still to be found in many places in and around Kyŏngju. The other is Buddhist remains in bronze and stone. Korea is rich in stone and there are numerous stone sculptures, stone pagodas and stone foundations of ancient temples. Some bronze and some gold Buddhist images have also survived. From these two principal sources we are relatively well informed about this remarkable period.

Tombs and burial objects

With the unification of the country by the Silla Dynasty a change took place in the construction of tombs. The tomb before unification was the so-called block stone structure, which had actually no tomb-chamber in the true meaning of the word, as the wooden coffin which served as a kind of tomb-chamber decayed easily. This particular construction often prevented the tombs from being looted, as it was quite difficult to reach the burial objects from outside. However, it was unsuitable for a family grave. As the outer coffins decayed easily, and there was also no entrance, no second burial in the same tomb was possible. To overcome this difficulty, a second exactly similar tomb was made beside the old one and constructed like the twin tombs of which one can see so many examples in Kyŏngju to-day.

From the beginning of the Great Silla period, however, tombs were constructed with a tomb-chamber using cut stones: probably the method was taken from Koguryŏ's mounded tombs, which had an entrance and a chamber built with stone slabs. This type of tomb from the Great Silla Dynasty is usually found at the foot of hills or upon the hills themselves. Large mounds like those of King Muyŏl and Kwenung, and the tomb ascribed traditionally to Kim Yu-sin, are each situated at the foot of a mountain and are believed to be tombs with stone chambers. In contrast to the earlier tombs of stone block construction from which we have splendid burial objects, no important objects from the Great Silla period have been uncovered. This may be because the stone chamber tombs were easily broken into and robbed. It is also true that no archaeological investigations have been done on any important tombs of the Great Silla period, because the notable large tombs are also believed to have been robbed of their contents long ago. The Tomb of the Double Funeral Beds, for example, which stands close to tombs of block stone construction in Kyŏngju, was excavated in 1953 by the National Museum of Korea and proved to be from the early Great Silla period, but the burial objects had been taken away by thieves long ago, leaving only a couple of potsherds.

ARCHITECTURE

Pulguksa

PLATE P. 95

The most important Buddhist remains in Korea today are the temple of Pulguksa and Sŏkkuram cave, both dating from the reign of King Kyŏngdŏk (742–764). Pulguksa (Temple of the Buddha Land) is located twelve kilometres to the east of Kyŏngju, at the foot of Toham mountain, and is one of the most ancient of existing Korean temples. The wooden parts of the temple buildings are without exception of the Yi period (1392–1910). But the foundations are from the Silla period, together with two pagodas, a stone lantern and two large images. The temple is built on relatively high double platforms, which are believed to have been surrounded, or at least fronted, by a moat over which were the two bridges (the Blue Cloud Bridge and the White Cloud Bridge)

FIG. 9 – Śākyamuni stūpa, Pulguksa, Kyŏngju. Great Silla Dynasty, 8th century. Height 7.38 m

leading to the stairways and platforms. These bridges symbolically connect our earthly society with the Buddha Land. The platform with its wall has been repeatedly restored, the last time in 1924, and has lost much of its original flavour, but the whole stone structure of platforms and bridges is in perfect harmony with the temple, even though the wooden buildings on the platform are only about three hundred years old, and are by no means architectural masterpieces. The whole complex is unique in the Far East.

When the visitor steps up to the platform after crossing the two bridges, he faces the Main Hall of the temple. In front of the Main Hall are two stone pagodas, of which the right one (as seen from the Main Hall) is called the Śākyamuni FIG. 9 stupa (Sŏkka-t'ap) and the left one the Prabhūta-ratna stupa (Tabo-t'ap). The Śākyamuni stupa, about 7.5 metres high, is simple in form, and has three storeys of fine proportions erected on double platforms. The name Śākyamuni stupa indicates that this pagoda was made to enshrine *śarīra* (relics) of the historic Śākyamuni Buddha. It is surrounded by eight round stones with lotus designs carved in relief. These stones are arranged in a square which symbolizes the holy domain inside; or else each round stone may indicate a seat for any Bodhisattva who might come to adore the Buddha's *śarīra*.

FIG. 10   The Prabhūta-ratna stupa is about 10.5 metres high and has a much elaborated form, of which there is no other example in the Orient. Four stairways on each side lead to the platform on which four corner pillars and one square central pillar support the next storey, which is octagonal and can be divided into three parts: roof, body and base, each of exquisite elegance. The reliquary was no doubt placed under the roof and within the pagoda body, where it is decorated and protected by upturned lotus petals. The fact that, while the first storey of the pagoda has a relatively simple shape, the second storey has square and octagonal railings and inverted lotus petals indicates that the core of the pagoda lies here. The first roof has a simple square shape, but the upper roof is octagonal; above it is a finial that has remained intact.

This kind of temple plan, with two pagodas in front of the Main Hall, seems to have been introduced from T'ang China and is also typical of the temples of the Nara period in Japan. The temple plan of Pulguksa, though nine-tenths of the wooden structures listed in old records have been destroyed, can still be reconstructed from the remaining foundation stones. The middle gate, the

PLATE 8 – Pulguksa, North Kyŏngsang province. Great Silla Dynasty, 8th century. *Cf. p. 92*

pagoda on either side, the lantern, Main Hall and Lecture Hall were all aligned on a north–south axis and the so-called corridor encloses the important parts of the temple. The corridor runs outward from the west and east sides of the middle gate, then turns north, enclosing the two pagodas and the Main Hall. Though it is not very clear, because some foundation stones are missing, the corridor seems to turn inwards again, until it reaches the east and west sides of the Lecture Hall. In the middle of the eastern and western sides of the corridor there are branches of the corridor which lead to the east and west sides of the Main Hall. This middle corridor was not always present in temple plans of the Silla period.

On the left of the main stairways two more stone bridges, similar to the Blue and White Cloud Bridges, lead to a small relatively low platform on which stand an entrance gate (Anyang-mun) and Nirvāna Hall (Kŭngnak-jŏn) with a beautiful stone lantern in front of the Hall. Judging from the remaining foundations this part of the temple was also constructed according to a specific temple plan. But there are too many missing foundation stones to allow us to draw definite conclusions on this point. In the Nirvāna Hall are two large heavy gilt-bronze seated statues: Amitābhā Buddha, 1.65 metres high, and Vairocana Buddha, 1.83 metres high, with their usual *mudrā*. The Vairocana Buddha was originally in the Main Hall, but was moved in 1915 to the present building to be seated side by side with the Amitābhā Buddha. Both figures are very realistic, but have long ears. Their faces have a quiet and gentle air. Until a few years ago they were painted over with white plaster and created a very strange impression. Now that the plaster has been taken off, they wear entirely different expressions.

Sŏkkuram Anyone who visits Pulguksa usually climbs up the hill behind the temple for a little more than half an hour to see Sŏkkuram, the cave-temple, which according to old records was constructed at the same time and by the same minister, Kim Tae-sŏng. The cave-temple houses what are probably some of best stone sculptures of the period in the Far East. Japan has preserved a number of excellent Buddhist sculptures of the period in bronze and wood, but none in stone like these in Korea. No doubt the Koreans got the idea from China, where there are many important caves like Yün-kang or Lung-men — but Sŏkkuram is an artificial cave, covered with earth and only seemingly a part of the hill-side.

PLATE P. 99 Sŏkkuram was restored twice in modern times, from 1913 to 1915 and from 1920 to 1923 by the Japanese Government-General of Korea. Because of insufficient studies of the cave prior to the restoration, we are no longer in a position to say for certain what was its original form. The present form, especially the antechamber, is based very much on imaginary reconstruction and was done rather carelessly. We deplore, as do Japanese scholars, the fact that the well-intended restoration spoiled such an important monument as Sŏkkuram. Connected with the rather small antechamber by a short passage-way, the Main Hall was separated by two octagonal pillars from the rest of the cave. In all probability there was also a gate between the antechamber and the passage-way. The Main Hall is round in shape and the ceiling is domed. Within the rotunda sits a majestic Śākyamuni Buddha, about 3.5 metres high, carved in granite, oriented to the east with the *mudrā* 'calling earth to witness'. The entire wall of Sŏkkuram is lined with granite slabs on which a whole entourage of the Buddha is represented in relief. First, eight Parivāra figures are lined up in the antechamber, four figures on each side, of which one is facing towards the Main Hall. These figures are somewhat stiff and in relatively low relief. Walking through the antechamber towards the passage-way the pilgrim will be faced on both sides by two powerful guards (Vajrapāni) in high relief. With raised fists, they defend the sacred area from the intruder. In the passage-way between the main chamber and antechamber stand the four guardian Deva Kings, two on each side, trampling on demons. All these figures — the Parivāra figures, Vajrapāni and the four guardians — are protectors of the Main Hall and, passing the octagonal pillars, one enters the cave, the Buddha's world. On either side two Devas, one on each side, are represented. Next are two Bodhisattvas, also one on each side. As a rule these two flanking Bodhisattvas to Śākyamuni should be Mañjuśri and Samantabha-

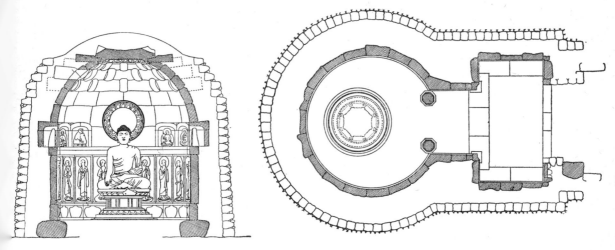

dra. Next to these two Bodhisattvas are ten arhats, five on each side. As usual they all are shaven and have lean, ascetic faces with the long noses of Aryan Indians. They are turned towards one another as if in discussion. In the centre at the back, behind Śākyamuni Buddha, is an outstandingly beautiful sculpture of the eleven-headed Bodhisattva Ekādasamukha. Above these chief figures in niches are eight seated figures of which seven are Bodhisattvas and the last one is Vimalakīrti. Two niches are now empty, the figures probably having been stolen. The execution of these figures is no less refined and beautiful than that of the chief figures.

Sŏkkuram has a total of thirty-seven figures, given their proper places according to their function and rank in the Buddhist pantheon. The architecture is cleverly designed to produce subtle effects by the way the light falls on the individual figures. It also gives the pilgrims space to admire, and walk round, the main figure so that they can see its noble profile. All the figures on the wall are in gentle movement and produce constantly varying impressions according to the various times of the day and month. Sŏkkuram is a splendid architectural achievement and one of the most remarkable sculptural masterpieces in all Asia.

The main Buddha of Sŏkkuram, Śākyamuni, is seated facing toward the east in eternal watch over the Eastern Sea. It is believed that here the main Buddha is facing east to defend the Silla Empire against Japanese pirates. There are many indications that Buddhism in Silla had strong patriotic aspects. For instance, the temples of Sach'ŏnwangsa and Kamunsa were built, so say historical records, to help Silla's defence against aggression.

Kamunsa was located right on the coast of the Eastern Sea about 16 kilometres from Sŏkkuram. The *Samguk Yusa*, one of the oldest Korean historical records, says about Kamunsa: 'King Munmu wanted to defeat the soldiers of Japan, so he began the construction of the temple. Before completing it, he died and

FIG. 11

Kamunsa

became a sea dragon. His son, Sinmun, became king and completed the temple in the second year of K'ai-yao (682). Under the Golden Hall a hole was dug toward the Eastern Sea so that the dragon could enter the temple and crawl around in it. The place where the bones (of the late king) were preserved, in accordance with his will, was called Taewang-am (the Rock of the Great King). The name of the temple is Kamunsa. The place where later the dragon appeared was called Yigyŏn-dae.'

The temple itself was burned down long ago, but the foundation stones and two giant stone pagodas in front of them remain. The archaeological excavation on the site of the temple and the restoration of the western pagoda has shown that the above historical record was not entirely fantastic; there was evidence which showed that the stone floor of the temple was actually constructed so as to make it possible for a dragon to crawl in under the floor.

The temple of Kamunsa has almost exactly the same plan as that of Pulguksa. It has two pagodas in front of the Main Hall. The corridor encloses the whole temple, as in the case of Pulguksa, and there is also a middle corridor. Our great concern, however, is with the relics (śarīra-container) which were found in the third storey of the pagoda and have thrown new light on the Buddhist art of the period.

The purpose of the pagoda in front of the Main Hall of a Buddhist temple is to enshrine the śarīra of Buddha or some well-known Buddhist monk. The so-called śarīra was in reality a tiny crystal-like object the size of a grain of millet. This was usually put in a glass or crystal bottle, which in turn was placed in an elaborate container often embellished with all kinds of decoration.

PLATE P. 102

In the western of the two pagodas of Kamunsa we found a bronze case to enshrine the śarīra-container. On the four sides of the case are sculptures of four guardian gods, one on each side. The lower parts of two of these figures are damaged, but on the whole they are well preserved. The guardian god of the north, Vaiśravana, has strikingly similar features to some figures on the wall-paintings found in Turkestan by Le Coq, Aurel Stein and others. The guardian in armour is standing on a fat little devil and holding a pagoda in his right hand. No doubt the frequent travels of Korean monks to China and India explain this interesting Turkestan influence.

FIG. 12

The śarīra-container within the case rests on a bronze platform with a railing. On each side of the base of the platform are two niches, each with little figures. Inside the railing sit four small figures playing music at each corner of the platform. One has a flute, the second a cymbal, the third a zither, and the last a drum. The śarīra rests in a crystal bottle under a cover richly decorated with lotus-petals. Between the railing and the centre of the platform are four small standing figurines, flattened in shape, rising out of lotus flowers. This is the so-called Aupapaduka, rebirth in the Land of Buddha by transformation through the lotus flower. The scene on the platform symbolizes the Land of Buddha where the śarīra rests, surrounded by divine musicians playing music, guarded and worshipped by gods outside.

There are still in South Korea more than two hundred stone pagodas, which

PLATE 9 – Buddha in cave-temple at Sŏkkuram, Kyŏngju. Great Silla Dynasty, 8th century. *Height of Buddha including pedestal 5.15 m. Cf. p. 96*

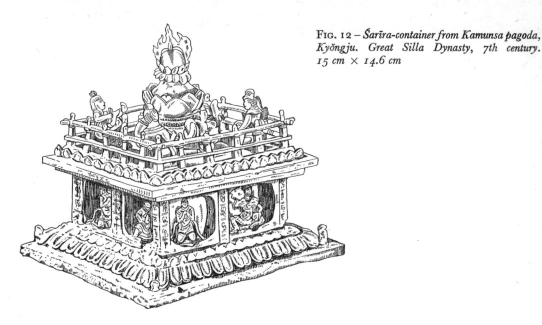

were originally erected in temple precincts. Today most of the temples have gone, leaving only pagodas in the middle of rice-fields or at the foot of mountains. At these pagodas, as at the pagoda of Kamunsa, bronze Buddhist figures have often been found. We believe that many of the small bronze statuettes preserved today probably came from stone pagodas.

Pagoda of Kuhwang-ni and its finds

The pagoda of Kuhwang-ni in Kyŏngju preserved two beautiful pure gold Buddhist figures together with a long bronze casket which contained the relics. The inscription, with the date 706 A.D., mentions only one Amitābhā figure, but there were two Buddhist images, neither of which concurs with the measurements mentioned in the inscription or has the usual characteristics of Amitābhā. The first one is a standing figure on a pedestal in lotus form, height approx. 13.5 cm. The right hand is raised in a gesture of blessing, the left grasps a part of the long robe. The halo is executed in open-work. Judging from the expression this figure seems to be slightly earlier than the other seated figure.

PLATE P. 103

The second image is seated and consists of three parts: the figure of Buddha, the lotus pedestal, and the complex aureole. The base and the figure are hollow cast. The whole statuette reflects rather the influence of T'ang China and we are fortunate to know the date 706 A.D. when both images were placed in the pagoda. The style fits excellently into the general scheme of the early 8th century.

Besides the two golden Buddhas the large bronze casket contained a śarīra-bottle with śarīra (the bottle was broken), a small golden box, a small silver box, many small glass beads including bead bracelets, two mounted cups in gold and two in silver, some gold strings, a flat piece of glass, several as yet unidentified glass objects, and many pieces of bamboo. How all these things were grouped together inside the bronze casket was difficult to reconstruct, as it was filled

FIG. 13 – *Rubbing of the great bronze bell, Kyŏngju. Great Silla Dynasty, 8th century. National Museum of Korea. Greatly reduced*

with dirt inside and all the objects were lying about in disorder. In any case the finds from both the pagoda of Kuhwang-ni and of Kamunsa were excellent examples of how śarīra were installed in the stone pagodas of the early Great Silla period. A comparative study of similar finds in Japan is most desirable.

One of the best known objects in Kyŏngju is the big bronze bell now at the Kyŏngju branch of the National Museum of Korea. The bell has a very long inscription. It was originally at the ancient temple of Pongdŏksa and was cast in 771 A.D. during the reign of King Hyegong. It has a diameter of 2.28 metres and is 3.35 metres high.

Great bronze bell
FIG. 13

Korean bells have entirely different features from Japanese or Chinese bells, which have a decoration of cord in such a way as to divide the surface into many sections, or, to put it another way, to look as if the bell were tied with cords. Korean bells seem to have been developed independently and have no such cord decoration on the surface.

The Kyŏngju bell has an arabesque pattern at the top and bottom; around the crown there are four squares, each supplied with nine nipples. Below are two pairs of flying angels, facing each other with incense-burners in their hands. They are set upon lotus flowers and the stalks of the flowers and the angels' draperies appear like flying clouds. These graceful angels, beautifully cast in bas-relief, have made the bell world-famous.

PLATE 10 – Vaiśravana, Guardian God of the North. From Kamunsa near Kyŏngju. Great Silla Dynasty, 8th century. *National Museum of Korea. Height 21.5 cm. Cf. p. 98*

PLATE 11 – Buddha. Gold statuette on gilt-bronze pedestal. Found in pagoda of Kuhwang-ni in Kyŏngju. Great Silla Dynasty. *National Museum of Korea. Height 12 cm. Cf. p. 100*

IV. KORYŎ DYNASTY

HISTORY Silla society began to disintegrate towards the end of the 8th century A.D. There were frequent quarrels among the nobles about the succession to the throne and as a result there were as many as twenty kings during a period of about a hundred and fifty years, many of whom were assassinated.

But the disintegration of Silla became acute from the time of Queen Chinsŏng (887–897). The main cause of trouble was discontent among the peasants who suffered most from the luxury of the nobles and the general demoralization of society. They were separated from their land and became slaves of the nobility. Some became robbers and joined various organized bands which began to threaten the state.

Among these bands the one led by Kung'ye was most powerful. But Kung'ye was very ruthless, and one of his followers named Wang Kŏn turned against him and proclaimed himself king in 918. He founded the Koryŏ Dynasty, which was to rule Korea for about five hundred years. In contrast to other armed rebels of those times, he was very lenient in his treatment of the defeated ruling class of Silla, and even gave his own daughter in marriage to the last king of Silla. But officially the last Silla king surrendered to him in 935. As already stated the transfer of power took place peacefully, and no destruction occurred in the Silla capital.

Buddhism The dominant religion was Buddhism. It was no longer considered foreign, but had become deeply rooted in the soul of the people. The printing of the huge Buddhist Tripitaka took four generations. As was the case with Silla Buddhism, such a tremendous enterprise as printing the whole Tripitaka was connected with a worldly desire: to protect the country by securing the help of Buddha. With the same idea in mind many new temples were built. Kaesŏng alone had at least seventy. Many Buddhist ceremonies took place on a grand scale and were attended by all the royal and noble families.

Geomancy Besides Buddhism and Confucianism, which also began to gain in strength, there was another traditional Oriental idea which dominated Koryŏ society more than any other religious belief for many hundreds of years. This was geomancy. According to this theory geographical environment, the location of cities, palaces, living quarters, and even graves of ancestors had a direct influence on people's destiny. If a country had its capital in the right geographical environment, it would prosper. The fortunes of a man depended on the location of his house or of the graves of his ancestors. Palaces, official government buildings, temples, and private houses were erected according to geomancy. For example: Manwŏltae, the place where Koryŏ's palace was built in Kaesŏng, was chosen in accordance with these principles.

Movable type Among the many things Koreans are still proud of today is the invention of movable metallic printing type during the Koryŏ Dynasty. The use of movable type was certainly an epoch-making invention, as Korea's great neighbour China was still using only block printing. The idea of type as such originated in China. A man named P'i Sheng, of the Sung Dynasty, is said to have made printing type of clay mixed with glue. But actually these Chinese clay types were never widely used and remained an interesting novelty.

The Koreans, on the other hand, made metallic movable type some time in the latter part of the 12th century or in the early 13th century, two centuries earlier than Gutenberg in Europe, developed the technique steadily and printed many learned books. This important aid to cultural activity contributed a great deal to the intellectual development of Korea in later centuries. In fact movable type printing was more and more widely used thereafter; government publications in particular were in later days printed by movable type made of wood or bronze.

This does not mean that Koreans stopped block printing altogether. Block printing might seem to have been less efficient than type printing. But this was not always the case. In the printing process the type had to be lined up in glue placed on a board, and was easily disarranged by the pressure used in the printing process; it therefore had to be corrected and re-aligned after each impression. In addition the surface was not always evenly flat as in block printing. Block printing has, on other hand, its own strong point: once the laborious job of engraving was completed the printing process was extremely easy and the blocks could be kept for many hundreds of years, like the thirteenth-century Tripitaka blocks which are still at Haein-sa.

As a small country Korea needed many kinds of books, but only a limited number of copies of each, for the small number of scholars and officials; for that purpose type printing was ideal, and thus type printing made such great progress in Korea by the end of the Koryŏ Dynasty and early Yi Dynasty.

Unfortunately no example of the type-printed material of the Koryŏ Dynasty has survived. The earliest extant example of bronze type printing is to be dated 1403, eleven years after the fall of the Koryŏ Dynasty. There is, however, one surviving example of printing by movable wooden type which predates bronze type by six years. It was used for printing citations for people who earned merit by their assistance in establishing the new dynasty.

The Koryŏ period may be divided into three different phases in order to examine its politics and culture. The first phase covers about one hundred years (918–1031) during which time the dynasty was consolidating its power. To the north the state of Liao was beginning to invade neighbouring countries, including Koryŏ, for whom defence became a serious problem. THREE PHASES

During the second phase Koryŏ had to fight the Chin, who had won control of Liao in China, and eventually Koryŏ had to surrender (1126). In spite of these desperate struggles Koryŏ maintained close contact with the Southern Sung, and received great cultural stimulation from them. The famous Koryŏ potteries attained their highest glory about this time.

In China, meanwhile, the Mongols replaced the Chin and invaded Koryŏ with

PLATE 12 – Kyŏngch'ŏnsa pagoda. Koryŏ Dynasty, 14th century. *Now in Seoul. Height 15.38 m. Cf. p. 108*

a huge military force such as had never been seen before. The Koryŏ king decided in 1232 to move the capital to Kanghwa Island, which was located barely half a mile away from the mainland but could not be conquered by the Mongols, who had no seamanship even across such a narrow channel. Kanghwa is a small island and the Koryŏ court stayed there for thirty-eight years, until 1270. During these years Kanghwa was transformed into a second Kaesŏng with all kinds of luxury. Palaces, mansions, and temples were constructed and there was a continuous round of feasts. Some of the finest celadon wares were produced and the tremendous undertaking of printing the Tripitaka was carried out with greatest care.

The refugee life of a government, however, could not continue indefinitely, and because of increasing difficulties in the country, King Wŏnjong left the island in 1270 to face the facts as they were; he went back to Kaesŏng and placed the country under complete Mongol domination. From this year until the end of the dynasty, during which time Koryŏ had to accept Mongol interference in all its domestic affairs and even to follow Mongol customs in daily life, we designate as the third phase of Koryŏ history.

Two different architectural styles prevailed in Korea during the Koryŏ period. The first is called Chusimp'o, which seems already to have been widely in use for some time; it underwent some modification during the Koryŏ Dynasty. The Chusimp'o of Koryŏ has some similarity with the Tenjikuyo in Japan, which actually means 'Indian style', though in reality it has nothing to do with India. Tenjikuyo was obviously brought to Japan from the coastal provinces of South China during the Southern Sung Dynasty. It is difficult to say in what way the Chusimp'o style of Koryŏ was influenced by contemporary Chinese architecture. ARCHITECTURE

The distinguishing feature of Chusimp'o style is that all the bracketing which carries the beams of the eaves springs directly from the top of the pillars, so that the weight is borne by the axis of the column. In the second, Tap'o, style, there are more brackets. A beam is laid across the top of the pillars, and more brackets are placed on this beam, some of them over the spaces between the pillars. These brackets then bear the weight of the eave beams themselves. The number of brackets varies according to the width of the bay.

Bracketing was originally a mere technical device to support the heavy eaves, but it also became an ornament to the building. As such it became one of the most important artistic parts of buildings in the Far East and often characterized a certain style and period.

The Chusimp'o style, in addition to the difference in bracketing, had a difference in the interior of the building. It had a simple beamed ceiling exposing the roof and brackets. Therefore the wooden parts were usually highly decorated. In the Tap'o style an extra ceiling made of wood concealed the roofing and bracketing. Most of the extant Koryŏ Dynasty buildings are of the Chusimp'o type. The Main Hall, Muryangsu-jŏn, of Pusŏksa in North Kyongsang province is probably the oldest still preserved. The building bears a calligraphic inscription

Pusŏksa

dated 1376, but the actual date of construction seems to have been a century and a half earlier.

It is a relatively small building. The columns show entasis like the columns of the Kondo in the Horyuji at Nara, Japan. In the interior is a double row of columns supporting the inner cross beam. The floor is of brick. The entire building gives a feeling of great simplicity with the gentle rotundity of its beautifully curved columns.

Pagodas
PLATE P. 106

Many stone pagodas have survived. A typical and rare specimen is the ten-storeyed pagoda of Kyŏngch'ŏnsa which originally stood near Kaesŏng, but has now been re-erected in the garden of Kyŏngbok Palace in Seoul. According to the testimonial inscription, the pagoda was erected in 1348 in honour of the emperor, empress and crown prince of the Yüan Dynasty, which was then the suzerain power of Koryŏ. It has the pillar-like slenderness and carpentry details which we often meet in some monuments of the Yangtze region. It is made of grey marble and has, on the surface of every storey, sculptured Buddhist figures, flowers and animals. It is a unique example of the Yüan type of stone pagoda in Korea. It is very possible that Yüan craftsmen worked on this pagoda. There is another similar one in Pagoda Park in Seoul. But this one is of a much later date and obviously a copy of the first.

FIG. 14

Another small pagoda from North Ch'ungch'ŏng province is also now in the Kyŏngbok Palace grounds. It was built to contain the ashes of the priest Hong-bŏp in 1017. The first pedestal is octagonal, while the second, much more complicated pedestal has up-turned and down-turned lotus petals as ornaments and supports a slightly flattened stone ball.

SCULPTURE AND
PAINTING

Buddhism enjoyed unprecedented wealth and prosperity. Splendid Buddhist temples were constructed throughout the country and many Buddhist images were made. But the golden age of Buddhist art had definitely passed with the end of Great Silla and such beautiful images as we have seen from that period were never made again.

Of the few remaining Buddhist sculptures we have the great life-size Amitābhā in the Muryangsu-jŏn of Pusŏksa as a vestige of the glorious past. The figure is of clay, which is made durable by having hempen cloth worked into it to bind the substance. It faces east and has a wooden halo. The facial expression is rather stiff, but on the whole it is well balanced and has a refined dignity which can seldom be seen in Koryŏ figures. The drapery is very free and the execution is skilful, resembling that of the sculpture of Sung and Yüan China. The wooden halo has a design of honeysuckle moulded on it in the clay and hempen cloth technique, but its border has a flame design carved in the wood. It is a rare work to be preserved from this period. Beyond any doubt the figure was contemporary with the Muryangsu-jŏn itself; that is to say, it is a work of the middle phase of the Koryŏ Dynasty.

Painting

The Koryŏ Dynasty annals mention many names of good painters, but especially that of Yi Nyŏng, during the reign of King Injong (1123–1146). He visited Sung China and his painting was very much admired by the famous artist Emperor Hui-tsung. It is to be assumed from this and other literary sources that

many Korean artists visited China to get new inspiration and to study technique so that Koryŏ paintings were constantly influenced by China. The best known artist of Koryŏ is, however, King Kongmin (1352–1374) who is said to have executed very delicate paintings. Among many paintings by his hand the following titles are recorded in literature: Śākyamuni coming out of the mountains, a portrait of the princess Noguk (his wife), Dharma crossing the sea on a reed, and the Afang Palace. But none of these works has been preserved. Only one painting attributed to him has survived: 'Hunting in the Tien Shan Mountains'. This painting is now cut up into several parts: two parts of it belong to the Tŏksu Palace Museum of Fine Arts and one part to the National Museum of Korea, while yet another portion is in the library of Seoul National University. Unfortunately the condition of the painting is very poor, but one can distinguish the delicate and free handling of mounted hunters in a hilly landscape, and is reminded of some Yüan landscapes and paintings of horses.

Many kings of the Koryŏ Dynasty about this time were married to Mongol princesses, and many of them spent a number of years at the Yüan court. King Chungsŏng (1309–1313), for instance, lived almost the entire period of his reign in the Yüan capital and invited to his house, which was called the Pavilion of Ten Thousand Books, noted scholars and painters, among others Chao Meng-fu, the famous Yüan painter. Under these circumstances it was only natural that Koryŏ painting should always have been greatly influenced by contemporary Chinese painting.

Wall-painting   The oldest Koryŏ painting is, however, the wall-painting of guardian gods and Bodhisattvas preserved in the Chosa-dang of Pusŏksa. It is painted on a blue-green ground in reddish-brown colour with simple and graceful brushwork. The figures are beautifully balanced and the colour is delightful. No doubt this wall-painting is of the same date as the building of the Chosa-dang, which was constructed in 1377.

There are a few more Buddhist paintings of the Koryŏ Dynasty, some preserved in Japan, some in various museums in America and Europe. Most of them are from the end of the dynasty and seem not to represent the best painting of the period, but still show some freedom in brushwork of subtle rhythmic lines, with an archaic quietness in facial expression.

DECORATIVE AND   The Koryŏ Dynasty left to posterity very little sculpture and, as we have seen,
APPLIED ARTS   few paintings. Its strength lies rather in decorative and applied arts. In the Koryŏ tombs which were frequently opened by robbers searching for previous burial objects various works of art of extreme importance were sometimes found. A bronze *chŏngbyŏng*, or water-sprinkler, belonging to the National Museum of Korea, is of unusual beauty, with beautiful inlaid decoration. The major decoration shows an idyllic scene of willow-trees, with ducks and geese partly in the water. All the decorations are inlaid with silver. As the bronze body has developed a powdery green patina, the white silver-inlaid designs now stand out more distinctly and delicately.

Ceramic ware   Among all Korean works of art the ceramic wares of the Koryŏ Dynasty are the most popular and widely known. A Sung Dynasty Chinese scholar said that the colour of Koryŏ wares was among the most wonderful things in the world: 'The books of the Academy, the wines of the palace, the ink-stones from Tuan Chi, the ink of Huichou, the white peonies of Lo-Yang, the tea of Chien-chou, and the secret colour of Koryŏ are all first under Heaven.'

Hsü Ching   Similarly, a Chinese scholar named Hsü Ching, who accompanied the Sung envoy to Korea in 1123, describes in his famous travel account Koryŏ ceramic wares as follows: 'The ceramic wares are green (*ch'ing*) in colour and are called "kingfisher-coloured" by the people of Koryŏ. In recent years they have been made with great skill, and their colour is specially fine. There are melon-shaped wine-jugs with small lids surmounted by ducks seated on lotus flowers. There are also bowls and dishes, wine-cups and tea bowls, flower-vases and hot-water bowls, all copied from Ting ware... Only the wine-jugs are of novel and original design. There are incense-burners shaped like lions which are also "kingfisher-coloured". The animal crouches on top supported by a lotus. This is the best and most striking of all the ceramic vessels; the others generally resemble the old Pi-se ware of Yüeh-chou and the new ware of Ju-chou.'

This brief passage written about eight hundred years ago by a contemporary Chinese scholar tells us a great deal about Koryŏ ceramic art. It gives many clues to various problems in regard to the development of Koryŏ wares.

Both in China and Korea the five centuries from the beginning of the tenth century to the end of fourteenth constituted the golden age of ceramic art. In China during this period fine celadons and white porcelains were produced at such famous factories as Yüeh-chou, Ting-chou, Tz'u-chou and Ching-tê-chên. At first the ceramic art of the Koryŏ period was influenced by that of Sung China, combining classical style with remarkable proficiency in technique. The elegant shapes, rich colour and unique inlay of Koryŏ pottery stand out as major achievements in this field.

The development of Koryŏ pottery may be divided into four periods:

Four periods of Koryŏ pottery

(a) *Transitional period.* This period covers the beginning of the Koryŏ Dynasty, comprising roughly the tenth century, when the so-called Silla pottery and low fired greenish, dark brown glazed wares were made. Examples of it are very scarce. By the end of the century the prototype of celadon ware had made its appearance. The brownish-yellow jar covered with an olive glaze of pre-celadon type in the collection of the museum of Ehwa Women's University bears an inscription dated 993 which suggests that true celadon may first have been made only in the 11th century.

(b) *Period of Chinese influence.* From about the end of the tenth century Koryŏ pottery began to reflect the influence of Chinese celadon, both in the shape of the vessels and in the technique. This period lasted about 150 years. The wares have a light greyish and brownish-green colour; they especially recall Yüeh wares. Towards the end of the period a quiet undecorated but beautiful celadon glaze appeared, and in the early part of the twelfth century white porcelain and painted celadon were also produced. Influences from Ting-chou, Tz'u-chou and Ching-tê-chên are clearly recognizable.

(c) *Period of distinct Korean wares.* By the twelfth century Koryŏ ceramic art had become independent of Chinese influence. This period lasts about a hundred and sixty years, from the reign of Uijong (1147–1170), when the first inlaid ware was made, until the end of the reign of Ch'ung'yŏl (1275–1308).

The typically Korean celadon with inlaid technique was first made under King Uijong and continued to be made until the end of the dynasty. But the best glaze, decoration and shape were produced some time between 1150 and the end of the thirteenth century. Various kinds of decoration were applied, especially cranes and clouds, willow-trees and ducks, which can be called typically Korean. White porcelains, celadon with under-glaze iron, and black wares were also produced.

(d) *Period of degeneration.* The time from the beginning of the fourteenth century to the end of the dynasty can be called a period of degeneration. By the end of the thirteenth century a fresh wave of influence from Yüan China had reached Korea. This found expression in novel designs and methods of decoration, but it undermined the native tradition. With the decadence of the nation, the brilliant achievement of Koryŏ celadon ware had become a thing of the past by the end of the fourteenth century. In shape, glaze and feeling, Koryŏ wares were deteriorating rapidly so that none of the pieces of this period can be called good, although besides pure celadon wares inlaid wares, white porcelains and black Koryŏ wares also continued to be made.

Koryŏ porcellaneous wares can be divided into groups according to different methods of manufacture, decoration and glaze.

Plain celadon　This is celadon without any decoration on the surface. But wares with incised or relief decoration are usually considered as closely linked to this group. This type was manufactured in greater quantity than any other wares throughout the whole Koryŏ period. Early celadon clearly reflects Chinese Yüeh wares of the Five Dynasties and Sung periods, and shows great affinity in decoration and motifs with them. It has a dark brownish-green colour. Soon, however, the distinctive and beautiful Korean bluish-green glaze was developed, which was called 'kingfisher-coloured', *pisaek* (Chinese: *pi-se*). It originated in the late 10th century and continued to the end of the dynasty.

PLATE P. 113　The wine-jug with incised decoration in the shape of a lotus bud has the typical celadon colour, although the surface of the lower part disintegrated slightly during the long period it was buried in the tomb, so that its original beauty suffered slightly. Pottery in this particular shape is rare, and this object can be classified to the earlier wares of the 11th century. From the period when this wine-jug was made to the middle of the 12th century celadon wares made rapid progress, as Hsü Ching rightly recorded in his travel account.

PLATE P. 115　The potters produced celadons not only with incised or impressed decoration, but also vessels in human or animal form. The water-dropper for use with an ink-stone made in the form of a monkey holding its baby in its arms is an excellent sample of its kind. The eyes and nose of the adult and the eyes of the baby are painted in under-glaze iron. The quality and colour of the celadon is superb. It is a product of the best period of Koryŏ porcelains, before the invention of inlaid wares.

PLATE P. 116　Another example of the kind is the water-dropper in the form of a duck holding a twisted lotus-stem in its bill. The eyes are marked with under-glaze iron. This typical bluish-green coloured duck of the first half of 12th century was much admired by Hsü Ching. The feathers are so delicately and realistically modelled that no sculptor could hope to model them better than this Koryŏ potter.

Inlaid celadon　The technique of inlaying porcelain was invented by Korean potters. This was a method of decoration in which the pattern was first incised and then filled in with white or black slip. Any excess slip was smoothed away and the vessel was fired. After this it was covered with a celadon glaze and re-fired. According to some authorities, however, only a single firing took place and there was no preliminary low-temperature firing. Sometimes iron or copper oxides were used for additional decoration: the copper produced a reddish colour after the firing, while the iron produced a rust colour. This technique was probably developed about the middle of the twelfth century and was not yet in production when Hsü Ching visited Koryŏ in 1124.

PLATE P. 117　The first datable inlaid ware was found in a tomb with an epitaph bearing a date corresponding to 1159. This bowl, however, has already reached the height of inlaid technique, and it has therefore been assumed that this inlaid technique was commonly applied at a much earlier date than 1159. However, as Hsü Ching did not mention in his travel account the existence of inlaid ware in 1123,

PLATE 13 – Wine-jug with lid. Celadon glaze, modelled and incised decoration. Koryŏ Dynasty. *National Museum of Korea. Height 29 cm, diameter at base 20 cm. Cf. p. 112*

the invention must have been made some time between the two dates, probably soon after Hsü Ching's visit.

It should be noted that in the case of this bowl a special inlaying technique was applied. The bowl was decorated inside with elaborate reverse inlay in white. This means that the actual pattern is not inlaid, but the white inlaid part forms the ground for the pattern. This reverse technique shows clearly that this celadon bowl demonstrates a very advanced stage of development.

The inlaid wares came into full flower in the latter half of the 12th century and excellent wares also continued to be produced in the first half of the 13th century. All the extant inlaid wares of the highest quality were produced during a period of little more than one hundred and fifty years.

PLATE P. 118   The water-sprinkler can be classified as one of the best of all Koryŏ inlaid wares. One never meets anywhere a better colour than this bluish-green. All the typically Korean decorations – willow-tree, reeds, lotus and ducks—are represented here in white inlay, with the exception of the duck's eyes.

White porcelain   This technique was known from an early date as a result of the importation of Sung white wares. Koryŏ white porcelain exhibits either the bluish tone of Chinese Ying-ch'ing or the ivory colour of T'ang ware. Incised or impressed decoration was the rule, but sometimes open-work designs or inlaying were employed. Western scholars long questioned whether any of the white porcelains found in Korea were actually made there, but unfired white porcelains dating from the Koryŏ period were eventually found at a kiln-site; this proved that they were made in Korea.

PLATE P. 119   The white *maebyŏng* is unique in having inlaid celadon panels in each of the six lobes of the vase. The inlaid designs in the panels are willow, reed, heron and peony, all motifs which characterized the 12th century. The doubt that Koreans ever produced white porcelains during the Koryŏ Dynasty can also be dispelled by this white porcelain, with panels inlaid with such typically Korean motifs. The form of the vase is slightly distorted by too high a temperature in firing. Is this because the clay used for white porcelain cannot resist the heat usually required for celadon wares? At any rate, this piece is a unique combination of inlaid celadon ware and white porcelain.

Painted celadon   With the decline of the Koryŏ celadon wares in the latter part of the 13th century, northern Chinese Tz'u-chou pottery of the Yüan Dynasty came into Korea and many painted Koryŏ wares were produced. Typical in this case is the fact that the same celadon glaze was applied to Korean painted wares. The colour is usually yellowish-dark green. This type continued to be produced until the end of the dynasty.

Iron black ware   This is often mistaken for black glazed ware. It was made with the same greyish clay as that used for ordinary celadon. However, it was first coated with iron pigment before application of the glaze. Some pieces are plain, without decoration, but others have an incised pattern showing through the iron pigment, with the result that the grey colour of the body stands out against the dark background and often assumes a green tone owing to the glaze being of

PLATE 14 – Water-dropper, used to dilute ink, in the form of a monkey holding its young. Celadon glaze, modelled and under-glaze iron decoration. *Chun Hyung-pil Collection. Height 10 cm. Cf. p. 112*

PLATE 15 – Water-dropper in the form of a duck. Celadon glaze. Koryŏ Dynasty, 12th century. *Chun Hyung-pil Collection. Length 12.9 cm. Cf. p. 112*

the celadon type. This type is said to have originated in the late 12th century and disappeared in the early 14th century.

Iron glazed ware   The red and brown colour of this pottery is caused by the high percentage of iron in the glaze. Usually the surface was left plain, without decoration. There are some examples with a pattern made by scraping away the background and filling this in with white slip.

Black glazed ware   This is pottery with a thick glaze of black or dark brown colour, known by the Japanese name *temmoku*. It is not quite certain when this type of ware was first made. Judging from the existing examples, they may have originated in the late 12th century and continued to be made until the end of the dynasty.

Miscellaneous ware   Pottery with glazes of various other colours was also made during the late Koryŏ period. A few examples are known where inlaid celadons were gilded: that is to say, the designs were outlined in gold over the glaze. It was believed

PLATE 16 – Bowl. Celadon glaze, inlaid decoration. Koryŏ Dynasty, mid-12th century. *National Museum of Korea. Height 6 cm, diameter 16.8 cm. Cf. p. 112*

that this was in fashion during the early 13th century for roughly fifty years. There are also specimens which have designs painted in thick white slip so that the decoration appears embossed under the glaze. Other types of ware were sprayed with iron glaze or coated with a layer of lacquer, and a few specimens of marbled ware have also been found. However, celadon was without question the main product throughout the period.

PLATE 17 – Ewer or water-sprinkler. Celadon glaze, inlaid decoration. Koryŏ Dynasty, late 12th century. *Chun Hyung-pil Collection. Height 36 cm, diameter at base 9 cm. Cf. p. 114*

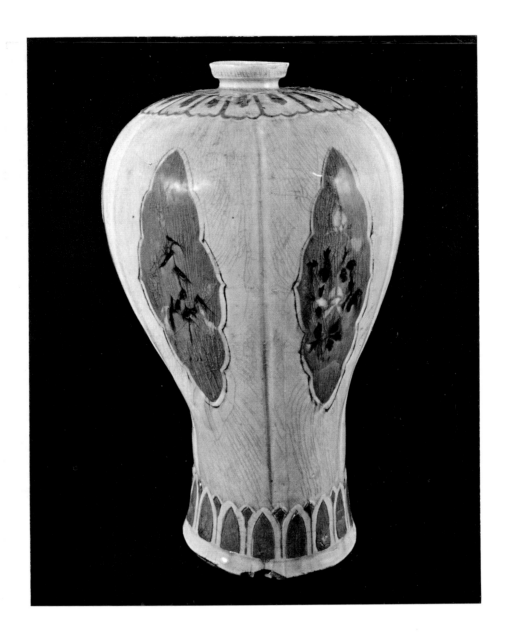

PLATE 18 – Vase, probably from Puan. White porcelain; six inlaid panels with celadon glaze. Koryŏ Dynasty, 12th–13th century. *Tŏksu Palace Museum of Fine Arts. Height 28.7 cm, diameter at base 10.4 cm.* *Cf. p. 114*

and Confucianism the only suitable subject for a literary man. Koreans today take great pride in the Korean alphabet, devised under the direction of King Sejong and promulgated by him in 1446; it is widely regarded as being the most scientific system of writing in general use in any country, almost perfect for writing the Korean language, and the finest product of the Korean intellectual genius. However, the Confucians called it 'women's writing' or 'common people's writing', and many scholars of Korean literature now feel that there was very little in the Korean language which could really be called literature until very recently, that in fact Korean literature under the Yi Dynasty was Chinese literature.

Non-Buddhist art The chief source of artistic impulse and imagination in Korea had been, beyond doubt, Buddhism, and every branch of fine arts has been connected with Buddhist belief. Now that Buddhism was stripped of its traditional favour, worldly-oriented Confucianism, with its examination system and strong bureaucratism, dominated intellectual society, and left little room for free-thinking creative artists. No great art could be produced in such a society. All the artists were dependent on government officials and survived at the mercy of the *yangban* class. The Office of Arts, the chief pool of Yi Dynasty artists, mainly painted portraits of *yangban*, enjoying thereby only a meagre possibility of existence.

ARCHITECTURE While only a handful of examples of Koryŏ Dynasty architecture has been preserved many structures, religious and profane, have survived from the Yi Dynasty. There are city gates, palace buildings, Confucian shrines, schools and temples. Representative city gates are the South Gate (1396) and East Gate (1869) of Seoul, the South Gate (1394) of Kaesŏng, the Pot'ongmun (1756) of P'yŏngyang and the P'altalmun (1796) of Suwŏn, among others. Of all these the South Gate of Seoul is the most impressive and representative building of the early Yi Dynasty. The lower part of the gate was made of granite blocks and the two-storeyed pavilion stands on it. It is a tap'o-style building, like all other Yi Dynasty buildings, and seems to have been restored twice during its long history. There are indications that the style of the roof was changed by later restoration.

Palaces in Seoul There are several palaces in Seoul, the Kyŏngbok Palace, Tŏksu Palace and Changdŏk Palace being now the most important. The Kyŏngbok Palace was constructed in the third year of Yi Sŏnggye (1394), surrounded by a palace wall and composed of nearly one hundred small and large buildings. It was, however, burned down during the Hideyoshi invasion by the irate citizens and remained in ruins for nearly two hundred and fifty years. The whole palace was rebuilt by Prince Regent Taewŏn-gun in 1867. Today most of the buildings have been torn down, leaving only a few of the important ones.

The Kŭnjŏng-jŏn (Throne Hall) is the most stately looking and largest building remaining from the Yi Dynasty. It is built upon double-tiered platforms of dressed stones, which are surrounded on all four sides by carved railings and have stone steps at the centre of each side. The central and main stone steps in front of the Throne Hall are elaborately decorated with phoenix designs, symbols of royal power. Just below the steps in the front yard are two lines of ranking stones for civilians and military. The interior of the hall is impressively decorated with a dragon in the centre of the ceiling, and the whole building gives an impression of dignity and grandeur; close observation, however, shows that the details of the building were worked rather crudely and with little care. Originally the palace had a magnificent central entrance gate (Kwanghwa-mun) in front of the Throne Hall. That gate was moved to the east side of the palace so that the ugly modern building of the Japanese Government-General of Korea might be built on its site, and the gate itself was unfortunately burned down during the Korean War in 1951.

Many Confucian shrines and schools were constructed throughout the country *Confucian shrines* but most of them were lost during the Hideyoshi invasion. They were usually buildings of great simplicity, lacking in imagination.

The Taesŏng-jŏn, the Confucian shrine of Seoul, is perhaps the best preserved one-storey building on a single platform. It served for the worship of Confucius and his chief disciples. The building is almost without decoration, except that the wooden part is painted red.

Many Confucian school buildings were formerly the private houses of notable scholars and are useful for the study of private house construction in the Yi period.

In contrast to Confucian buildings, which were constructed everywhere, Bud- *Buddhist temples* dhist temples were practically expelled from the cities and survived only in the remote countryside. During the Hideyoshi invasion even the few remaining temples were burned and were not able to be reconstructed later. But Buddhism still retained some spiritual appeal for the people and financial means to resist the disasters of the time.

These financial resources came from the land and forests Buddhists still owned. Many of them kept a great number of buildings and supported hundreds of monks and nuns, who protected the works of art of the dynasty; we should feel grateful that many cultural relics were handed down in these Buddhist temples. The Buddhist temples were always located in scenic spots. The main building is as usual the Golden Hall with an image of the Buddha and, to the left and the right of it, are living quarters for the monks. The main entrance is in front of it. No strict temple plan was observed during the Yi Dynasty, and larger temples had many more buildings: the Hall of Maitreya, Hall of Bhaisajyaguru, Hall of Arhats, and Hall of the Mountain Spirit, all of which were built on stone platforms. The pillar of the earlier period has usually a little entasis; the bracketing system is more complicated than in the Koryŏ period, and is usually richly painted. Ornaments were applied to the wooden parts of the interior, and sometimes to the whole ceiling.

A large number of Buddhist temples of the Yi Dynasty throughout Korea has preserved very interesting representative architecture, which is still in good shape. The Hoji Gate of Sŏgwangsa, Anbyŏn, South Hamgyŏng province has a style linking Koryŏ and Yi. It combined an old simplicity with the more modern decorative manner. The Store House for wooden printing-blocks of the Koryŏ Tripitaka, Haein-sa, in South Kyŏngsang province, is technically interesting for its method of keeping wooden materials free of moisture. The

Kakhwang-jŏn of Hwaŏmsa in North Chŏlla province is a grand double-roofed building.

Pŏpchusa in North Ch'ungch'ŏng province has a building called the Palsang-jŏn, which is in reality a five-storeyed wooden pagoda. This is the only extant wooden pagoda of the Yi Dynasty and has interesting features comparable with those in many wooden pagodas of Japan.

SCULPTURE AND PAINTING

It is most regrettable that the Yi Dynasty has left little sculpture of importance to posterity. A few Buddhist statues of considerable beauty can be seen in various temples; but they are rather stiff and show little of the artistic flavour found in earlier works in Korea.

Some remarkable stone stelae with winding dragons sculptured on the upper part have been preserved. These, too, can hardly be considered as masterpieces of the time. It can be said with the degradation of Buddhism Koreans lost a great deal of their artistic inspiration. Whatever was created in spite of their unfortunate circumstances was destroyed during the Hideyoshi invasion.

Paintings of Muryangsa and Yongjusa

The Buddhist temples usually have some religious paintings hanging on the walls of the main hall. Most of these paintings are from the latter part of the Yi Dynasty and show little artistic merit. Nevertheless the large painting of Maitreya at Muryangsa near Puyŏ, 13.5 metres wide and 7.5 metres high, is an excellent painting and serves as mural covering for the entire wall. It is painted with remarkable finesse, yet with vigour, in magnificent colours, and can be praised as representing the best Buddhist art of this dynasty. It is a pity that this kind of painting has seldom been preserved.

The mural of Yongjusa, near Suwŏn, Kyŏnggi province, is a very interesting and quite unique painting of this kind. The three different Buddhas (Bhaisajyaguru, Śākyamuni and Amitābhā), seated side by side in the centre, are surrounded by Bodhisattvas and other attendants. Two Deva Kings appear to the left and right, and some attendants are depicted, on a smaller scale, behind the other figures. The painting is unique in so far as the figures are modelled with chiaroscuro, to suggest a third dimension as in western painting. The painting is traditionally attributed to Kim Hong-do, but on no conclusive evidence. It certainly must have been painted some time in the 18th century after Korea had come into contact with the West.

Mural of Unhaesa

Unhaesa near Taegu possesses a large mural on reddish-brown coloured hemp painted with gold. Śākyamuni Buddha is sitting in the centre surrounded by Bodhisattvas and Deva Kings. The painting is executed entirely by subtle graceful gold lines and has its own particular charm.

This type of painting seldom remained untouched by monks of later periods. Korean monks have strange customs of re-gilding statues or re-touching paintings as a gesture of devotion. This is why Buddhist sculptures are so often ugly, sometimes even painted white with plaster. In the same way Buddhist painting

PLATE 19 – Portrait of Cho Mal-saeng (1394–1447) by an unknown artist. Hanging scroll, ink and colour on silk. Late Yi Dynasty. *Tŏksu Palace Museum of Fine Arts. Length of scroll 1.80 m, width 1.05 m.* Cf. *p. 127*

suffered by repeated re-paintings that obscured the lines and expressions the figures originally had.

There is in the collection of the Tŏksu Palace Museum of Fine Arts a hanging scroll of Bhaisajyaguru with two attending Bodhisattvas, painted in gold on a dark background. It is painted, like the mural of Unhaesa, with fine and sensitive lines, and the figures make a noble impression.

Much early Buddhist painting has been preserved in Japan. No doubt it was taken there by the so-called Waegu, the Japanese pirates who raided Korea for many hundreds of years. Or it may be that the paintings were taken by Japanese generals during the Hideyoshi invasion. One such is the hanging scroll of Bhaisajyaguru with ten Bodhisattvas and other attendants on dark blue hemp, preserved at Entsuji on Koyazan, Japan. It is also painted with gold, and all the details, including the figures and drapery, are almost identical with the painting in the collection of the Tŏksu Palace Museum of Fine Arts, so that both paintings must have originated from the same artist.

Profane painting   Painting in China is closely associated with Confucian scholarship. So it was also in Korea. A good Confucian must excel in three different skills: poetry, calligraphy and painting. Most important of these three skills in Korea was poetry. Actually under the examination system of the Yi Dynasty the candidates were examined primarily in poetry. Whoever composed good poems and wrote them in excellent calligraphy could pass the highest examinations in the country. To him all the roads to higher positions were open. Calligraphy is correctly considered as an art form, and many Koreans have reputations as good calligraphers; but since the standards of calligraphy are as purely Chinese as the standards of the literary works written calligraphically, we will not dwell on this subject in this survey, which is an attempt to describe only what is purely Korean in the art produced in Korea. Of those three skills painting was the least appreciated in Korea. As in China, Korean scholars regarded painting as an approved scholarly hobby, and they looked down on the professional painters attached to the Office of Arts.

The Office of Arts   The Office of Arts, Tohwasŏ, was the governmental bureau to which all the professional artists belonged. They were recruited from the *chungin*, the middle-class people, after an examination of their skill. Taejŏn T'ongpyŏn mentions in detail what kind of test candidates for the Office of Arts had to go through and how much they were paid.

They had to select two subjects from among the approved categories of bamboo, landscape, figure, animals and flowers. Of these five different subjects bamboo was considered the most important. Landscape came second, figures and animals third, and flowers last. Why bamboo was considered the most important is not clear: probably bamboo painting required special skill in making powerful brush-strokes.

A good painter was accorded the rank of second class of the sixth *p'um*, which means that he was paid no more than a skilled labourer. Actually the duty of a member of the Office of Arts was not to paint anything creative, but to produce portraits of the kings, members of the royal family, and nobles or ancestors to order. The plate on page 125 is a good typical example of the formal official PLATE P. 125 portraiture produced by these men. Because no painter could be paid more than they were, they considered it a great honour to become members of the Office of Arts; a successful career painter could later become a *hyŏn'gam*, or county magistrate, which was the highest possible government job open to a member of the Office of Arts. With such low esteem in society there was little possibility of developing great art, and most of the members of the Office of Arts were just mediocre portrait-painters with no great artistic talent. There were very few exceptions.

Korean painting in the Yi period was always under strong Chinese influence *Subjects* and the subject matter of Korean painting is similar to that of Chinese painting. Landscapes, figures, animals, fish or the so-called Chinese 'Four Gentlemen' (bamboo, chrysanthemum, orchid and plum-blossom), were commonly painted in Korea just as in China. But typically Korean birds like the wild goose, magpie and bush warbler were also favoured subjects. For figure-painting they preferred T'ang costumes, as in the southern school of China, but they did also paint people in Korean costume. For landscapes the Diamond Mountains were the most favoured subject. They frequently painted bird's-eye views of cities like P'yŏngyang, Seoul and Pusan. One often meets in screen paintings views of palaces or towers in thick pigment. Interiors of rooms with books and furniture, or scenes of anniversary feasts or other jovial festivities were frequently painted, and there are also paintings showing official ceremonies or royal processions, with Chinese characters on them indicating the names of the participants for commemorative purposes. Animal paintings have survived: tigers, horses, oxen, dogs or sheep. But most animal paintings were poorly done, with few exceptions. Later in the eighteenth century genre painting became popular, and this continued to the end of the 19th century; depicting scenes from the everyday life of the common people, they were rich in humour and vitality.

As painting in general was regarded simply as a hobby for the gentleman *Materials* painter, while professional painters had such a low living standard, they were not even able to use good materials for their painting. Fine Chinese-made paper was seldom used and Korean paper, although very strong, was not entirely suitable for delicate painting. Silk or hemp were very often used, and paper dyed dark blue for painting with gold or silver.

The Korean houses of the common people were not fit to accommodate good paintings. Because of the cold winter, they were generally low buildings and the rooms were small, with little space on the walls for paintings. This circumstance may have contributed greatly to the fact that good large paintings were seldom handed down in private families. Palaces or Buddhist temples were the only places where such paintings were kept. But during the Hideyoshi invasion most palaces and temples were burned down with all the paintings in them.

There are few painters of the early Yi Dynasty whose works have been handed *Early period* down to the present day. Kang Hŭi-an was one of them.

Born in 1419, he passed the state examinations and entered the 'Chiphyŏn- *Kang Hŭi-an* jŏn', the academy to which all the scholars of the time were attached. He was one of the scholars who helped King Sejong to invent the Korean alphabet. He served three kings—Sejong, Munjong and Tanjong—and for a short while also King Sejo, who usurped the throne and sent his predecessor, his own nephew Tanjong, into exile and afterwards had him killed. Kang Hŭi-an participated in the famous unsuccessful plot to restore the boy-king Tanjong and was arrested by Sejo. His close friend, the famous scholar Sŏng Sam-mun, before he himself was executed, urged Sejo to save Kang Hŭi-an, for he was such a fine scholar and might be useful to him. So Kang Hŭi-an escaped execution. He visited China in the suite of an envoy, and his painting and calligraphy were very much admired by Chinese scholars.

His painting faithfully followed the tradition of the Chinese school; it is obvious that he had seen many old paintings in China and was greatly influenced by those of the Sung Dynasty rather than by contemporary Ming paintings. The famous Japanese Sesshu lived at about the same time as Kang Hŭi-an, and there is a certain similarity in their brushwork. Kang Hŭi-an excelled in all three scholarly skills: not only in painting, but also in calligraphy and poetry. That is why he, together with his noble and distinguished characters, is considered a shining example of the scholar-painter in Korea. Only three paintings certainly done by him have been preserved. The Tŏksu Palace Museum of Fine Arts treasures two small paintings: 'Scholars Crossing a Bridge' and a fragment of a large painting 'Arranging Plum-blossoms in a Vase'. Both are painted with a firm and powerful brush and remind one of works by Ma Yüan or Hsia Kuei. It is a pity that the condition of the paintings is poor.

PLATE P. 129   There is another painting, 'Sage at Rest on a Rock', in the collection of the National Museum of Korea. In this painting one feels to a greater extent the influence of Ming China. The artist used a strong, yet soft, wet brush.

An Kyŏn   A contemporary of Kang Hŭi-an, An Kyŏn, is at least as famous as and possibly even a better painter than Kang. But An Kyŏn was a member of the Office of Arts and not a scholar like Kang Hŭi-an. The Tŏksu Palace Museum of Fine Arts has one large painting: 'Boating at Chŏkpyŏk', 1.60 m. by 99 cm., which has no signature but is attributed to An Kyŏn. This painting has a remarkably fine composition and shows a grandiose landscape executed with strong and energetic lines. It must be by the hand of a great master of the style of the old school of China. It has no seal and no signature, but no one except An Kyŏn could have painted a picture of such magnificence.

Two more paintings are in the collection of the Tŏksu Palace Museum of Fine Arts: 'A Winter Landscape' and 'An Autumn Landscape'. Although they also have neither seal nor signature, the masterly control of the misty atmosphere surrounding the boats could only be rendered by a great master such as An

PLATE 20 – 'Sage at Rest on a Rock': painting by Kang Hŭi-an (1419–1465). Album-leaf: ink on paper. Early Yi Dynasty. *National Museum of Korea. 23 × 15.8 cm. Cf. above*

Kyŏn. The best of the extant works by An Kyŏn is the 'Wandering in a Dream in the Garden of Peach-blossoms', which is now in Japan. It is a long scroll including appreciative comments by almost all the scholars of the time. The painting alone measures 1.37 m. by 45.7 cm. It depicts an imaginary landscape and is said to have been painted at the request of Prince Anp'yŏng, who was the younger brother of King Sejo and a gifted man of letters, widely respected for his culture. Prince Anp'yŏng strolled in a dream in the Garden of Peach-blossoms such as was described by the famous T'ang poet T'ao Yüan-ming. Ever since T'ao wrote his famous account, 'the Garden of Peach-blossoms' meant an imaginary country, a Chinese equivalent of Shangri-la. Prince Anp'yŏng is said to have asked An Kyŏn to paint the dream. Magic mountains, misty valleys, blossoming groves and an inviting empty cottage are delicately drawn with fine and sensitive technique. This painting is no doubt the best existing work of all the Yi Dynasty painters.

Era of King Sejo What makes this painting historically more valuable is the fact that all the famous scholars of the period wrote appreciative comments on it, especially those who participated in the plot against Sejo mentioned above, who are still considered the noblest personalities of the Yi Dynasty. King Sejo killed not only his royal nephew but also the six faithful and famous scholars who attempted to restore the ousted king. Sejo left a very bad reputation to posterity. But he was an able politician and greatly consolidated the foundations of the dynasty. He completed the Kyŏngguk Taejŏn which codified the organization of Korea as a Confucian state with a centralized administration.

Yi Sang-jwa Yi Sang-jwa, who was active during this period of great difficulty for liberal and scholarly-minded people, can be singled out as an outstanding man who continued in the style of the old masters. He was originally the slave of a *yangban*. From his childhood he showed a talent for painting, and therefore was made a free man by special order of King Chungjong and admitted as a member of the Office of Arts. He painted portraits of the king and many well-known politicians of the time. A painting 'Moon Viewing' by Yi Sang-jwa is in the collection of the Tŏksu Palace Museum of Fine Arts and has often been displayed in major exhibitions as a representative painting of large size from the sixteenth century.

Madame Shin No woman of the Yi Dynasty has more fame as painter, calligrapher and poet, as ideal daughter, wife and mother, than Madame Shin Saimdang. Her achievements were remarkable in such a rigidly Confucian and male society as Yi Korea. Her speciality was delicate plant, flower and insect life. She caught the essence of nature in these subjects and expressed her sensitivity in harmony of lines and colour. The Tŏksu Palace Museum of Fine Arts possesses two representative works by her hand: 'Wild Geese with Reeds' and 'Wild Duck at the Stream'. Simple, clear, in full movement, and yet realistically portrayed, the birds perch amidst quiet natural surroundings in an autumn landscape. They recall the work of Ming artists. Madame Shin's fame and respect is, however, not due merely to the excellence of her painting. Artistic quality was, after all, in a Confucian society only an approved and appreciated skill for scholars.

What mattered more was her personality combined with her taste for beauty and purity, her wide knowledge, her observation of nature, her devotion to her parents, husband and sons and not least her influence upon others. She was born the second daughter of the scholar Shin Myŏng-hwa and on her mother's side was the great-granddaughter of Ch'oe Se-hyŏn, whose official rank was *ch'amp'an* or vice-minister. She was married to Yi Wŏn-su, a young official of the rank of *kamch'al* (inspector of the censorate). She read as a child all the Confucian books, and could write essays and poems with ease.

She also did household work, sewing and embroidery very well. She had four children; her third son was the famous scholar and statesman Yulgok, no doubt the most original thinker of the Yi Dynasty. According to a story recorded on the memorial stone in honour of Yulgok, Madame Shin dreamed of a dragon before his birth. A dragon symbolizes the birth of an unusual man. Madame Shin died in 1559 at the age of forty-eight, and her name remains to this day an example of perfect womanhood. The famous Confucian scholar and statesman Song Si-yŏl (1607–1689) even wrote appreciative comments in the warmest words for her painting of butterflies on autumn grass.

Yi Chŏng (1541–?) belonged to the royal family and was also called Chung-sŏp. *Yi Chŏng* His artist's name was Tanŭm. 'There was nothing in the artistic field he could not do; he was good at poetry and calligraphy, but was especially famous for painting bamboos. During the Hideyoshi invasion he was wounded in the right arm and after it was cured he could paint even better'—so runs one account. In early life Yi Chŏng enjoyed princely rank, with plenty of leisure for scholarly and artistic work. There is a comment for an album of paintings by Yi Chŏng: 'We opened the album and found that not only were the bamboos as good as formerly but even better — Chung-sŏp asked me to write a preface criticizing his work. Seeing the painting of the thinly spaced bamboo, I liked it; but the one of densely grouped bamboo I did not dislike either. I felt that I could hear it rustling even though it was silent. Although the colour was not life-like (it was black and white), yet the painting looked real and I seemed to feel the fresh breeze blowing...'

Several bamboo paintings by Yi Chŏng have been handed down. The one in the collection of Chun Hyung-pil is especially good, and the comments by Yi Chŏng's friend fit the painting perfectly. Bamboo, together with chrysanthemum, orchid and plum-blossom is a favourite subject for the scholar-painter. They symbolize the refined characteristics of a gentleman with spiritual firmness.

The paintings of the first half of the Yi Dynasty had generally been influenced by the paintings of Yüan China, but from the second half onwards some painters were influenced rather by Ming artists; this was understandable in view of the frequent and cordial relations between the two countries.

Almost contemporary with the painter Yi Chŏng there lived another and *Yi Chŏng* younger Yi Chŏng (written with different Chinese characters), who deserves to *the Younger* be mentioned here first as an artist who belonged to the second half of the Yi Dynasty. This younger Yi Chŏng, who had as his artist's name Nae-ong, was

born in 1578, sixteen years before the outbreak of the Hideyoshi war. He died
at the age of twenty-nine. His father Sunhyo, grandfather Paeryŏn and great-
grandfather Sŏbul were all renowned artists. Growing up in artistic surroundings, Nae-ong was able to make a fair painting at the age of five.

When he was ten, he had already painted landscapes and figures, as well
as Buddhist paintings, just like a mature artist. At the age of eleven he felt
attracted to the beautiful landscape of the Diamond Mountains, went there
and never came back home. He wandered in the Diamond Mountains from one
Buddhist temple to another, and painted mostly landscapes and religious subjects. Like most Korean artists, he was fond of drinking, and fell ill of it, and
died young. He left very little work, but the Tŏksu Palace Museum of Fine Arts
treasures a painting on paper, 'Sailing Homeward'. Using only a couple of wet
brushes, he gives a wonderful picture of a fishing-village by a stream after a
shower. The brush-stroke is typical of the style of the southern Chinese school.
In the same collection there is another landscape. In the foreground is a
village seen in a somewhat foggy atmosphere. But the high mountain in the
background is already plunged in solitude at the approaching evening hour.
There is absolutely no stiffness; in mood the whole painting reminds one very
much of some old master of the southern school.

Yi Chŭng   Yi Chŭng (Hŏju) was another remarkable artist contemporary with the two
Yi Chŏng. He was born in 1581 to a concubine of a member of the royal family.
Because of his illegitimate birth he was not able to get a high government post
and ended in a minor official position, as *chubu*. During his childhood he learned
to paint, and one day he disappeared from home for three days. When he
was found again, he got a beating from his father and, as the tears fell on the
ground, he painted a bird with them. As he grew older he concentrated his
energy on painting. Although critics agree that Yi Chŭng belongs to the great
masters of the period, his paintings were 'not magnificent enough and lacking
in sensitivity, though large and carefully and painstakingly executed'. The
Tŏksu Palace Museum of Fine Arts has a landscape painting on a grand scale,
but it lacks precisely that certain refined sensitivity, although it is detailed and
has a mood of dreamy tranquillity.

17th century   In the seventeenth century Korean painters were gradually developing a
typically Korean flavour and trying to liberate themselves from tradition-bound
Chinese painting. But Korean painters never became completely free from
Chinese influence, and failed to create an independent Korean style of painting
as the Japanese so successfully did.

Kim Myŏng-guk   Kim Myŏng-guk, whose artist's name was Yŏndam, should be mentioned first in
this connection. 'He had a rare personality and individuality, free and unbound,
never paid any attention to the traditional manner and was good at both figure
and landscape painting. He showed particular skill in using thin ink and light
colour. He specialized in 'breathing a spirit of life into his figures' and never
used unnecessary decoration. He was open-minded and fond of making jokes.
He always painted when he was completely drunk. Only then did his spiritual
quality emerge and his thoughts express themselves in his brush. All his

PLATE 21 – 'Dharma' by Kim Myŏng-guk. Hanging scroll: ink on paper, signed and sealed. Middle of Yi Dynasty, first half of 17th century. *National Museum of Korea. 83 × 58 cm; reproduced back to front.* *Cf. p. 134*

masterpieces were done under the stimulus of liquor.' Such is his personality as recorded in the book called *Wanamjip*. Anecdotes about his drinking habits are endless.

One day a monk came and asked him to paint a scene of hell. He brought a large piece of silk for the painting and many rolls of cloth as payment. Kim Myŏng-guk gave the cloth to his wife. 'Buy wine with this and let me get drunk for many months.' When the monk returned after a couple of days, Myŏng-guk said: 'You must wait until I get the inspiration to paint it.' This was often repeated until one day he got very drunk. He sat in front of the silk, gathering his ideas, looked at the silk for a while, and completed the entire painting in a few minutes. The palaces of the dead, the figures of devils were awe-inspiring. But those who were pulling, punishing, burning and torturing the sinners were all monks and nuns. The monk saw it and cried out in amazement. Kim Myŏng-guk laughed and said: 'You monks in your whole life do nothing but wicked things. You are leading the people astray. Who should go to hell if not you people? But if you want me to finish the painting, then bring me more wine. I will alter it.' When the monk brought more wine, Kim Myŏng-guk laughed and painted the silk. The figures that had been bald-headed were given hair, those who had no beards and those who wore black clothing were painted with bright colours, and in a minute the whole painting obtained such brightness and charm that no additional touch was needed. The monk was pleased and said: 'You are truly a divine painter.'

Those who wanted pictures from him stood a better chance if they brought him fine wine. All these stories tell eloquently what kind of personality Kim Myŏng-guk was. He never used many strokes or too much time for a painting. The 'Dharma' in the collection of the National Museum of Korea is an excellent sample of his work. Hardly twenty strokes and maybe no more than two minutes were needed to make this vivid painting.

PLATE P. 133

Kim Myŏng-guk was born as one of the middle class and was attached to the Office of Arts in a teaching capacity. Nothing, however, is known about his early life, family, or dates of birth and death. He was active during the reign of Injo (1623–1650). He once went to Japan as one of the artists a Korean envoy took with him. 'Whoever had a chance to get in touch with him wanted to get a painting. And whoever got a painting treasured it like a jewel.' It is believed that his personality and his painting left a great sensation behind in Japan; many Japanese artists imitated his technique of 'one-stroke' painting. On the other hand, he hardly could escape the criticism that he was too careless in painting and emphasized the exotic treatment of subject.

18th century: new trend in scholarship

At the beginning of the eighteenth century, during the reigns of Yŏngjo and Chŏngjo, Korea had so far recovered from the disaster caused by the Hideyoshi invasion that a regeneration of Korean culture took place. On the continent the new power of the Manchus was firmly established and in Japan a new ruler took a conciliatory attitude to Korea.

When a relatively tranquil atmosphere had finally been restored, a strong new wave of western culture reached Korea. It was through Ming China that

Koreans first heard of the West. During the reign of Injo (1623–1650) a Korean envoy to Ming China brought back western fire-arms, binoculars, watches, atlases, astronomical literature and Christian books. The contact with Christianity and western science had thus started in the 17th century and the Korean concept of the world began to change. Korean scholars gradually became critical of the orthodox Confucianism of Chu Hsi and dissatisfied with government policies; they demanded a fundamental reform of the administrative organization. This new trend was called *sirhak*, meaning a 'science based on fact and utility'. The scholars of this group expanded their activity to the field of geography, natural sciences and the like.

The new intellectual climate gave artists more opportunity to pursue their calling freely, and in fact the eighteenth century was a century of stability and renaissance for Korean art. The first great artist of this century was Chŏng Sŏn, (artist's name Kyŏmjae), who is generally recognized as one of the best landscape painters of the Yi Dynasty. No other painters have left us so much work. The large painting of the Diamond Mountains which was shown at the Exhibition of Korean Arts in Europe and America is one of his representative works. The Diamond Mountains are actually situated in the north-eastern part of Korea and are famous for their crystalline formation. In this painting Kyŏmjae used an unusual technique by making repeated fine vertical lines to depict the unique rock formation of the mountain. From the standpoint of Chinese painting these brush-strokes running vertically are against all the rules. Yet the effect of the painting is magnificent; the needle-pointed peaks and deep valleys of the Diamond Mountains could never find a better artist than Kyŏmjae to paint them. Kyŏmjae was the first man to liberate Korean painting from Chinese patterns, and create a typically Korean style, and lead it along an independent course. He always painted the real landscape which he himself saw and studied carefully and seldom took an imaginary landscape as a subject for his painting. He painted directly from nature, choosing only Korean scenes and Korean life. His painting has sometimes had the reputation of not being refined and sophisticated enough, or of being very peasant-like. The home-spun Korean painting of Kyŏmjae differs very much from Chinese idealized landscape; it smells, as Koreans usually jokingly say, of *kimch'i*, the typical Korean food, a kind of pickle. This is what makes Kyŏmjae the leading landscape painter of the Yi Dynasty.

Kyŏmjae was born in 1676, as the son of old and impoverished parents, and died in 1759, after serving at the Office of Arts over a period of fifty years. Although his family belonged to the *yangban* class, he eventually achieved the official position of *hyŏn'gam*. He was associated with all the prominent personages of the time. The older he became, the better was his painting. He continued to paint until his death (1759).

'Mount Inwang' was also exhibited at the Exhibition of Korean Arts in Europe and America. It is dated 1751. This means that it was done when the artist was 75 years old. In this landscape Kyŏmjae used massive ink strokes with a wet brush until the mountain was painted black. This style of brushwork is

Chŏng Sŏn

PLATE P. 136

135

not common in Chinese painting, especially in painting mountains, yet the whole work gives a wonderful impression of a wet mountain after rain. Mount Inwang is situated in the western part of Seoul and dominates the city.

Kyŏmjae taught painting to younger people. His best pupil was a man named Shim Sa-jŏng (1707–1769) who was usually called by his artist's name: *Shim Sa-jŏng* Hyŏnjae. Though he is supposed to have received most of his artistic treatment of subjects and ideas from Kyŏmjae, his painting somewhat lacks originality and vigour. His brush has not Kyŏmjae's vivid expressiveness. But he seems to have been a man of inner harmony and uprightness and his painting is always balanced and free from exaggeration. The Exhibition of Korean Arts in Europe featured a painting of his, 'Landscape in Rain'. It follows, as was the case with some of his other works, Chinese models. In one instance he himself said that he had used the style of Shen Chou of Ming China.

He originated from a *yangban* family, who had been distinguished for many generations, but died in such poverty that his friends and relatives had to collect money to bury him. He is said to have been skilful in painting from his early childhood and not to have laid his brush down until his death. He is considered one of the ablest masters of landscape-painting in Korea after Kyŏmjae.

Another remarkable landscape painter was Yi In-mun. He served as a member *Yi In-mun* of the Office of Arts, and was born in 1745 and died in 1821. He often used a dry brush and applied heavy pigment in the form of water-colour. He sometimes tried western perspective by painting distant objects on a smaller scale.

The painting on page 136 is part of his long horizontal scroll 'Mountain and *PLATE P. 136* Stream Without End'. This subject was often painted by various Chinese artists. Here Yi In-mun seems to have portrayed the Korean landscape, which is rich in granite outcrops of all kinds. This painting was primarily done in ink, but here and there the artist added a few touches of colour.

Kim Hong-do is probably the most widely known painter in Korea, under his *Kim Hong-do* artist's name of Tanwŏn. A man of universal talents, he is said to have been a very handsome and carefree man, and never to have followed any model in his painting. He is known to have painted figures of immortals, and his genre painting of the lower classes of Korean people is especially treasured. But he also left a great number of landscape paintings, executed with a powerful brush, though later he departed from this style and developed one of his own, choosing subjects mainly from Korean scenery and life. His genre paintings are rich in humour, yet display great realism.

The year of his birth is usually given as 1760, but judging from inscriptions on some of his paintings and from other literary sources, there is some doubt as to this. He was a member of the Office of Arts and later received the position of

PLATE 22 – 'Mount Inwang' by Chŏng Sŏn (1676–1759). Horizontal scroll: ink and colours on paper. Middle of Yi Dynasty. *Sohn Jai Hyung Collection. 80 cm × 1.38 m. Cf. p. 135*
PLATE 23 – 'Mountains and Streams without End' (detail), by Yi In-mun (1746–1825). Horizontal scroll with seal: ink and colour on silk. *Tŏksu Palace Museum of Fine Arts. 44.5 cm × 8.80 m. Cf. above*

PLATE 24 – 'Immortals' by Kim Hong-do (1760–?). Album-leaf, ink on paper. Late Yi Dynasty. *National Museum of Korea. 27 × 48.8 cm. Cf. p. 137*

PLATE P. 138

hyŏn'gam. This painting shows one of his pictures of immortals in the collection of the National Museum of Korea. Several immortals are depicted holding the different animals which are their attributes. It is painted largely after Chinese models and is probably not his best work. But one can see that he has an enormous power and freedom in his brushwork seldom seen in other artists. Tanwŏn was also the first man to choose subjects for painting from everyday life, which has made him popular among Koreans until the present. Korean artists, like artists everywhere, are Bohemians, and Tanwŏn was no exception. One day a man came to sell a very lovely plum-tree, but Tanwŏn had no money to buy it. So he did a quick painting for an admirer who paid Tanwŏn three thousand *yang*. He immediately went out and bought the plum-tree for two thousand *yang*, and then with eight hundred he bought wine and gave the remaining two hundred to his wife to buy rice and firewood, which was enough only for one day.

Shin Yun-bok

Next to Tanwŏn, and probably even better than Tanwŏn in genre painting is Shin Yun-bok, who is generally known by his artist's name, Hyewŏn. Hyewŏn was born in 1758 and is believed to have died about 1820. Both he and his father held military positions, but he also served at the Office of Arts. He often painted frivolous scenes of Korean life which seem to have offended the sensibilities of the Confucian-oriented upper class. The painting on page 139

138

PLATE 25 – Portrait of a girl,
by Shin Yun-bok (1758–?).
Hanging scroll with inscrip-
tion, seal and signature; ink
and colour on silk. Late Yi
Dynasty. *Chun Hyung-pil
Collection. 1.14 m × 45.7 cm.
Cf. p. 140*

PLATE P. 139   is of a girl, probably a *kisaeng*, or singer and entertainer, with a coil of braided hair bound with a purple ribbon. She wears a white blouse and blue skirt, and is holding in her hand three reddish-white beads. Except for the hair style, this is still today the dress of women in Korea. Hyewŏn is here using extremely delicate and sensitive lines as well as gentle colours to portray a young Korean beauty. There is a whole album of genre paintings by Hyewŏn in the collection of Mr Chun Hyung-pil. In all the paintings there, women were included, shown in scenes of everyday life or with special emphasis on their relation to men, which was a new subject in painting.

Pyŏn Sang-byŏk   Probably about the same time as Hyewŏn there was a member of the Office of Arts who was called by his nick-name Koyang'i, in Korean 'cat' or 'strange fellow', because he painted with great skill animals and birds such as hens and sparrows, especially cats. But he also painted many good portraits of notable people of the time, so that he was called Kuksu, the best painter of the country. His real name was Pyŏn Sang-byŏk and his artist's name was Hwajae. Nothing is known about the dates of his birth or death. But after long service at the Office of Arts he got the official position of *hyŏn'gam*. 'Cats and Sparrows' in

PLATE P. 141   the collection of the Tŏksu Palace Museum of Fine Arts is probably one of his best. Two cats are shown, one on the ground and one poised uncertainly on the trunk of the tree, while six alarmed sparrows are scattering through the branches. No one among Yi Dynasty painters could better catch and express animal life than Pyŏn Sang-byŏk.

CERAMIC WARE   Korean ceramic art changed together with the dynasty. The delicate, refined and beautifully coloured Koryŏ wares gave way to the rather simple robust forms and direct unsophisticated style of the Yi Dynasty.

But how can we classify the history of the development of the Yi Dynasty wares themselves? It is very difficult to draw a dividing line between the different periods within the dynasty. There are few dated objects. Korean potters often made one and the same type of ware over many centuries, using the same clay and the same type of kiln, and the wares were also manufactured by the same families. This is especially the case with the wares produced in the country-side in kilns not operated by the government, but by private enterprise.

There are two basic types of pottery among the Yi period wares: the first is called *punch'ŏng* ware, and is actually a transformation of Koryŏ celadon, while the second is white porcelain and is also derived from the white porcelain of the Koryŏ period. Some scholars like Asakawa have divided Yi Dynasty pottery roughly into three periods. According to Asakawa, the first hundred years after the beginning of the Yi Dynasty (1392–1495) can be considered the period of punch'ŏng. Many kilns were constructed throughout South Korea. Those of Kyeryŏngsan, Koryŏng, Sangju, and Chinju were the most notable

PLATE 26 – 'Cats and Sparrows', by Pyŏn Sang-byŏk. Hanging scroll: ink and colour on silk, signed. Late Yi Dynasty, early 18th century. *Tŏksu Palace Museum of Fine Arts. 94 × 42 cm. Cf. above*

ones. Of course, some white porcelains and blue and white wares as well as a few under-glazed copper and black glazed wares were also produced.

During the second period of about one hundred and fifty years—roughly from the reign of Prince Yŏnsan to that of King Hyojong (1495-1659)—blue and white wares were produced in quantity and a few under-glazed iron and under-glazed copper ones were also produced.

The third period of about two hundred years (1659-1868) was the flowering period of blue and white wares; punch'ŏng wares of inferior quality were manufactured only in the countryside. The last fifty years could be called the period of degeneration.

But drastic changes in Yi Dynasty pottery were brought about by the Hideyoshi invasion, which caused great damage to the ceramic industry. Numerous kilns were destroyed and the potters themselves were seized and carried off to Japan. The technique of making white porcelains managed to survive, but punch'ŏng wares failed to re-appear in their old form. Therefore it is safer to divide the history of Yi ceramic wares into two periods, with the Hideyoshi invasion as the dividing-line. During the first period, which covers roughly the two centuries from the late fourteenth to the end of the sixteenth, there was a steady development in ceramic art. Following in the tradition of Koryŏ celadon punch'ŏng ware was produced in large quantities; likewise, white porcelain, plain or with under-glaze decoration, progressed steadily, influenced strongly by Ming blue and white.

The Hideyoshi invasion interrupted its development. After that punch'ŏng wares were only made near Pusan for export to Japan; other kilns making other types suffered heavy losses. The Yi court had difficulty in finding kilns to supply

Punwŏn ceramics for its own use, and a large government-run kiln was operated at Punwŏn near Seoul to meet the court's needs from the seventeenth to the nineteenth century. The major production was blue and white wares.

The Japanese invaders not only destroyed potteries and kilns, but also kidnapped many Korean potters and put them to work in Japan making the tea-bowls that were already highly valued there. It was in this way that the foundation of the Japanese porcelain industry was laid.

After the Japanese invasion white porcelain with under-glaze blue became the main product of the Yi potters. Various other types, such as porcelain with under-glaze iron brown and copper red decoration, were also produced. In 1883 the Punwŏn kilns were turned over to a private company as a result of the financial straits of the government, and Japanese potters were employed to modernize the plant. This hastened the decline of the Yi pottery tradition.

Punch'ŏng ware Punch'ŏng is the abbreviation of *punjangch'ŏng sagi*, which is written with five Chinese characters meaning 'powder', 'dressing', 'green', 'sand', 'vessel', the last two of which make a common Korean word for ceramic wares, *sagi*. The first and the third characters together to make punch'ŏng, literally meaning 'powder green'. The same two characters were also used in Chinese to designate another type of ceramic ware, quite different from Korean punch'ŏng.

PLATE 27 – Rice-bowl with lid. Punch'ŏng ware with celadon glaze. Muan district. Yi Dynasty, late 14th–early 15th century. *Chun Hyung-pil Collection. Height 16 cm. Cf. p. 144*

Punch'ŏng ware is made of the same greyish clay as Koryŏ celadon, though it is somewhat coarser in texture. The surface is covered either partially or completely with a brushed coating of white slip. Sometimes, instead of using a brush, the potters placed the vessel in a large tray filled with white slip. The vessel coated with brushed slip shows traces of swift strokes with a broad brush. It is this kind of brush-mark that exhibits the carefree artless character of Yi pottery in the highest degree. Most of the teacups treasured by Japanese teamasters belong to this category.

There are also specimens without an overall coating of white slip: instead, tiny floral patterns or just dots were stamped into the surface, and these stamped patterns filled in with brushed white slip after the general style of the inlaid celadon ware of the Koryŏ period. The excess slip was wiped off, leaving the pattern filled with the residue. Sometimes a bold design was incised freely in the body and carefully filled in with white or black slip, a technique identical with that of inlaying Koryŏ celadon (Japanese: *mishima*). A typical example of PLATE P. 143 this ware is the bowl shown on page 143. It is a covered bowl used for holding rice. The decoration was made by incising the pattern very lightly but broadly into the body and filling with white slip. The design consists of a peony arabesque encircling the lid and bowl, with one large peony in the centre of the lid. But there are examples in which the stamping and inlaying technique were used together. This is, in short, a hasty superficial way of inlaying decoration. The result was far inferior to the earlier work of the Koryŏ Dynasty. The pattern is often confused and the effect impaired by traces of excess slip which could not be entirely removed.

There are also some other variations, such as designs of flowers, fish or birds on a white body, or made by scraping away the white background in sgraffito style so that the pattern stands out (Japanese: *horihakeme*).

Punch'ŏng ware in general is nothing but a modification of Koryŏ celadon. The application of white slip and the overall decorative pattern were employed to distract the eye from the poor, greyish-blue tone of the body and glaze; however, it should be admitted that the pottery is novel in type and entirely characteristic of the period. The exact date when punch'ŏng ware first appeared is uncertain, but it was being produced in fully developed form in southern Korea at the beginning of the fifteenth century, and it continued to be made until the end of the sixteenth century.

PLATE P. 145 There are punch'ŏng wares painted in under-glaze iron with brushed slip which can be considered a continuation of painted Koryŏ ware. The wine-jar shown was produced at the Kyeryŏngsan kiln and is a good sample of this type. It is pear-shaped with a contracted neck and trumpet-mouth and is covered with broad brushed slip, which has a rather yellow colour. On the side is a freely *Black glazed ware* painted design of a fish and two lotuses in black.

As in the Koryŏ period, so also during the Yi period a black glazed ware (*temmoku*) was continuously produced throughout Korea.

Relatively few pieces have survived, but a number have been excavated from Kyeryŏngsan and other sites. Early black glazed ware has a rather less

PLATE 28 – Wine-jar. Punch'ŏng ware, decorated with brushed yellowish slip. From Kyeryŏngsan. Yi Dynasty, 15th–16th century. *Yi Hong-kun Collection. Height 28.7 cm, diameter 16 cm. Cf. p. 144*

shiny glaze with a simple tone, and is therefore more favoured by connoisseurs.

White porcelain White porcelain was produced throughout the entire period. While punch'ŏng ware died out almost completely after the Hideyoshi invasion, white porcelain continued to be produced to the end of the dynasty. More than punch'ŏng ware, white porcelain can be considered to represent Yi pottery as celadon ware represents Koryŏ. Abundant varieties of white porcelains were produced over a long period and are much treasured by Korean people. They were derived from the white porcelain of the Koryŏ period and most of the best white porcelain was produced at Punwŏn.

The plain white porcelain of the first period is characterized by a robust form, thick potting and by the solid texture of the white colour. We no longer see the *ying-ch'ing* bluish tone or the ivory tone of the Koryŏ white wares. During the second period, however, the tone became slightly bluish-white and has been likened to that of clear water.

Blue and white ware Punch'ŏng wares were originally made only for the common people, and not for the upper class. They were produced everywhere in the country and only a few specimens were presented to the court. Plain white ware was produced primarily for ceremonial purposes, and there were numerous kilns for it throughout the land. But the blue and white wares were for a very long time made exclusively in Punwŏn, and no other kilns were allowed to make them until the Punwŏn government kiln became a private enterprise. How far the origin of blue and white wares goes back it is difficult to say, but probably as far as the early fifteenth century. It seems to be likely that the technique of early Ming blue and white reached Korea early in the dynasty. At the beginning of the fifteenth century white porcelain with under-glaze blue decoration was being produced in Korea with the aid of imported cobalt. After cobalt ore was discovered in Korea in 1464, indigenous material was used for decoration.

There are some blue and white wares preserved from the pre-Hideyoshi period. Their number is, however, extremely limited, and blue and white came into full bloom only after the invasion, as the country gradually recovered from the disaster. Many excellent wares were produced after the kilns were established in Punwŏn. But cobalt was a very expensive material; the potter used it only very sparingly and in many cases applied it only to a small area of the surface. In 1754 King Yŏngjo even prohibited the use of blue and white porcelain by the common people, indicating that the wares were at that time regarded as luxury products.

PLATE P. 147 The vase on page 147 is a very fine example of blue and white. It has an unusual shape, with a wide mouth and swelling sides. The under-glaze blue designs are bold and extremely free, showing a youth fishing in a stream among rocks with orchids growing from them and two ducks approaching. The porcelain is of superb quality and the painting on it is no doubt by the hand of an extremely gifted potter or even a professional painter.

White ware with under-glaze iron decoration While cobalt was used sparingly, other pigments, such as iron brown, were utilized extensively. Though under-glaze iron was probably used in the first period, most of the surviving examples are from the post-Hideyoshi period.

146

PLATE 29 – Vase. White porcelain, with blue under-glaze painting. From Punwŏn. Yi Dynasty, 17th–18th century. *Chun Hyung-pil Collection. Height 25.3 cm, diameter at base 11.6 cm. Cf. p. 146*

A good example of this class is the jar on page 149. The body is grey, but is PLATE P. 149 traditionally considered as akin to white porcelain. It is decorated with a very abstract pattern of a dragon and clouds, painted in under-glaze iron. The bold sweep of the brushwork and the rich brown of the iron pigment produce an effect that evokes the admiration of modern potters, working with complete freedom to express their own concept of beauty. The chemical action of the iron is such that it appears to eat into the glaze.

White ware with under-glaze copper decoration

Copper red was also used to paint designs. There are also some examples where copper red and blue were used together. Most Yi white porcelain with copper red designs belongs to the second period and was made at Punwŏn.

Besides the above-mentioned wares, various minor products with black, yellowish-brown, azure and opaque glazes were produced at different kilns in Korea.

PLATE 30 – Jar. Greyish-blue porcelain decorated with iron under-glaze. Yi Dynasty, 17th–18th century. *Tŏksu Palace Museum of Fine Arts. Height 36 cm, diameter 37.4 cm. Cf. p. 147*

TIBET
BY
PETER H. POTT

INTRODUCTION

A description of the art of Tibet confronts the author with a number of special problems which cannot be solved easily. Firstly, what is understood in this case by the general term 'art'; secondly, how are the geographical limits of Tibet to be determined? Moreover, it is impossible to treat the theme purely in the abstract; much will have to be elucidated by means of examples. The choice of these is limited, and the author must in most cases add that neither their origin nor their age can be precisely determined or correctly estimated. The number of objects known in the West must be taken to be extremely limited; this applies particularly to those to which definite dates can be assigned as regards their origin and the period of their creation.

Approach to Tibetan art

During recent decades interest in that group of works of art which are customarily grouped together under the collective term 'Tibetan' has evidently greatly increased, although the majority of these objects have never crossed the boundaries of that most inaccessible country, distinguished by its mystic character. Most of these works of art stem rather from the western part of China or the southern frontier areas such as Nepal, Sikkim and Bhutan. It is legitimate to ask how such a significant number of objects has none the less reached western collections. Two immediate causes were decisive in this respect. On the one hand, they were made available by the connection which England forced on Tibet in 1903 and 1904. This reached its climax in the 'Younghusband Expedition' which, after an initial peaceful penetration of the country, finally degenerated into military action with all the latter's side effects. On the other hand, the repercussions of the Chinese revolution of 1911, during which western Chinese and eastern Tibetan monasteries were plundered in large numbers, contributed particularly to the dispersion of numerous treasures in the West, partly by way of India and partly by way of Japan. In the West they formed the basis of collections of so-called Tibetan art, which were in some cases extensive, especially in France. There is considerable difference in value between the individual works which we owe to the two events mentioned. In the course of the first action those centres in particular which had offered resistance were plundered after the conquest. As a result many very valuable pieces were removed and, after remaining for years in the possession of members of the army, mostly ended up in the larger museums of western Europe. The second group is much more extensive and consists for the most part of works of very recent origin; for they came from an area which, as a result of political upheavals, had repeatedly fallen victim to looting. Furthermore, we must also take into account the very extensive manufacture of objects which, until the outbreak of the Chinese revolution, were produced in such centres as Peking. As a result of the disappearance of the people who had formerly commissioned these works, the bronze-founders now tried to support themselves by putting their craft at the disposal of foreigners. They quickly adapted themselves to the demands of tourists; but the expert supervision by specialists who had formerly scrutinized the commissioned work in detail ceased to operate, so that very soon many works of low quality which were quite worthless from a ritualistic standpoint came on to the market. All these aspects must be borne in mind; and this makes it difficult to draw a precise line in time and space in dealing with the art of Tibet.

It is legitimate to ask why Tibetan art enjoys growing popularity. Many of its products undoubtedly reveal a high degree of specialized ability and skill on the part of the unknown craftsmen who produced them. Admittedly, it must be added that the majority of these objects can only be correctly appreciated as works of art by those with a fundamental knowledge of the culture to which they give expression. Furthermore, much of the material that has reached western collections in fact exemplifies nothing more than a skilled specialist ability which can lay no claim to be described as true artistry. It appears therefore that it is not primarily the true artistic value of those objects which has aroused interest. Their rarity may be partly responsible; but a much more certain reason is the aura of mystery which seems to veil everything emerging from this country of the 'supernatural', with its many unproven tales of wonder. In reality, however, the mysterious plays only a modest role; for from an artistic viewpoint only a very small group of objects exerts an impact of compelling fascination, and these reveal at the same time such a mastery of form that they can be regarded as true artistic treasures without any reservation at all. On the other hand, there are only relatively few genuine works of art amongst those objects in which the mysterious aspect is predominant. As they clearly have reference to a mysterious side of life they can certainly be of such interest to initiates that, despite all aesthetic inadequacies, they become desirable objects, but certainly not works of art.

It is therefore clear that in treating this theme it is hardly possible to determine the precise geographical origin of any particular object or to decide by reference to our own standards which object can be considered 'true art' and which as a work of artistic craftsmanship. Above all, certain general characteristics of so-called Tibetan art must be outlined, and the function which this art fulfilled in the environment in which it was created must be borne in mind.

Tibet can certainly lay claim to an art of its own, which may undoubtedly be less interesting than that of India and China, but is still attractive enough to compete with the latter. This art is so narrowly interwoven with the special form of the later development of Tantric Buddhism that the typical characteristics of this form of Buddhism, frequently known in Tibet as Lamaism, must be understood in order that the art which emerged from these conditions may be appreciated and valued. The art of Tibet is indeed primarily an art with a purpose. The artist created a work for ritual use. Beauty was of subordinate importance, in so far as it was conditioned by the power of expression with which the artist succeeded in embodying in his work the tradition handed down to him and the formal language of symbols. The artist is therefore not motivated by an impulse to produce a work of art but merely executes a commission to produce an object for meditative practices or for the extensive rites of Lamaism. In a certain respect the production of the work can in itself be an exercise in meditation; in this case the artist must make himself so familiar with the object he is producing that he brings it forth entirely from his own self, and yet he must do this in such a way that not only does a universally valid specimen emerge but each detail can be ritually justified; otherwise the result cannot serve the desired end. In this way the production of works of art is completely committed. Any freedom in the creation of form would signify imprecision, which would make the object invalid for its intended function and which would have rather a disturbing than an inspiring effect as soon as the object were used for purposes of meditation. If we as outsiders wish to learn to understand and appraise a work of art of this type we must first become aware why the work was produced in this way. Only then can we in some degree judge the artistic value of the work.

If it is possible with some knowledge to apply aesthetic standards to Tibetan art, the latter still resists any attempt to consider it from a geographical or historical viewpoint. It is hardly possible to talk of an older or a more recent artistic trend. In general, no works earlier than the seventeenth century are known in western collections. It may be the case that the older works are usually distinguished from those of more recent date by a somewhat more careful execution and, where colours are concerned, by a more elegant and better defined scale of colours. But the differences are too slight to upset the general rule that Tibetan art as a whole shows itself to be an almost unchanging quantity. Thus its timelessness can be looked on as one of its typical characteristics. Favourable circumstances may have preserved an older work of art in excellent condition whereas an item of more recent date may perhaps have been exposed to influences which have caused it to deteriorate more severely under the impact of time, and in this way may give the impression of having originated at a much earlier date. The work of art may have been frequently used, or year after year the butter-lamps may have burned and smoked in front of it, thus giving it a special patina and aroma which might mislead even a connoisseur. Furthermore, a prosperous patron may have made it possible for the artist to employ the original precious colouring materials, as prescribed by the ancient rules, of a type which were not often available to the ordinary man; in this way, by reason of its elegance and craftsmanship, and also of the material employed, the work would give the impression of belonging to the 'golden age', whereas it was manufactured at a much later period than that object in which colouring materials of lesser quality had unmistakably been employed. Only in the most recent period, in the last fifty years for example, have objects been produced which, both through their poverty of execution and the low standard of the materials employed, display such clear characteristics of decadence that they can be recognized without difficulty as recent works. In these cases symbolic elements are often evident which are completely absent from older works, and their origin can be determined. This applies particularly to those works manufactured during the last fifty years in the small border state of Sikkim, which was under the clear and unmistakable influence of India and Indian culture.

The third general characteristic of Tibetan art was the anonymity of the creative artists. It is very rare that a signed work is encountered, and only in the last years of the Lamaist period of art do signed objects appear in a centre such as Peking. Here and there it is true that a number of monasteries do indicate the identity of the painter of their murals, but this is not because of a signature but because of the data contained in the *dkar-c'ag*, a document with a detailed description of a monastery, as is, for example, contained in a Baedeker. Such dkar-c'ag have been produced for quite a large number of monasteries. They were made with the help of printing-blocks and were duplicated for pilgrims to the monasteries. Where they are available they supply particularly valuable information about the periods in which the larger pictures and statues were produced, about the artists and the history of their origin. This in itself creates great difficulty in relation to our theme; for only a few research workers have the opportunity of seeking out these monasteries and examining these comprehensive works of art on the spot. For the most part we only know a large number of objects whose exact origin is uncertain and which were in most cases not sufficiently interesting to be mentioned in such a dkar-c'ag, even if we do have such a document at our disposal. In addition, the condition in which we would find these monasteries would no longer correspond to what the compiler of the document saw; for the political effects to which a large part of Tibet has been exposed during recent centuries have had as a result the repeated looting and burning of monasteries and palaces, so that they have always had to be rebuilt anew and re-equipped *in toto*. In very few cases have the original works of art been spared as though by a miracle.

As already mentioned, Tibetan art is of a highly committed character. Thus it is absolutely impossible to evaluate it unless one is thoroughly acquainted with the details of Lamaist culture. Tibetan art, however, is so closely interwoven with Tantric Buddhism that it is impossible to discuss and understand this art without analysing this unusual form of Buddhism, which remained preserved in Tibet after once extending over a large part of South-east Asia, including Indonesia and Japan. The degree of remoteness which characterizes this inaccessible high plateau of Central Asia resulted in the unalloyed preservation of a form of religion which elsewhere was lost through the penetration or imposition of other cultures. Tibet can therefore be regarded as the protector of the Bengali-Buddhist traditions of the eighth to the eleventh century, on which neighbouring countries such as Kashmir, Nepal and China exerted a moderate influence.

But Tibetan art also reveals a certain Central Asiatic influence. This is particularly prominent in the work in bronze, which reveals a propensity to exuberant forms and an extravagant use of gilt and inlaid work with coloured stones; this gives the whole of art the appearance of barbarian luxuriance. It may be the case that the garish colours of the Tibetan landscape inspired this flamboyance, but this may also express a certain naïve gaiety innate in the Tibetan people. The area that we know as Tibet is of such a geographic structure that it could only develop towards national unity with difficulty. Large parts of the country are unsuited to settlement; nomadic tribes roam over them in the search for grazing-grounds for their sheep and yaks. A settled population is met with on the banks of the great rivers in the south of the country. From time immemorial these peoples have been divided into small regional principalities whose rulers, like robber knights, were in a state of constant feud with each other. When *their* interests were at stake, the ordinary man all too often became the victim of a quarrel in which he had basically no interest. On only one occasion did one of these princes succeed in extending his rule over a larger area; and the first to rule over the whole country was King Srong-btsan-sgam-po. He had founded his kingdom in the middle of the seventh century and came to feel himself so powerful that he asked for the hand in marriage of a Chinese and Nepalese princess, and did in fact marry both. As these princesses were zealous followers of Buddhism, Tibet came for the first time into direct contact with that religion. This contact, however, only took a superficial form and remained limited to the immediate environment of the prince, who continued to tolerate, side by side with Buddhism, the old so-called Bon-po forms of worship. But in the history of Buddhist tradition he is regarded as one of the three great royal 'protectors of the doctrine' *(dharmarājā)*. The next great supporter of Buddhism in Tibet was King K'ri-srong-lde-btsan, his successor in the fifth generation who, although he also did not remove the Bon-po priests, was more interested in Buddhism and sent envoys to India to persuade the learned monks of the famous monastic universities of Nālandā and Vaisāli to come to Tibet and spread Buddhist doctrine. This was during the second half of the eighth century, i.e., at a time when Buddhism in its Tantric form had already taken root in these important Indian centres. The prince's concern was probably less to make himself familiar with the elevated moral teaching of Buddha than to acquire insight into the mysterious power which had emanated from this special mystical evolution and impelled princes from the whole of South-east Asia to send scholars to India to acquire the knowledge necessary to strengthen the power of each prince in his own territory.

The king's envoys were successful in inducing the famous scholar Śāntarakshita to leave India for Tibet, where he advised the prince to summon Padmasambhava from Udyāna to give further encouragement to the spread of Buddhism. Padmasambhava, an enthusiastic supporter of the Tantra school, laid the real foundations for the development of Buddhism in what was for Tibet its typical form. He was the founder of the first great monastery, which was established about 770 A.D. in Sam-yas (Sam-ye), some fifty kilometres from Lhasa. It was built on the model of the monastery and temple of Odantapurī in Magadha in India. This is the oldest monastery in Tibet and in it many ancient treasures are supposedly preserved.

Although Padmasambhava laid the basis of Tibetan Buddhism, this did not mean that the religion would henceforth exercise a decisive influence over the country. This point was not reached until several centuries later. The grandson of K'ri-srong-lde-btsan, the 'evil king' Glang-dar-ma, even waged a determined war against Buddhism. He was the eldest son of his father, who died in 817. He was followed on the throne by his younger brother, Ral-pa-can. In

Ral-pa-can Chinese sources of the T'ang period Ral-pa-can is described as weak and incapable, but the official Lamaist historians praise him highly. The monasteries received many privileges and their numbers rapidly multiplied. Under the leadership of noted scholars an almost incredible amount of translation work was undertaken by rendering the whole of Buddhist Sanskrit literature into Tibetan. This is the foundation of our knowledge of Tantric Buddhism, which only became accessible through these Tibetan translations. King Ral-pa-can, who is revered as the third great 'protector of the doctrine' *(dharmarājā)*, was to a high degree under the influence of his advisers; he favoured the monasteries in such a way that the country became impoverished and the lesser princes and nobility were pushed into the background. The abbots of the great monasteries, on the other hand, won status for themselves in a sort of feudal system. This had as consequence that King Ral-pa-can was murdered by rebels in 835 A.D., and

Glang-dar-ma this enabled his elder brother Glang-dar-ma to seize power. The histories make short shrift of this king. Chinese sources portray him as a drunkard and a ladies' man as well as being suspicious, cruel and tyrannical. They also make mention of repeated uprisings against his arbitrary rule. The fact that he is portrayed in an even worse light by the official Lamaist sources needs no further emphasis. The *Bod-kyi-rgyal-rabs*, one of the most important chronicles, reports that he was not originally chosen king because he 'had a monkey's head and was ugly and stupid'; for this reason Ral-pa-can was appointed in his stead. After the murder of the latter and Glang-dar-ma's seizure of power, the chronicle continues, 'he ruled righteously for six months, but towards the end of the Iron-Bird year (841) the sacred doctrine was darkened; he now reigned for another six and a half months in a sinful way. Altogether his power lasted for one year and half a month. In the year of the Dog (Water-Dog: 842) he was killed by the "Bodhisattva" dPal-gyi-rdo-rje (Śrīvajra).' Other sources make it clear that he devoted all his efforts to uprooting Buddhism. The foreign (Indian) pandits were driven out and the native scholars had to take refuge in the most remote parts of the country. Libraries were burned, statues overturned, monasteries looted and temples walled up. As was only to be expected, some reaction had to follow such a violent rule. As already mentioned, this took place in the form of a ritual murder by the monk dPal-gyi-rdo-rje whereby, however, the dynasty of Srong-btsan-sgam-po lost its central power and Tibet once again collapsed into a series of small principalities, strongly conscious of their complete autonomy. In the course of time the great monasteries regained their influence, which soon had a much stronger impact on the general run of events in Tibet than the highly localized and limited power of these petty potentates. This inaugurated an epoch in which a theocratic government gradually developed in Tibet. Once again great scholars, as for example the famous Atīśa, streamed into Tibet from India to encourage the further development of the Buddhist community, and in the twelfth and thirteenth centuries the power of the monasteries developed to an unprecedented extent. In the year 1270 A.D. the first Mongol emperor of China, Kublai Khan, summoned the abbot of the great Tibetan monastery of Sakya (Sa-skya) to his court and had himself instructed in one of the highest Tantric consecrations. He then conferred on him sovereignty over Tibet; thus for the first time, a dignitary of the church assumed the first secular government of Tibet. This first period lasted from 1270 to 1345 and was a time of prosperity for many monasteries. In 1345, however, the power of the Sakya hierarchy was broken by King Chang-chub Gyal-tsen, who founded the second great monarchy in Tibet. Although he also supported Buddhism, he limited the power of the monasteries. In the meantime Chinese influence, which had grown considerably during the rule of the Sakya hierarchy, was greatly diminished under the rule of the Sitya Dynasty. This lasted almost three centuries, and the era is described as one of peace and prosperity. But in 1635 the prince of Tsang in Central Tibet revolted against the government and succeeded in seizing power for a few years. In 1642, however, the whole country was conquered by Gushi Khan, prince of the Oelöt Mongols, who had intervened at the request of the Dalai Lama in order to bring the country under the authority of the dGe-lugs-pa or Order of the Yellow Hats, founded by the great reformer Tsong-k'a-pa, 'the man from the onion valley'. The latter was born in *Tsong-k'a-pa* 1358 in the province of Amdo in north-eastern Tibet and was to be the founder of the great monasteries of Ganden (dGaldan) and Sera, which together with the powerful monastery of Drepung ('Bras-spungs) were to form the 'three pillars of the state'. As an important reformer Tsong-k'a-pa introduced a strict and ritualistic form of worship and in particular encouraged a more precise observance of the rules governing the life of the monks. Whereas the monks of the so-called unreformed sects wear a red hat, Tsong-k'a-pa introduced the yellow priest's hat for the dGe-lugs-pa, also known as the Order of the Virtuous. In the West his order is therefore known as the Order of the Yellow Hats, whereas the order founded by Padmasambhava is generally described as the Order of the Red Hats, in spite of the different sects into which it is divided. Tsong-k'a-pa's successor in the hierarchy was his supporter Gedundub (dGe-'dun-grub), who founded the famous monastery of Tashi Lumpo (bKra-šis-lhun-po). On his death in 1474 there emerged for the first time the theory that his soul had sought out a new body and found it in a child whose birth took place at approximately the time of his death; in this way the theory of the incarnate Lama was introduced. Many monasteries soon took over these theories and since then many hundreds of so-called Tul-ku Lamas (sPrul-sku-bla-ma) have been known.

The line of Dalai Lamas was continued by dGe-'dun-grub (1391–1478), the *Dalai Lamas* successor of Tsong-k'a-pa. The title of a Dalai Lama Vajradhāra, 'the All-powerful Lama, Bearer of the Thunderbolt', was admittedly only given to the third of this line, Sönam Gyatso (bSod-nams gya-mts'o), by the Mongol ruler Altan Khan for his efforts in converting the Mongols to Buddhism. The fifth in the line, Lob-sang Gyatso (bLo-bzang rgya-mts'o), began construction of the great monastery palace of Potala in Lhasa. It was built on the spot where the fortress of King Srong-btsan-sgam-po had once stood. This Dalai Lama, 'the Great Fifth', who regarded himself as the incarnation of the Bodhisattva Avalokiteśvara, decreed that his old teacher, an abbot of the great monastery of Tashi Lumpo, be looked on as a reincarnation of Amitābha, the Buddha of Boundless Light, who is regarded in the pantheon of Buddhism as the intellectual father of the Bodhisattva Avalokiteśvara. On the basis of this declaration, which was to retain its validity even in later incarnations of the hierarch of Tashi Lumpo, many Tibetans attribute greater spiritual authority to these priests than to the Dalai Lama who, apart from his spiritual duties, also exercised secular powers over Tibet. In reality, however, the Dalai Lama only busied himself in exceptional cases with secular matters of government. This task was for the most part handed over to a 'regent' *(sde-srid)*. The holders of this office included many strange figures.

Regents The best known regent was probably Sangs-rgyas-rgya-mts'o, who ruled Tibet with a firm hand. He was chosen for this purpose in 1679 by the 'Great Fifth'; for many years he kept secret the death of the 'Great Fifth', which took place in 1682, and would not allow the latter's reincarnation to assume the succession until 1696. This reincarnation was at the time already a young man who had seen something of life and would enter history as a gifted poet — the only poet of Tibet, as it happens, who composed erotic love songs. He had no inclination for his sublime task, and in 1702 decided to renounce his privileges. Although the regent agreed to this, the situation could not last, all the less so when the Mongol ruler Lha-bzang Khan of the Qośot family attained power in 1700 and sought to form an alliance with the Chinese Emperor K'ang-hsi, the most important emperor of the Manchu Dynasty.

Chinese rule The years 1705–1750 were hardly happy, for little by little the country fell completely under Chinese rule as a consequence of the struggle waged by China against the Junkars. In 1717 a horde of Junkars invaded Tibet; Lha-bzang Khan tried to save 'the holy city', but failed and forfeited his life. A petty Tibetan prince, P'o-lha-nas, however, succeeded in escaping alive, planning a counter-attack and assembling rebels against the extraordinarily cruel rule of the Junkars. The Chinese emperor sent him some support, with the result that the Junkars were once again driven out, but only after they had plundered the country and utterly laid waste numerous ancient monasteries. It was natural therefore that P'o-lha-nas, because of his loyalty, should be entrusted with the administration of Tibet under the supervision of the Chinese emperors. After the death of K'ang-hsi at the end of 1722 his successor Yung-chêng followed a moderate policy vis-à-vis Tibet. This was a period when the country had not yet settled down again to peaceful ways. This policy failed, and in the years 1727–1728 a civil war broke out in which the country once again suffered great damage. The eventual victor was P'o-lha-nas, principally because he was able to assure himself of the support of the powerful monasteries and recognized the supremacy of the Chinese emperor. From 1729 to 1747 he ruled the country, first as vice-regent and then for all practical purposes as an independent prince.

Shortly before his death, however, the tensions between individual Tibetan princes increased again, and his son and successor, 'Gyur-med-rnam-rgyal, could only maintain his position until 1750. On November 11, 1750 he was murdered in the residence of the Chinese Amban, which brought about a new period of troubles, murder and incendiarism. But now the Emperor Ch'ien-Lung (1736–1795) intervened ruthlessly to re-establish law and order and Tibet only retained a nominal independence. In name the secular government of the country remained reserved to the Dalai Lama, but in reality Tibet was ruled by agreement with the Chinese Amban through a ministerial council. In the latter the representatives of the great monasteries played a certain part, as did also the regents who represented the Dalai Lamas, who were often under-age. This situation lasted unchanged for almost a century. But at the end of the nineteenth century new power relationships emerged in the Far East between Russia, Great Britain and China. The thirteenth Dalai Lama, bLo-bzang T'ub-ldan, who possessed a certain political astuteness, more or less tried to play these great powers off against one another. He recognized the inner weakness of the Chinese Empire at the end of the Ching Dynasty, and at first allowed himself to be induced by the Buryat tribesman Dorjeff to follow a pro-Russian policy, while Great Britain tried to protect the northern frontier of its Indian empire. British policy moved progressively further in this direction, leading to the 'Younghusband Expedition' of 1903 and 1904, during which Lhasa was occupied and the Dalai Lama took refuge in Mongolian territory. But the British were not interested in a permanent occupation of Tibet, and after they had come to an agreement in Lhasa with a provisional government they withdrew their troops from the country. Shortly afterwards, in 1907, Great Britain and Russia settled their existing differences in Asia and created a balance of power. But for Tibet this signified a sort of power vacuum which a weakened China could now exploit to re-establish its sovereignty over Tibet. This took place in such a cruel manner and was combined with such incredible ruthlessness that the Dalai Lama fled from Tibet, to India, where the British offered him protection in the neighbourhood of Darjeeling. This reign of terror lasted several years; both the Tibetan population and the monasteries suffered unspeakably, and once again there was large-scale looting. The outbreak of the Chinese revolution in 1911 caused the troops to be withdrawn from Tibet, whereupon the Dalai Lama returned to Lhasa and at first pursued a policy that was friendly to Great Britain. Russia was excluded, for in the Russo-Japanese war the weakness of the Russian Empire had been made manifest. Various agreements were concluded by which Tibet was granted a certain degree of independence and the frontiers between China, Tibet and India were determined. Although Great Britain recognized their validity they were never ratified by the Chinese government, so that the position of Tibet remained somewhat obscure. At the same time it became clear that Great Britain would not plunge into new adventures on account of Tibet whereas the power of China was gradually becoming re-established. It is therefore not surprising that the thirteenth Dalai Lama did not dare to stick to his pro-British policy. The

Modern times

whole situation, as it developed after the emergence of the Chinese People's Republic, made it clear that China was in a position to force its will on Tibet, and this it did with proven ruthlessness in 1950 and 1958. The successor of the thirteenth Dalai Lama once again had to flee Lhasa and to seek refuge in India, while the old Tibetan Lamaist culture fell victim to thorough destruction at the hands of the Chinese. In view of the present international situation it must be doubted whether there is any real prospect of a revival of Tibetan civilization; it seems that it belongs to a closed past. The products of this civilization have thus become archaeological objects which are of importance for the study of the past but are without relevance to the present. In this way the last offshoot of Bengali civilization of the ninth and eleventh centuries has ceased to exist.

We have described in relative detail the political evolution of Tibet because it has influenced to a high degree the art of the country. As a result of repeated revolutions and revolts much ancient work has been lost. But fresh political influences have evoked new forms, especially in the application of architectonic ornamentation and architecture, and also in the decorative elements of painting. Much of this is inaccessible to us, for it is located in a country to which entry is completely barred. As a result a survey of Tibetan art must more or less ignore architecture as well as the plastic arts — and this includes the powerful stucco figures in the important monasteries and the great metal images which constitute their treasures. In the main we shall have to devote ourselves to those items which have left the country in one way or another; and even here we shall have to concentrate particularly on the religious art of Tibetan Buddhism, the so-called Lamaism, and occupy ourselves less with popular art. Only a few examples of the latter, in the form of metal work and delicately decorated articles of daily use, have reached western collections and can be used for our research.

Finally, we shall only be able to spare a few words for the executive arts, such as dance and music, which were so important to the ordinary Tibetan. We are comparatively well informed regarding the demon-dances — which should really be described as mystery plays. On the other hand, the popular dances and their music are a less well-known field, which unfortunately lies outside our scope. For this reason we must not hesitate to point out that our descriptions are necessarily limited and therefore one-sided.

I. BUDDHISM IN TIBET

By origin Buddhism is an Indian doctrine of salvation which in the course of
time has become a world religion and, particularly through the favour of
princes, has spread through large parts of Asia. This doctrine was proclaimed
by Śākyamuni, described as 'the Buddha', i.e., 'the Awakened One'. It is
generally thought that he lived between 560 and 480 B.C. and that he preached
in the central part of the Ganges plain as well as in the hilly countryside
bordering it to the north. This is a continuation of the huge Himalaya range and
forms the present frontier between India and the mountain state of Nepal.

In Kapilavastu, a place not far from the frontier situated in present-day Nepal,
the future Buddha, Prince Siddhārtha, was born. He was the son of the petty
king *(rājā)* Śuddhodana, of the Śākya family, and of Queen Māyā. Legend has
it that he emerged from the right side of his mother while she was breaking off
a branch from a tree with her right hand; she was staying at the time in
Lumbinī Park, a country palace not far from Kapilavastu. This theme is
treated again and again in Buddhist art, as much in the older representations of
Gandhāra as in the art of Nepal and Tibet.

The Buddha

PLATE P. 177

The young prince Siddhārtha grew up at the court of his father, where he
tasted all the pleasures of a princely life and received instruction in all the royal
virtues and accomplishments. His father, however, noticed with alarm that the
young prince evidently found no satisfaction in this life, although he excelled
in all the arts appropriate to the son of a prince. After the birth of Siddhārtha
the king learned from a prophecy that the prince had a great future before him
and would either become a mighty ruler of the world *(cakravartin)* or a great
sage *(tathāgata)*. The king, whose main concern was to have a capable successor
as ruler over his growing empire, did his utmost to keep his son apart from anything that might seduce him from his princely duties or incline him towards a
life devoted to reflection and meditation. But in vain. Despite all the father's
efforts to protect his son from the disturbing aspects of life, the young unpre-
pared prince came into contact with old age, sickness and death. When he then
met a beggar monk to whom these could obviously mean nothing, the prince
decided to renounce his courtly life and secretly left the palace overnight. He
went into the forest, discarded his princely garb, cut the long hair on his head
and wrapped himself in the simple garment of a beggar monk. He sought instruction from different penitents and ascetics, but their teachings could not
satisfy him. He therefore decided to become an ascetic himself in the hope that
meditation might show him the way to higher insight. But no matter how much
mortification he imposed on himself, he was not successful in sharing in this
higher insight. Finally, when he had almost completely consumed himself
through fasting and mortification, he recognized that this path would not lead

PLATE I – Ratnasambhava, the Dhyāni-Buddha of the South, on his throne, surrounded by the eight
Mahābodhisattvas. Nepalese painting in a characteristically Indian tradition going back to the 10th
century.

Curiously enough, the Dhyāni-Buddha, as well as the eight surrounding Mahābodhisattvas, is shown
with the attributes of a Bodhisattva. The style is strongly reminiscent of those miniature paintings met
with in Indian palm-leaf manuscripts which probably reproduce certain temple statues. The work
stands out through the beauty of its lines and colours as well as through its temple background, whereby it can at once be recognized as a very old work. From G. Tucci, *Tibetan Painted Scrolls*, Plate E

him to supreme salvation. Yet he felt that the time of his illumination was near. He broke off his ascetic practices and again took nourishment in the form of a broth which was prepared for him by the girl Sujātā. When he again felt strong enough, he went to the sacred fig-tree which grew in the vicinity of Gayā. Under this tree he made himself a seat out of holy *kuśa* grass and rested on it so that he might plunge himself in his last profound meditation. But, as legend has it, he had first to take up the struggle with Māra, the Indian god of lust, who in Buddhism is the embodiment of evil. But neither the weapons of Māra's hosts nor the seductive arts of his enticing daughters could hold him back from his meditation. Māra had to lay down his weapons and now Siddhārtha received the *bodhi*, illumination, in which the highest insight revealed itself to him and he was transformed from a Bodhisattva, i.e., a being which bears within itself the nucleus of illumination, into a Buddha, an 'Awakened One'. He had thereby come to share in the supreme salvation. After a short hesitation he decided to help others to find the way to salvation by proclaiming his doctrine. In the Gazelle Park not far from Benares, he delivered his first sermon to five ascetics. They had once been his followers but had left him when he broke off his ascetic practices. With this there began for the Buddha a life as wandering priest, during which he gathered around him an ever-growing following. In different places he received gifts from wealthy merchants and other prosperous people. The Buddha was acknowledged by them as a spiritual leader and they affirmed the value of his teaching, although they themselves pursued their social duties as before. As so-called *upāsakas* they provided the material means to support the monastic order and looked after the upkeep of its members. In accordance with an age-old Indian custom a garden of rest was put at the disposal of wandering ascetics and their disciples in which they might find relaxation. In this way, during these years of preaching and wandering the first Buddhist community was founded. Very soon the 'three jewels' *(triratna)* — the Buddha, his doctrine *(dharma)* and the community of monks *(sanggha)* — were looked on as the three fundamentals of Buddhism. The teaching of Buddha is for the most part contained in sermons in which he answered the questions of his followers. In the oldest of them, especially in the stories, Buddha's favourite disciple Ānanda and the couple, Śāriputra and Mahāmaudgalyāyana, are prominent figures. The first of these is frequently encountered in written texts, but the other two, represented as his acolytes, are often met with in the plastic arts, making gestures of reverence and renunciation. Apart from these figures, the group of *sthaviras* or 'elders' is prominent. These consist of sixteen 'apostles'; in Tibet their number was increased by two more who were later sent out to spread the doctrine in neighbouring countries.

In order to understand the teaching of Buddha it is necessary to be familiar with two typically Indian conceptions of life. In one there is reflected a deep-rooted consciousness of the transitoriness of all things; in its ultimate consequences this leads to a complete turning away from this world, to its renunciation. The other is based on a belief in an eternal cycle of reincarnation *(samsāra)*, according to which each existence already contains within itself the germ of the next. Thus

PLATE P. 179

Buddhist doctrine

each being remains caught in this cycle, and man can only free himself from it by following the right path leading to salvation.

The kernel of the doctrine proclaimed by Buddha is formed by the four sacred truths: of suffering, of the origin of suffering, of the removal of suffering and of the path which must be followed to achieve this. That is the eight-fold path of right belief, right decision, right word, right deed, right living, right striving, right thinking and right meditation. The man able to follow this path to the end with confidence in the doctrine, to act in accordance with Buddhist ethics and to sink himself in deep meditation, can reach a stage of Enlightenment known as Nirvāna. This represents complete release from all ties to an earthly life. The man who reaches this stage is described as *arhat*, as 'reverence'. With the help of Buddhist teaching it is possible to escape the perniciousness of existence. It leads to freedom from the endless cycle of reincarnation, for it releases man from every bond with earthly affairs. It is not easy to follow this path, but through upright striving and loyal obedience to Buddha's teaching the monk can follow this path to the end and thus share in the supreme salvation.

Buddha often employed parables in his sermons, and many of his stories contain descriptions of events from his previous existences. As man, in the Indian view, is enclosed in a cycle of reincarnations the deeds of this life determine the character of his next existence. Only a Buddha who has broken through this cycle and is no longer bound to an earthly life can recollect his earlier forms of existence and may thus derive from them a lesson with which to enrich his followers.

The so-called *Jātakas* or birth-narratives form an extensive and colourful narrative material which, as well as the life-story of Siddhārtha himself, was often used as a source for the decoration of buildings and paintings.

In this way the Buddha passed his life, frequently known by his supporters as Śākyamuni, meaning the sage of the family of Śākya, and often described by his opponents as Gautama, the wandering preacher. He died when he was about eighty and entered the so-called *parinirvāna*. This took place in Kuśinagara, the present-day Kasia which, like his birth-place, is situated in the mountainous frontier area between India and Nepal. The Buddha died, deeply mourned by his followers, after giving his last instructions to his disciples. He told them that

PLATE 2 – Amoghapāśa, an eight-armed manifestation of Avalokiteśvara, joined by Sudhanakumāra and Hayagrīva *(left)* as well as Tārā and Bhrkutī *(right)*, Scroll-painting in old Nepalese style; the signature dates it to 1436 A.D.
This is not only an old and particularly beautiful work but is a striking example of that representational art which was still under the strong influence of the miniature painting in Indian manuscripts. The figures in the picture are unrelated to one another. There has been no attempt to integrate them into the landscape. The inscription shows that the work was produced on behalf of Bhikshuśrī, his wife Jirulakshmī and their children. The figure supposedly reproduces the Amoghapāśa of the Mahābhuta temple in Bhatgaon in Nepal. At the end of the inscription the wish is expressed that Bhikshuśrī may enjoy a long and healthy life, keep his children and his prosperity, have a constantly increasing number of descendants, grow old and harvest all the fine fruits of his pious deed, as the books lay down. Bhikshuśrī and his wife and children can certainly be recognized among the figures below.

167

FIG. 3 – *Wall-painting of the so-called 'mgon-khang'*

his words, his declarations, the deep foundations of a higher truth remained with them, that they had the laws which he had established for all mankind, and that from now on these must be their principles.

Buddhism in India   Buddhism was originally an Indian doctrine of salvation such as had been repeatedly proclaimed in that part of the world. However, it acquired predominance because its undoubtedly very profound ideas were taken over by a number of powerful rulers in India proper. It was they who gave the impulse to the erection of the first great monumental buildings which have come down

to us from the history of Buddhism. Furthermore, owing to their connections with other rulers, Buddhism could spread far beyond India. The first great protector of Buddhism was King Aśoka Maurya (268–226 B.C.), whose empire extended over the largest part of India. It is to him that is ascribed the erection of numerous memorial buildings, especially the so-called *stūpas**. These were large massive buildings in the form of a semi-circle around which ran a processional path, surrounded on the outside by a railing or balustrade.

* Cf. D. Seckel, *Buddhism*, frontispiece.

Although no single stūpa can definitely be ascribed to Aśoka, numerous such monuments have been excavated and restored in India. This type of building reached Tibet much reduced in size and to some extent in a divergent form. It was of stone with a wooden top, very common in the countryside but in many monasteries made of precious metal. Not only were relics of the Buddha preserved in them but also the remains of monks and princes. They stood out clearly in the countryside and ultimately became a sort of landmark erected at important points or at places whence the road branched off to a high-lying monastery. Although they frequently have a special significance from the architectonic standpoint, probably symbolizing the construction of the world from the elements, they no longer have anything in common with the original construction: a monument erected over the relics of the Buddha.

FIG. 1

FIG. 2

The second great protector of Buddhism in India was King Kanishka of the Kushān Dynasty. This dynasty ruled over a powerful empire that not only extended over India proper but also included large parts of Central Asia. At that time Buddhism spread by way of the old trade routes from China to the Black Sea, and along the Silk Route bordering on Tibet. As Tibet lay on a forbiddingly high plateau it was avoided by the caravans linking east and west. In the Kushān era, which lasted from the beginning of our reckoning to 220 A.D., Buddhism underwent an unusual transformation, expressed not only in Buddhist teaching but also in the art which it inspired. The view gained ground that each man was a Bodhisattva, i.e., a being bearing within himself the seed of Enlightenment. As such he had the possibility of 'awakening' to the salvation of mankind and preaching the doctrine. This new teaching, which was less concerned with release from the cycle of reincarnation, but had as its aim the preparation of man for a future existence as a Bodhisattva, is known by its adherents as Mahāyāna, i.e., the Great Vehicle. It is also known as Bodhisattva-yāna, 'the vehicle of the awakening being'. On the other hand, the original form of Buddhism was termed Hīnayāna, the Lesser Vehicle or the Pratyeka-buddhayāna, 'the vehicle of the man who awakes himself'. In the realm of simple piety this thought is expressed in the legend of the Bodhisattva Avalokiteśvara. The latter incorporates a creature who on the way to salvation reached the threshold of Nirvāna, but then saw in a vision the suffering of all earthly creatures who had not yet been granted release. He swore an oath in which he renounced all the bliss promised to him until the moment when all mankind should have been released. He thereby became Mahākarunika, the great merciful one, who fulfils his tasks in the world for the sake of ordinary mortals, instead of withdrawing into the abstraction of beatitude as he was entitled to do. The Dalai Lama is regarded with good reason as the reincarnation of this Bodhisattva; the pious Buddhist will, when he is in need, implore this Bodhisattva Avalokiteśvara in particular, that 'liberator from the eight dangers', as he is also known. He is shown in this form in one of the oldest Tibetan representations in the cave-temple of Tun-huang, which lies at the most extreme north-easterly approaches to Tibet. In Mahāyāna, belief in the great Bodhisattvas is only part of a system in which, side by side with the

Hīnayāna and Mahāyāna

Fig. 1 – *Stūpa drawn on reverse side of a 'thang-ka'*

human Buddha-priest, several more theoretical Buddhas were created, integrated into a hierarchy of gods, aligned in the direction of the prevailing winds and recognizable by certain deviations in the position of their hands, the colour and the details of their thrones, etc. For example, the two hands of the Amitābha, the meditative or Dhyāni-Buddha of the West, lie in his lap, in an attitude of reflection, whereas Akshobhya, the Dhyāni-Buddha of the East, makes a gesture as though trying to touch the earth, etc. It seems strange to us that these varying gestures also symbolize certain important events from the life of Śākyamuni, the historic Buddha-man, so that it is often particularly difficult to discover whether a certain picture portrays a Dhyāni-Buddha or the historical Buddha at a certain phase of his life. These difficulties are repeatedly encountered in Tibetan art and can only be solved with the help of tiny details or an inscription.

In about the year 220 A.D. the power of the Kushān was thrust back from India to northern Afghanistan; this had as sequel an Indian time of troubles. But in about the fourth century the new powerful Gupta Dynasty arose. Its capital, Pātaliputra (Patna), was the old Magadha, which had once formed the centre of the empire of the Maurya Dynasty. At this epoch the Buddhist art of India reached its culminating point. It was distinguished by the flowing mobility of the garments which clung closely and transparently to the image of Buddha. A delicately worked circlet of rays often decorated his head. This form spread all over India proper, and from the south-east of the country made its way throughout the whole of South-east Asia.

Although the power of the Gupta Dynasty soon weakened again and new principalities formed in India, Gupta culture did not succumb to the deterioration in its political position. Buddhism and its art continued to develop; in this a particularly important part was played by the monastic universities in the area of Magadha. The most important of these was the powerful monastery of Nālandā, which lies somewhat to the south of Patna, and attracted many thousands of Buddhists in quest of knowledge from all the countries of Asia. Inscriptions from the ruins of this extensive university show that numerous princes, even some from Indonesia, erected hostels here so that the monks from their countries might be assured of fitting accommodation. It was also to this university that King K'ri-srong-lde-btsan sent his envoys to seek out scholars prepared to give Buddhism in Tibet a stronger foundation.

From these universities new views spread concerning the deeper values of Buddhism, and these gradually became universally acknowledged. In the Mahāyāna more and more importance was attached to the view that, apart from Buddhist doctrine, method also had a part to play, i.e., through the consistent observance of certain rules under the supervision of an experienced

Fig. 2 – *Symbolism of the stūpa in Lamaist cosmology*

171

teacher, and by following the path of specific mystical practices, supreme insight would necessarily be attained. No longer was an inner moral ripening at stake. Instead, growing importance was attributed to progressively advancing mystical development; this, it was thought, could be furthered by ritual acts in full conformity with sympathetic thought. This meant that whenever a symbol was employed in this mystical process an action referring to this symbol could further the inner process of mystical development. In the so-called *Tantras* — meaning literally textbooks or manuals — which were in reality mystical writings only accessible and comprehensible to the initiated, this system of method was further elaborated. It is for this reason that this later form of Buddhism *Vajrayāna* is known as Tantrayāna or also as Vajrayāna, for the symbol of the method was the *vajra* — the sceptre-shaped thunderbolt. This system attributes the unfolding of definite supernatural powers to the acquisition of higher mystical knowledge and insight. In practice the desire to exercise these powers often led to application of the method, which had as consequence a type of magical practice. The princes of numerous South-east Asian countries sent monks to these universities in order to strengthen their position, so that they, the monks, might acquire this knowledge and then use their secret powers to support the influence of their rulers. Those princes who had once been initiated into Tantric doctrine and then did not use it as a means to strengthen their power, must have been rare.

The system of gods employed in Tantrayāna is unusually complicated and gives the outsider the impression of being very obscure. It can be understood only after acquiring a certain insight into the particular background features of Tantrayāna, in which the different figures have a special and sharply defined task to fulfil. For this reason they often present a form which is quite incomprehensible to the non-initiated eye and can easily give rise to all kinds of misunderstandings and erroneous judgments, creating the impression that they are poor degenerations. This Vajrayāna was introduced by the great 'magician' Padmasambhava into Tibet, where it took root. Elsewhere, however, it collapsed, as much because of uninformed use of the texts and the resulting mixture of symbol and rite, as because of external influences, such as the challenging intervention of Islam with its opposition to any form of 'idolatry'. Because Tantric Buddhism played such a large part in Tibet, we shall examine its system of gods and the concealed background of its mystical basis.

In Mahāyāna we have already met a number of figures who may be described from a certain point of view as divine. Side by side with the historical Buddha and the Buddha of the next world-epoch, Maitreya, there had already crystallized out of Mahāyāna a system of Dhyāni-Buddhas — those 'meditative' Buddhas of the different points of the compass, and also of the eight great Bodhisattvas, those beings who bear in themselves the germ of Enlightenment

PLATE 3 – One of the eighteen Sthaviras or elders, those disciples of Buddha who travelled in foreign countries to spread the doctrine. *J. C. French Collection, British Museum*

and have set themselves the task of helping mankind to attain release. These Future Buddhas, which can be recognized by their princely Indian garments — was the Buddha before the *bodhi* not the son of a prince? — are now accompanied by feminine beings, the Tārās, who also wear Indian princely garb and stand side by side with the Bodhisattvas, and even the meditative Buddhas of the different points of the compass. What is strange is that these figures generally do not appear individually, but in groups which are arranged in precise geometrical systems, usually known as *mandalas*.

Mandalas   At the basis of the mandala lies a certain order which is revealed in everything: in the picture of the cosmos, of man, in the structure of the system of gods, etc. Everything that exists emerges from a germ-cell *(bīja)* which at the moment of creation is divided into two halves, one conceived of as masculine and the other as feminine. The world of appearances stems from the separation of these two elements. If the original state of things is to be re-established then the two elements must reunite and lose their identity in each other.

The system of gods expresses this basic thought in different ways. A mandala can be so constructed that it occupies the complete picture by an uncommonly elaborate system of triangles emerging one from the other. In the course of meditation these must be reduced to forms that become more and more simple until two triangles are all that remain; they are interlocked and finally dissolve in a single point. Such a mandala, however, can also be composed of several divine figures arranged around a central figure, which in its turn forms part of a more centrally placed higher figure, until everything is absorbed in a single central high figure. This embodies the Creator or the creative principle, which makes itself known in this manner. Occasionally such groups are united in a composite figure with numerous heads, arms and hands, producing at first a confusing impression. Only an expert can 'dissolve' such a figure into a series of separate images which together again form a mandala. The highest union, which is at the same time the symbol of the highest bliss, can also be reproduced by the absorption of the masculine and feminine principle in a divine figure depicted in bodily union with its feminine complement *(Śakti)*. All too hastily this was burdened by Lamaism with the stigma of moral decay. Such figures, however, were not intended to be seen by inquisitive ignorant outsiders but were only destined for those who had been taught to understand such portrayals by the method of, and under the direction of, their personal instructor.

The Tantric system of gods has another peculiar feature which cannot easily be expressed in a summary form and has only too easily provoked rumours about the practices of unscrupulous priests. We are referring to the demoniac interpretation of certain sequences often representing highly placed divine figures which must appear to outsiders only as demons. They are termed 'protectors of the sacred teaching', but their true meaning is only compre-

Symbolism   hensible to the person who has been initiated in the most remarkable symbolism employed by the mystical method in its final and highest phase. This method teaches that two paths must be distinguished — the right and the left path, that man must not tread the left path until he has first trod the right path and then only under the leadership of an experienced teacher. In the case of the right path the way leads through progressive inner purification to the dissolution of all bonds which fetter man to his earthly existence. The man who achieves this is able to reach Nirvāna, the state of 'the extinguished self', in which all human impulses are suppressed and all earthly fetters discarded. In traversing the left path not only are all human impulses suppressed, but this path leads to a complete destruction of all such feelings by means of a process in which 'one's own self' (the ego), which is composed of eight human dispositions and feelings, is completely extinguished and thereby can be absorbed into the primal principle. According to Lamaist teaching, it is only by means of this process that the stage of complete assimilation to the highest principle is attained, enabling man to participate in supreme salvation. In order to attain such a state by this special method, a rare symbolism of destruction is employed: in Tibet it is the destruction which attacks the human body after death.

This artificial destruction of the corpse is based on the fear, common everywhere in India, that a demon might use the dead body in order to assume a human shape and thus wreak evil in the world of man. In India this led to the burning of corpses which was, of course, impossible in a country such as Tibet owing to the lack of combustible material. A different procedure is therefore employed. The corpse is taken to a remote place where it is immediately dismembered and thrown to the vultures, who fulfil their task with the necessary speed. It is only the corpses of the highest monks which are occasionally burned; for it is supposed that a man who has reached a certain stage in his mystical evolution can burn his own body in the hour of death by means of his internal glow *(tejas)*.

From this traditional method of destroying corpses there developed in the mystical method a symbolism which represented the obliteration of one's own ego, consisting of the eight elements, in a journey along the eight sacred burial-grounds. These are sometimes inhabited by a group of three diabolical beings; one is masculine, the other feminine, and the third is looked on as the result of their union. These beings now carry out the desired destruction. The eight sacred burial-grounds symbolically complement the eight sectors of the human heart in which the ego, one's own self, has its seat. The description of the pilgrim's way along the eight sacred burial-grounds and of the horrors that take place there fill the non-initiate with revulsion. It is even worse, however, if a believer on the left path confuses, as a result of inadequate support from his instructor, what is symbolic and what is part of the ritual action. This can lead to horrifying practices which have led to the collapse of Buddhism in Bengal as well as Java and Sumatra. In Tibet, however, this method was better preserved, although even here the knowledge of its profound and genuine foundations was certainly not communicated to the thousands of monks who once inhabited the numerous monasteries of the country. It should be obvious why this form of Buddhism allows the instructor such an important role. The instructor must himself know and grasp the method in all its profundities and have practised it in every detail. It is his task to test the applicant in relation to the presuppositions of the method and to determine to what degree he is fitted to follow it. At the same time he must protect the applicant from heedless advances which exceed his capacity for understanding. The instructor must be fully aware, through innate sympathy with the candidate, whether the latter has sufficient insight to be able to determine what is symbolical and what is ritual action. For the execution of an action with symbolical meaning can, in accordance with this view, further the inner process to which the symbolism refers. Ritual action in a burial-ground would in this sense favour the desired process, in which the destruction of one's self is completed against the background of the symbolical burial-ground. The physical union with a feminine partner described and formed as Śakti should not only symbolize attainment of the highest union but can also be employed as a method of reaching the desired loss of identity. It should be quite clear what problems are posed by this, and also the extent to which the direction of an experienced teacher is necessary to preserve the requisite or desired separation between symbol and reality. In Tibetan history the reformation of Tsong-k'a-pa, the founder of the dGe-lugs-pa Order (also known as the Order of the Virtuous or Yellow Hats) does not only signify the exile of all the remarkable diabolical figures from the Lamaist pantheon but also the correction of the abuses which had resulted from inappropriate and inexpert use of the direct method. From now on it was essential, before employing this method, to have first traversed the right path in detail. Only then was one permitted, under reliable guidance and with repeated examination, to tread the left path. The supernatural powers thereby acquired must only be permitted to contribute to further intellectual and mystical development, and not at all to the acquisition of earthly power or secular privileges. It is worth noting at this point that there is repeated mention in Tibetan literature of mystics and saints to whom certain supernatural powers are ascribed. These stories are often regarded as narrations of true events. It would be more correct, however, to look on them as descriptions of certain steps in the mystical development of the person concerned; for it is to this that the stories refer, and not to the miraculous aspect of an action as such.

Tibetan literature also has numerous examples of the failure of a ritual action which yet goes hand in hand with supreme mystical consecration. There is a celebrated story in a work ascribed to the outstanding magician Padmasambhava. It tells of a monk who had spent a whole year in complete isolation in a monastery cell *(mgon-khang)*. His object was to prepare himself for the offer of the mandala sacrifice which accompanies the highest rites of consecration. At the beginning of the ceremony everything seemed to be taking a favourable course. The sacrificial butter was burning evenly and the lamps were smoking with a constant flame. Finally, the grimacing countenance of Mahākrodha (Bhairava, the figure of supreme terror) emerged. When the magic dagger *(p'ur-bu)* began to waver — sign of the annunciation of the godhead — and other favourable omens became visible, the guardians of the divinity began to kill large numbers of people whom they had chosen as sacrifices to Mahākrodha.

FIG. 3

PLATE 4 – The birth of the Buddha in the Lumbinī Park at Kapilavastu. Gold bronze, Nepal, 19th century.
According to legend Buddha emerged from the right side of his mother, Queen Māyā, while she was in Lumbinī Park breaking a bough from a tree with her right hand. This moment is fixed by the representation in a manner which strongly recalls the art of Gandhāra, fifteen hundred years earlier. The work is a good example of the survival of the iconographic tradition. *Cf. p. 163*

Then the feminine half of the god (Śakti) intervened and demanded of the monk that he expiate the sins of the guardians. Instead of offering himself as a sacrifice, the monk answered that this was not his task. By allowing himself to be induced to speak, he destroyed the result of his actions. He did not know what to do with the heaped-up corpses and Śakti reproached the guardians who, however, would not be satisfied and demanded that Śakti withdraw. The mistake that had been made caused everything to fail: the mandala clouded over, the molten sacrificial butter would no longer burn, the lamps began to smoke and the grimacing devils began to weep. Everything threatened the monk with disaster; when he tried to escape from the mandala, a great whirlwind blew up, making him a woeful sight and hurling him to the ground.

If it is desired to reach the highest aim by the direct method, then there must be thorough preparation for the intellectual ordeals imposed. To a certain extent the study of the apparitions described in the texts and absorption in them contributes to this. To prepare pictures of these alien diabolical beings demands great care in order that a result which approaches as closely as possible to reality be achieved. This can only be to one's advantage, for in the hour of ordeal one's visions will be less fearsome; the diabolical figures will be recognized and appropriately honoured.

Death and reincarnation The Tibetan mystic not only experiences these hours of ordeal in the final phases of his intellectual development; they enter the life of every Tibetan at the moment when he prepares to leave this world. In the Buddhist view there is a short interval between the moment of death and reincarnation in a certain class of animate beings. Whereas the simple doctrine declares that the hierarchy of reincarnation is determined by the relationship of good and evil actions carried out in the life that has ended, the lama of esoteric initiation is familiar with a method which will help him, by certain actions and thoughts, to create the prerequisites for possible reincarnation in a higher position than is foreseen in the law of *karma* (the result of the sum of good and evil actions). None the less,

PLATE 5 – Episodes from the life-story of Siddhārtha, the Buddha. Detail of a scroll-painting from central Tibet, end of the 18th century.
The scenes shown, executed with fine brush-strokes, and grouped around the central figure of the Buddha and two Bodhisattvas, depict different important events in Buddha's life. At the extreme right the 'fourth encounter' of the Future Buddha can be recognized: the encounter with a beggar monk which causes Siddhārtha to renounce his princely life. Slightly to the left are depicted the departure of the prince from his loyal servant Chandaka and his horse Kanthaka, both, according to legend, born on the same day as the Buddha. He is further shown cutting his long hair and laying aside his princely clothing to exchange it for a simple monk's cowl. Below, left, are shown episodes from his ascetic and meditative practices; slightly above, the preparation of the meal handed to him by the girl Sujātā, which revives the strength of the Future Buddha before he begins his last meditation. Above, somewhat to the right, the grass-cutter Svastika hands him a bundle of *kuśa* grass from which Siddhārtha makes himself a seat beneath the sacred fig-tree of Gayā. It is on this that he sits for his last meditation, which leads to the acquisition of *bodhi*, supreme insight. *Rijksmuseum voor Volkenkunde, Leyden. Cf. p. 165*

the sins of the past may weigh so heavily as to nullify all the efforts of the deceased to attain a higher position.

In the interval that lies between the onset of death and the choice of a new body, the spirit of the deceased reaches *Bardo*, that intermediate world between death and reincarnation. It is a strange world, one which has been seen and described by the mystics. A common Tibetan phrase has it: 'He who conducts himself rightly always lives happily, even in Bardo.' The initiated will not allow themselves to be frightened by the strange visions of the intermediate stage; they will rather be able to assure themselves of a better reincarnation. They may even be able to escape the eternal cycle of reincarnation *(samsāra)*. They have trained their spirit. As soon as it is released from the body it moves over, full of confidence, into the strange intermediate world which is awaiting it. When their last hour has struck they no longer need any support and the ritual on their death-bed is superfluous.

Laymen, on the other hand, are in a quite different position. But they are not left to their fate either, even if it is doubted whether the requisite ceremonies will have the desired result. During a man's struggle with death and as soon as he has breathed his last, the lama is already instructing the deceased in everything which his spirit in life had not been able to perceive and which he will now encounter. He explains to him the meaning of the strange figures and apparitions which will accompany his spirit in the intermediate period and attempts to quiet him. Above all, however, he does not rest from showing him the path that he must tread.

This is in no way unnecessary, for hardly has the spirit left the body than it enters on a strange voyage. Immediately after release it has an intuition of highest reality which manifests itself like a flash of lightning. If it is able to comprehend this illumination, it reaches Nirvāna. But this is not often the case. Usually the spirit, dazzled by the light, turns away as a measure of self-preservation and also because of erroneous understanding.

This is the first stage of Bardo, 'that moment in which death enters'. This stage, until the moment when the spirit is released from the body, is estimated to last three to four days. The end of this period comes when the dying man realizes that he is dead; for usually he does not immediately become aware of his new situation. For a few days he continues to converse with his former associates and is surprised that nobody answers his questions or notices his presence. His spirit is immediately disturbed: what can have happened? He sees his lifeless body which resembles his own, and is surrounded by lamas and members of his family. Is he perhaps 'dead'? At this moment his spirit is released and immediately follows the intuition of the highest light. During the second phase of Bardo, 'that transitional stage in which reality is comprehended', and which is said to last fourteen days, the spirit of the deceased is undoubtedly dependent on the leadership of an expert. The lama who is carrying out the ritual of death exhorts the spirit of the deceased to continue fearlessly on its journey for the sake of its salvation. It must not look round, for otherwise it would only try to avoid the dangers threatening it. Again and again it sees figures of great beauty and terrifying power. During the first seven days these strange figures have a friendly appearance, but from the eighth day onwards they turn bloodthirsty and terrifying. Unaware that there are no other demoniac apparitions than those springing from its own thoughts, heavy with the hallucinations of karma, the spirit wanders helplessly among these apparitions. It is hoped that it will follow the advice of the lama; if this is so, it can then tread the path of the initiated which will assure it reincarnation amongst the gods. But that man who in his lifetime has acquired no knowledge of Bardo and is full of grief at leaving his earthly existence can hardly profit from the lama's advice. He may not even hear it! Blind with anxiety and terror he hurries through this world, pursued by a horde of physical devils until, after the fourteenth day, he enters the third stage of Bardo, 'the transitional stage in which the search for reincarnation takes place'. The paths which lead to the higher forms of existence already lie behind him. Once again he roams through a wondrous world in which he looks out for a place able to offer him protection, a place whence he will no longer be ejected. At last he catches a glimpse of a grotto, a house or a castle, and enters one of them in the belief that here he will find shelter. But it is only a mirage, an illusory evocation of the womb of that being which will bring him back into the world; thus he chooses, confined by the law of his karma, an appropriate reincarnation and therewith seals his own fate.

The text of the Tibetan *Book of the Dead* describes in great detail the different diabolical and divine beings of which the spirit becomes aware during its stay in Bardo. They form an uncommonly interesting group and different artists have tried to give them shape. With almost infinite patience the artist has tried PLATE P. 240 to fix on canvas those figures seen and described by the mystics, and has used all his power to shape them in such a way as to stimulate the imagination. However improbable the description of their forms may be, he attempts to depict them in such a way that they mean something to the imagination. He himself will then not need to fear them, when his time comes and his own spirit enters Bardo. He will be able to say with a smile: 'I do not fear you, for I know you.' The man who is successful in this will see other worlds opening before him. It is thus manifest that these Bardo paintings, which depict all the figures of the intermediate period, are often executed with great care. But only rarely does the layman see these representations.

The monasteries have another means of familiarizing the lay population with *Mystery plays* the visions they will encounter after death: by devil-dances, as western travellers have described the mystery plays. Their content and purpose were incomprehensible to the travellers, but the beautiful and grotesquely shaped masks worn by the dancers on these occasions fascinated them. In reality they are mystery plays in the most literal sense of the word. They are performed by monks of a certain monastery and may only take place at fixed times, after thorough study. There is no question therefore of the dancers being possessed. Every step, every movement of the dance is carried out in precise accordance with the rules, and their correct observance is watched over conscientiously by the older monks and sages. The dance is accompanied by a recitation of the action that is being depicted and by a strange music which is undoubtedly suited to the evocation of a particular mood. There are several such dances, especially the New Year dances of the dGe-lugs-pa or Order of the Yellow Hats, and the dance of the 'Murder of the evil king Glang-dar-ma'. This takes place in different monasteries of the Order of the Red Hat on the tenth day of the fifth Tibetan month, the birthday of Padmasambhava. Enormous preparation is necessary, for the dances last several hours. The dancers prepare themselves ritually by a recitation in the temple. The dance itself is performed in the adjacent inner courtyard in the presence of the lay public assembled from far and near. The dancers often wear particularly precious clothing of Chinese silk and beautiful masks of carved wood or papier mâché which belong to the great treasures of the monastery. Whereas the layman sees in the dance or mystery play a representation of some historical event or other, it is possible on closer examination to discern that this is a secondary interpretation, behind which a very different meaning lies concealed. The mystery play is in fact most intimately connected with certain mystical imaginings, as already described. The layman merely sees how, for example, a priest may acquire supernatural powers by winning influence over the demons and then 'kills the evil king'; but the initiates understand that the whole action refers to the 'killing of one's own self', to the eight symbolical burial-grounds. It is therefore not surprising that the groups of eight demoniac beings which appear in these plays, and which to a layman are 'the terrifying defenders of the sacred teaching', are known to initiates as *krodha* or horrifying figures of the eight great Bodhisattvas, which will help them to acquire the highest insight. These dances are truly an impressive experience and a magnificent spectacle for anyone who has seen them in all their glory amidst the mountains of the Tibetan borderlands.

PLATE 6 – The Buddha encircled by the eight great Bodhisattvas sitting in the paradise of Sukhāvatī. Beautiful scroll-painting whose style reveals strong Chinese influence. Southern Tibet, beginning of the 19th century.
The Buddha is surrounded by the eight Mahābodhisattvas, whereby he can be identified as such; otherwise one would easily be tempted to think of the Dhyāni-Buddha Amitābha, especially as there is a pool before his throne in which the souls of the blissful are reborn. This suggests that we have here the paradise of Sukhāvatī, a motif which is less well known in Tibet than it is, for example, in China and Japan. At the foot, the Buddha Śākyamuni is once again shown, this time in the earthly realm as a wandering priest followed by some disciples. *Rijksmuseum voor Volkenkunde, Leyden*

II. ART AND ARTISTS

It has already been shown that Tibetan art is a committed and a commissioned art. Behind it there stands not the creative urge of the individual artist to form a work of art but the commission of a powerful individual to prepare a serviceable item for a monastery or a private chapel. The motives of those who give the commissions cannot be summarized under one heading but in certain texts different motives are adduced. In the Āryamañjuśrīmūla Tantra, for example, it is pointed out that a commission can be given in order to acquire spiritual merit *(punyasambhāra)* or even to achieve a certain magical end. In the latter case the concern is mostly with wealth or a long life. Very often representations of this type reveal in the lower corners of the picture the figures of Vaiśravana, the 'god of wealth', and of Mahākāla or Yama, the latter being the 'god of the kingdom of the dead'. At times a small figure depicting the donor will appear in a posture of humble homage in the main part of the picture. At times also, the text of a plea imploring protection and a long and happy life will be affixed beneath the picture.

However, if we try to acquire a more general view of Tibetan art and to analyse not only its externals but also its inner motives, it is clear that it can be divided into several groups which are most intimately connected with the aim for which it is created. Such a division can of course only be superficial, but does make it possible for us to appraise more correctly what we see. The

TYPES OF PAINTING

Decorative paintings

following types of paintings can be distinguished: decorative, instructive, meditative, contemplative and visionary representations.

The first group serves to decorate certain rooms, living-rooms, reception-rooms, libraries, etc. Representations of this type follow a consistent sequence as, for example, the picture series of the Tashi Lama or the Dalai Lama. But the principal representations are of Buddha surrounded by his favourite disciples, the eighteen Sthaviras or elders and the four protectors of the world. These occur in a series which is repeatedly met with arranged in various ways, in an odd number of paintings — often three, sometimes five or even seven. The figure of the historical Buddha occupies the centre, and the other representations are grouped on both sides in equal proportions. Sometimes the figure of the Buddha appears on each individual picture, and it is only the accompanying personages who change. In order that these individual parts may be shown in the right sequence, they often contain on their reverse an instruction in Tibetan script which indicates their correct place: e.g., 'right 3' means that this figure is to be hung in the third place to the right of the central portion.

The portraits to the right of the central panel are generally turned to the left, i.e., in the direction of the central panel. This at once suggests a method whereby the date of the picture sequence can be approximately determined. The most important figure always occupies the centre and is shown full-face, whereas the others are shown more or less in profile. Now the most important figure is in most cases the final figure in the order of hierarchs, whereas the remaining pictures indicate, so to speak, the spiritual order of descent. But because this most important figure must at a certain moment seek out for itself 'a new body', the sequence is later extended by a new portrait which in turn then reveals the figure depicted full-face, and so on. This procedure is at its clearest in the sequence of official depictions of the so-called Tashi Lama.

Certain sequences of representations of devils can also be included amongst these decorative picture series. They adorn the tantra-chamber of a monastery, and are usually pictures of the *drag-gsed*, the 'eight terrifying beings', a certain sequence of eight diabolical beings who to the layman are the 'protectors of the sacred doctrine'. But to the initiates of the Tantra school they signify certain emanations of the eight great Bodhisattvas who confer on man the help he needs on his path to esoteric knowledge. In this case the pictures have a thoroughly conventional character; for although careful attention is given to all the iconographic requirements, the works are not characterized by spiritual power. Generally speaking, we may say that these decorative pictures are undoubtedly executed with great technical skill, but they cannot be put on a par with genuine works of art. For this they usually lack an inspiring expressiveness. Moreover, there is an exaggerated elaboration of detail whose free formation is left to the artist. Such series were usually made in accordance with unchanging patterns from which preliminary impressions were prepared — woodcuts printed on canvas — or pounce patterns. A complete series of such models is known for the portraits of the Tashi Lama. It is therefore not fortuitous that those portraits are so stereotyped and sometimes have the same measurements; it is only the details shown in the background which vary. This category of pictures may be regarded as thoroughly conventional and stiffly formal.

To the category of instructive paintings belong those which show in the centre *Instructive paintings* a figure intended to serve the spectator as a model or to depict graphically an edifying tale. These are usually embodied in a series of short episodes arranged in a landscape around the central figure; in most cases the story moves clockwise around the central figure, beginning at the top on the right and ending at the top on the left. The life story of the Buddha takes first place in such works and forms the most important material. Early on a mythology developed describing the intervention of the gods in the existence of man. Supernatural powers were already attributed to Siddhārtha as a child. As a boy he not only excels all his fellow-pupils in knowledge but also his teachers; in every contest he not only overcomes his comrades by greater dexterity, but does this with the help of capacities which exceed those of the normal man: he can throw an elephant; he does not swim in water but hovers over it. There are no limits to the artist's fantasy when the struggle against Māra is depicted. The miraculous deeds ascribed to the Buddha, such as the 'great miracle of Śravasti' during which he overcame his opponents by dissolving himself in air, provided rewarding themes for the artist. But the main emphasis remains with the four great encounters in which Prince Siddhārtha, accompanied by his faithful charioteer Chandaka, meets in succession an old man, a sick man, a dead man and a beggar monk, all of which determines him to take leave of his princely life. According to legend it is only with the help of the gods that he is able to leave the palace of his father. He sits on his horse Kanthaka and leaves the palace in the depth of night while the sentries are sleeping. They hear no hoof-beats because the gods are supporting the horse's legs. In addition to this edifying story of Śākyamuni, the Jātakas or birth-narratives also offer rewarding material for these instructive pictures. Some of these have particularly impressed the Tibetans, especially the story of the pious prince Viśvantara whose good deeds went so far that he gave away all his possessions. When he was put to the test by the gods he even gave up his wife and children and, finally, even his eyesight so that he might benefit others. He is rewarded in the end for his good deeds and recovers his wife and family, his sight and his possessions. This story is repeatedly used for these edifying pictures. It also provided material for a mystery play which enjoys great popularity among the people.

Not only did the life story of the Buddha and the Jātaka narratives provide themes for these instructive paintings; the lives of saints and princes of the church fulfilled the same purpose. The saint himself occupies the central place with his life story unfolding around him. It is not always the more spectacular events which are shown but often visits to monasteries, certain controversies or even visions. In tiny gold lettering a quotation taken from the text of the biography is often added to the smaller scenes of the picture. It gives the necessary explanation and provides the narrator with a focus of reference. An 'expert' explains these pictures to the public; in doing so he adheres as closely as possible to the documented life story. In this case also there is no question of a free interpretation or reproduction of those events which were decisive in the life of a saint. We know of whole series of paintings which depict the life story of a Padmasambhava, of a Tsong-k'a-pa or even of a mystic such as Milaraspa, who became known for his lyrical songs and can always be recognized by the way in which he is shown: clad all in white, he sits in a grotto, his right hand to his ear, listening to the voices of supernatural beings. We are also familiar with instructive paintings of this type from the lives of certain historical, non-ecclesiastical dignitaries such as King Srong-btsan-sgam-po and the national hero Kesar. The legend of the latter is used in a popular epic in which many

PLATE 7 – Gilded bronze statue of the Dhyāni-Buddha Akshobhya. Lamaist bronze from eastern Tibet or western China. Middle of the 19th century.
Characteristic example of a bronze from the late period of Lamaism, in which the artist reproduced the details of head and hands with great care but already treated the remainder of the figure in a purely conventional manner. The sitting Buddha figure, his hands in the position of 'touching the earth' (bhūmisparśamudrā) probably does not depict the historical Buddha but the Dhyāni-Buddha of the East. The statue is manufactured by the *cire-perdue* process, whereas the lotus footpiece is executed in embossed technique. The gilding still retains the beautiful old hue from which it may be concluded that no use was made of alloys. *Rijksmuseum voor Volkenkunde, Leyden*

supernatural achievements are mentioned; hero-worship receives greater emphasis than the spiritual significance of the figure, who is entirely enveloped in myth.

Meditative paintings The meditative pictures are employed in the execution of meditative practices. These are in particular the so-called mandala paintings, which are immediately recognizable as such. They are formed in a strict geometrical pattern that is often two-dimensional, but in certain cases in such a way as to make the mandala appear three-dimensional, as a 'mountain of the gods'. Mandalas are cosmic symbols whose strict geometrical structure displays the order of the cosmos, and are always shaped in such a way that they build up the whole picture from a central point but must in meditation return to this central point. They are mostly arranged in a square; on each side are projections, known as gates, divided by diagonals into four parts differently coloured. In the centre there is an intricate rosette of outlines of lotus-leaves, which are filled with divine figures. Inside the rosette stands a divine figure and sometimes a book protected by a parasol or a *pajong*. The large square is also surrounded by several lotus-leaves, and the space between the square and the innermost circle filled with all sort of symbols of good fortune, such as banners of victory. Finally the whole composition is enclosed by a border of rainbows and flames; the latter serves the mandala as an outer border. Because a circular figure of this type is often shown on a long piece of linen, a great deal of space remains free above and below the mandala. On the upper side this is filled in by adding a number of figures of peace-loving gods and by the doctrine and method of the preachers, i.e., a series of saints and hierarchs who belonged to the sect of the person giving the commission. The names of these figures are frequently given. This sometimes makes it possible to determine approximately the age of the paintings; the dating of those figures who occupy the most important places can be derived with certainty from historical sources. The space beneath the mandala is almost always inhabited by three or five diabolical figures belonging to the sequence of 'protectors of the doctrine'. All these marginal figures generally stand out against a landscape background. They have a purely decorative value and serve at most as an introduction to meditative practice, which is limited to the mandala proper. Yet these subordinate figures can be executed with great skill and devotion, and they not infrequently contain masterly depictions in miniature.

Contemplative paintings The contemplative representations help the person of advanced spirituality to establish a spiritual world-picture. The painting no longer serves purely meditative purposes, but is the *point de départ* for the world-picture that is to be formed in his mind, and to a certain extent invented — one which springs from a single point and is finally offered to the supreme principle as a spiritual gift. In order to be effective as a *point de départ* it employs primarily symbolic representations which the non-initiated is usually unable to interpret. It also often happens that such pictures are constructed by the initiate himself in the course of contemplation and are destroyed after use. They therefore manifest a mysterious character which is not lacking in a visionary element, even if the representations are based on knowledge acquired through a theoretical discipline. The individual pictures of this type, known to the West mainly through reproductions, are testimony to an outstanding creative gift on the part of the unknown artist who sought to put all his energy into his work, to make it express his innermost feelings.

In the visionary paintings that stage is reached in which the initiate himself has seen the strange figures and now holds them fast in the picture that they may serve others for meditation and contemplation. The style of representation here attains a fantastic power of expression, not only because it has been completely mastered and its technique applied with the ultimate degree of refinement, but because a direct visionary element emerges from the paintings. However incomprehensible these figures may appear to our understanding, they yet speak to us as real and living beings. The peculiarity of the colours, which stand out against a completely black background, are a help in this. The figures seem to come away from the background. Tremendous technical capacity is demanded of the artist, for he must comprehend the whole figure completely before he can re-create it in the picture; the technique employed makes it practically impossible to erase an erroneous line.

Visionary paintings

It can be clearly seen how the artistic value of the pictures keep step with the varying requirements of religious purpose. Amongst them there are pictures of such suggestive power that, despite their incomprehensible forms, they evoke an impression of extraordinary beauty. Whereas the first groups of paintings mentioned were destined for a broad lay public, the last group belongs to the 'secret representations', i.e., they are paintings only of significance to the initiated and are not intended to be seen by the non-specialist. But as this is difficult to avoid over a period, such paintings have been given a double meaning. To the initiated the strange figures exercise immediate efficacy within the whole process of meditation which helps him to attain the higher stages of Enlightenment. To the non-initiated, on the other hand, these strange figures, with their often terrifying exterior, signify nothing more than those diabolical beings overcome by Buddha and now known as 'protectors of the sacred doctrine'. Their purpose is to deter enemies of the doctrine or, in case of necessity, to destroy them. It is for this reason that secondary myths have formed around these figures: i.e., legends devised for the non-initiated which will explain their unusual exterior but without sacrificing their genuinely mystical and symbolical meaning. It is precisely these legends that were the first to be noted down by western scholars who did recognize their strangeness but, generally speaking, failed to perceive the very different truth concealed behind them. Only too often, therefore, they rejected these figures as completely incomprehensible and were unable to apprehend the beauty with which they were depicted. It was only later that insight was acquired into their deeper meaning, and esteem for these strange representations has grown visibly. They not only reveal unprecedented symbolic intuition but also testify to the unexpected virtuosity of the unknown artist.

TECHNIQUE   After this survey of the different groups of paintings and of the factors at work in artistic appreciation, we will now turn to the artist and his technique.

The artist   The artist often belonged to no monastic order at all but had to be trained under the direction of experienced and qualified monks if his work was to serve the purpose for which it was created. Not only was the artist always bound by his theme; this also applied to composition, to the way in which physical proportions were reproduced, to the exact reproduction of all parts of the body, especially the face and hands, and even the attitude of the body, the way in which the human figure stood out from the background, etc. Only here and there was a small degree of freedom allowed him, particularly in respect of the representation of landscape in which, above all from the period of the Emperor Ch'ien-Lung onwards, figures were inserted. But even here his freedom was by no means unlimited, for it is precisely in such small details that a definite symbolism can be concealed. The consequence of all this is that the artist must be subjected to a rigorous training before he is in a position to prepare a work of any significance. This knowledge is first given to him orally; but he will have to practise for a long period to acquire the necessary manual dexterity required to draw lines with a firm and secure hand. It is only partly, however, a question of training under the watchful eye of a teacher who will, moreover, also instruct him in the preparation of his colours and his canvas. The artist must also be instructed in the sacred tradition as laid down in the different texts. These show him not only how he must prepare himself spiritually for his work, or how he may find out the appropriate time for the execution of different parts of

PLATE 8 – Story of the origin of the first depiction of Buddha according to a legend from the Divyāvadāna.

According to this legend Rudrāyana, the king of Roruka, gave to King Bimbisāra of Magadha a present of a beautiful suit of armour. The latter was so overwhelmed that he summoned experts to determine the value of the gift in order that he might make an appropriate gift in return. The experts, however, reported that the gift was priceless, and this distressed the king. But he remembered the Buddha who was present in his kingdom and decided to explain his difficulties to the Sublime One. Buddha advised the prince that he should have his, Buddha's, portrait painted and present it to King Rudrāyana. Bimbisāra immediately called the painters and commissioned them to prepare a portrait of the Buddha. But this task proved to be unusually difficult; the painters were so overwhelmed by Buddha's presence that they forgot their task. They requested the king to prepare a banquet for the Buddha so that they might observe him at leisure, but they also proved unable to use this opportunity. The Sublime One knew of their difficulties. He advised the king to spread out a cloth on which he would allow his shadow to fall. In this way the painters only needed to draw in the outlines of the shadow and could later colour in the flat surface. And that is what happened. Subsequently the painting was appropriately framed. King Rudrāyana was informed of the gift and requested to accept it in accordance with the prescribed ceremonial; and thus the king came into possession of the first portrait of the Buddha.

This episode is in part depicted here: top right, the suit of armour being presented to King Bimbisāra and valued; extreme left, in the centre of the picture, the artists observing the Buddha; further towards the centre of this part of the picture the king is holding his banquet, and Buddha is casting his shadow on the outspread cloth. Extreme right, in the lower half of the picture, the ceremonial procession can be seen in which the portrait of the Buddha was conducted to Roruka. In the centre, the picture is shown occupying the place of honour in the castle of King Rudrāyana. The required sacrificial gifts are being offered. Detail from a thang-ka. *Musée Guimet, Paris*

his work; he will also be taught in detail how he must conform to the accepted formal directives. These directives not only lay down technical rules whereby a good result can be achieved; they are also based on a certain cosmological idea only rarely understood by the outsider.

Navātala system

In drawing a figure one takes as one's starting-point a network of horizontal and vertical lines in which the span *(tala)* is taken as a unit of length, i.e., the span between the tip of the thumb and the tip of the index finger of an outstretched hand, which corresponds to the distance from the hair-line to the chin. This span is subdivided into twelve thumbs *(angguli* = fingers). In sketching pictures and other representations of the gods the starting-point is

FIG. 4

a certain division such as the *navātala* or nine-span system. In this the standing body is divided into nine portions, each one span in height. This construction of the figure in nine superposed layers coincides to such a degree with the nine-fold division of the world that it can be assumed that in the creation of the *navātala* system the analogy between the macrocosmos and the microcosmos was borne in mind. In other words, the regularity of an ideal world-picture was to be reproduced in a smaller body also constructed on an ideal basis. In this way the picture of the ideal man — and Buddha can certainly be regarded as such — was determined by this system. The application of the *navātala* system was therefore not determined exclusively by technical rules, even if the examples known to us, both from Buddhist texts and from artists' practice manuals, reveal how the problem of bodily proportions, and even of the smallest parts of the body, could be technically solved in a practical manner. There was not only instruction in how certain divine figures must be drawn, but many details were regulated to the last degree. What is surprising is the peculiar interaction between certain decorative elements in painting and those woodcut illustrations encountered in important Tibetan writings, especially in the celebrated text of the *Vaidurya kar-po*, a sort of universal encyclopaedia.

Block printing

In Tibet books are produced by block printing. For every page a woodcut is prepared which is immediately pulled on paper usually manufactured in Bhūtan from a sort of mulberry-tree. These blocks were carefully preserved and anyone who wanted a copy of a certain work procured the necessary paper himself. Because woodcut technique was employed in the printing of these books, efforts were soon made to supply such works with individual illustrations. To this extent they may be compared with Indian books whose first pages also often bear illustrations, although these works were written (cut in palm-leaves) and the pictures often painted with a delicate miniaturist technique of a type which we will also find in Tibet. What is surprising is that these illustrations have exerted an influence on the details of other paintings. In the artists' sketch books, in which preliminary work for larger paintings was carried out, we often encounter exact copies of illustrations from block prints. These for their part are taken from larger paintings which are shown *en miniature*.

Iconographic manuals are also known in Tibet. They reveal the whole system of gods of a certain temple in sequences of, at most, three godheads shown side by side. But the examples at our disposal are few in number and are of a relati-

vely late period. It may be assumed, however, that this method has been followed for centuries. The best known example is the pantheon of lSang-skya Hutuktu Lalitavajra, the famous Yellow Hat hierarch from Peking who lived at the time of the Emperor Ch'ien-Lung. It is a block print of a pantheon of three hundred gods which was prepared in Peking in 1790 on behalf of this highest authority of Lamaist Buddhism. This small book has one hundred folios, on each of which three gods are shown with their names in Tibetan; on the reverse of the following folio are the appropriate *dhārāris* or invocation formulae. At the end of the nineteenth century Pander came across a copy of this work in the famous 'Temple of Eternal Peace' (Yūng-huô-kūng) in Peking. A little while later it was published by Grünwedel. This is the first manual from which the numerous godheads met with in the Lamaist pantheon could be identified. Through a lucky chance we have recently learnt that this little book was produced from a painted representation of the complete pantheon. It was distributed over three painted scrolls, each of one hundred figures, which must have belonged to the famous Hutuktu Lalitavajra. They were stolen during the Chinese revolution; in the meantime two of its parts have turned up again in private collections. There is no doubt that the wood-engravers who cut the blocks for the handbook used these pictures as their model. There is such a coincidence of form, and the explanations on the pictures correspond so closely to those of the manual, that it can be asserted with certainty that the handbook was manufactured at the end of the eighteenth century on the model of an already existing painted pattern, for the general instruction of those artists chosen to copy such systems of deities for other monasteries.

FIG. 6

The same hierarch took great care in establishing precise rules for Lamaist iconography. For example, it was on his behalf that in 1748 a Chinese Lamaist text *(Tsao Hsiang Liang-tu Ching)* was prepared; according to the colophon, Wang Ai-yeiëh from Ho-shuo carved the blocks. This 'classical text of measurements for the preparation of representations' is ascribed to Śāriputra, one of the oldest disciples of Buddha, although the text has been greatly adapted. It is instructive, however, to quote a part of this text in order to give an example of the way in which one of the most complicated figures of the Lamaist pantheon was to be drawn. It is the eleven-headed, thousand-armed form of the Bodhisattva Avalokiteśvara, a figure who is regularly met with in Tibetan art.

The text gives the following description: 'There is a further form of this Bodhisattva and it is the eleven-headed, thousand-armed Avalokiteśvara. The measurements of the body coincide with those of the upright-standing Buddha. The frontal head corresponds to the size of a Buddha head, i.e., it is ten *angguli* high and has a friendly expression; the side-head to the right is blue, to the left red; the width of these side-heads corresponds to half the frontal head, if this half, calculated to the tip of the nose, is widened by one angguli. Of the following (higher) three heads, the middle is eight angguli high and yellow-white in colour; it has wrinkled eyebrows, whereas the two heads to the right and left are yellow and orange in colour, and their width corresponds to half the frontal head with the addition of a further six strokes. The frontal head of the third area is seven angguli high, red in colour and with a friendly expression, whereas the head to the right is green, and that to the left purple, and their width is again half the frontal head, each increased by five strokes from the nasal spread. The head belonging to the fourth area is the only fearsome one; it is six angguli high, dark blue in colour, and has a curled mane like that of a lion. The topmost head, red or golden, is that of the Amitābha. All the heads, with the exception of this one, have three eyes and the visible ears of the heads on the outside are joined with those of the centre.'

'The arms are drawn as follows. From the pit of the stomach (precisely in the centre between the two nipples) move six angguli upwards and from there one span *(tala)* to each side and mark a point. Three angguli upwards is the top of the shoulder, three angguli below — the armpit. From the marked point a (half) arc with a radius of fifty angguli is drawn to each side. This encompasses

PLATE 9 – Inlaid ornamental plaque of gilt bronze. The Buddha is sitting under the sacred fig-tree defying the temptations of Māra (Māradarshana). Southern Tibet, 18th century.
Buddha occupies the central point of the tableau, his hands gesturing towards the earth (bhūmisparśamudrā), whereby he evokes the goddess of earth as witness to the selflessness of his striving for salvation. The four daughters of Māra can be recognized; with their dancing they are trying to disturb the Buddha in his meditation. Māra and his supporters are hurling weapons through the air at Buddha, but they turn into flowers. The four corners of the tableau are occupied by the four guardians of the world. The small figures inlaid in silver depict heavenly beings who witness the great event and praise Buddha's steadfastness. *Rijksmuseum voor Volkenkunde, Leyden*

FIG. 5 – *Decorative motif on printed text of the Vaidurya-kar-po, a frequent ornament in representations*

the surface inside which all the arms must lie. None of the hands, even when the arms are outstretched, must break through this circle. The thousand arms are divided as follows: eight belonging to the Dharmakāya manifestation, forty to that of the Sambhogakāya and nine hundred and fifty-two belonging to Nirmānakāya. In order to draw these correctly, now describe inside the arc enclosing the hands six successive circles, the radius of each of which is four anguli smaller than that of the preceding circle. The portion lying within the smallest circle is now (on both sides of the body) divided into three equal sectors, in which three pairs of Dharmakāya hands with their attributes are drawn. The fourth pair lie closely folded on the breast. The next arc, lying between the innermost and the following circle, is divided on both sides into three parts, each of which is arranged in six segments. The two outer ends of each are lengthened by one further segment, and in each of these segments a hand is drawn; in this way the forty hands of Sambhogakāya are obtained, each of which bears its appropriate attribute (which are named in the text).'

There is next a description of the way in which the nine hundred and fifty-two hands of Nirmānakāya must be drawn. 'For this purpose the adjacent arcs are divided on both sides in turn into twelve, fourteen, sixteen, eighteen and

FIG. 6 – *Page from a manual dealing with the 84 'mahāsiddhas', or yogis, who — regardless of their profession — have obtained the highest degree of insight by employing exactly the method appropriate to their way of life. The number 84 is not fortuitous; it is used symbolically to denote 'innumerable' or 'general'*

PLATE 10 – Vajradhāra, the central figure in the later Buddhist system of gods. Bronze, Nepal, 15th century.

Vajradhāra wears the princely decoration of a Bodhisattva; his hands are folded on his breast; the right hand holds the *vajra* (symbol of the method) and the left the prayer-bell (symbol of the doctrine). The artless fold of the shawl around his shoulders and the simple design of the lotus cushion suggest the relatively early date of this piece. *Rijksmuseum voor Volkenkunde, Leyden*

twenty parts, each of which is again subdivided into six segments. In each of these segments a hand is now drawn, with the exception of the bottom-most fans of the arc, which are divided into twelve, fourteen, sixteen and eighteen parts. Each hand has an eye which is all-seeing.' The text next gives rules for the position of the legs, the shape of the feet, as well as the decoration and adornments of the figure, and mentions the antelope-skin which the Bodhisattva wears thrown over the left shoulder.

It is in fact the case that a figure with a thousand arms can be constructed in this way:

In the innermost circle	2×4	$= 8$ arms (Dharmakāya)
In the first arc	$2 \times 3 \times 6 + 4$	$= 40$ arms (Sambhogakāya)
In the second arc	$2 \times 12 \times 6 - 2$	$= 142$ arms
In the third arc	$2 \times 14 \times 6 - 2$	$= 166$ arms
In the fourth arc	$2 \times 16 \times 6 - 2$	$= 190$ arms (Nirmānakāya)
In the fifth arc	$2 \times 18 \times 6 - 2$	$= 214$ arms
In the sixth arc	$2 \times 20 \times 6$	$= 240$ arms
	Total	$1,000$ arms

In this way the text gives precise technical details of this strange figure, but without explaining them in the slightest. It is only from the names given to the types of hands in the three groups of the three *kāyas* that the symbolism hidden within this form can be deduced. The figure of the Avalokiteśvara with eleven heads and eight arms represents a simplified form of the same Bodhisattva, which has also attracted the attention of scholars. The following explanation was given to the curious. The Bodhisattva Avalokiteśvara was so saddened by the lot of the damned in the Buddhist hells that he repeatedly descended to them to convert the sinners and to release them that they might be admitted to the paradise of his spiritual father Amitābha, the Buddha of Infinite Light. But he was greatly grieved to see that for every soul which he released in this manner another one immediately took its place; out of despair at so much suffering and at the extent of evil in the world his head split into ten parts. Then his spiritual father caused separate heads to spring from the ten parts, to which he added his own, so that the Bodhisattva of Great Compassion might have eleven heads instead of one with which to devise means of saving mankind. This story is characteristic of a secondary myth in that it provides a pseudo-reason for the fact that the figure is adorned with eleven heads. But it does not explain why one of the faces has wrinkled eyebrows and another a diabolic exterior. The figure cannot in fact be explained in this way, for it is formed by combining a series of eleven individual figures. This series consists of a group of eight plus one of the same characteristics belonging to the sphere of Nirmānakāya, one from the Sambhogakāya which has a horrifying exterior, and a further being which, as Buddha, belongs to the Dharmakāya system, as is clear from Fig. 7. The composite figure of Avalokiteśvara with the eleven heads results from a concentration of this group into a single figure, a phenomenon often met with

PLATE P. 201

PLATE 11 – Multi-coloured wooden sculpture showing the Dhyāni-Buddha Vajrasattva in the garments and with the attributes of a Bodhisattva. Southern Tibet, 17th century.
Fine example of an old wooden sculpture of which only few are known in Tibet. The figure bears the adornments of a Bodhisattva– i.e., the Indian princely dress which leaves the upper part of the body exposed and clothes the lower part in a beautiful nether garment. The left hand, resting on the hip, holds the prayer-bell; the tip of the index finger of the right hand originally held a *vajra* which has been broken off. The crown or princely hair style is also slightly damaged. *Rijksmuseum voor Volkenkunde, Leyden*

in the Lamaist pantheon, especially in the case of the complex diabolic figures. What is surprising in considering the drawing and practice manuals of Tibetan painters is the extent to which they were trained in the precise reproduction of details, of ornaments, and even in the execution of certain decorative motifs. This is exemplified in the borders running round the aureoles encircling the peace-loving figures of the pantheon, and also in the wreaths of flame radiating from the demoniac figures.

But the texts not only give an exact description of the details of the figures to be shown; they also describe down to the last detail the whole happening that is to be reproduced. Now, the aim of these texts is not always to achieve a pictorial

PLATE 12 – Eleven-headed and eight-armed Avalokiteśvara; gold bronze from Sikkim, 19th century. The iconographic rules have been followed precisely in the production of this bronze statue; the radiant garland is characteristic of the art of Sikkim. The strange design of this Bodhisattva is explained by a secondary myth: Avalokiteśvara was so affected by the fate of those creatures who descended into hell because of their inability to do good that his head split into ten parts; he was constantly thinking how mankind might be redeemed. His spiritual father Amitābha thereupon made each part into a separate head and added his own so that the Bodhisattva might more successfully conceive of a means to help mankind. However, the true origin of the figure is to be sought in the concentration of a group of figures from a certain system into one composite figure. *Rijksmuseum voor Volkenkunde, Leyden.* *Cf. p. 198*

representation of the event. In many cases their aim is purely to describe a certain event or a certain situation so that the reader of the text can form an image in his mind and then experience it as vividly as possible. Thus details constantly recur which are not appropriate for pictorial reproduction but are thoroughly in keeping with the aim of imagining a certain event. It is of special interest, when once it has been possible to establish a direct connection between a certain painting and a certain text, to note what has actually been achieved on this occasion. Basically, it is only in such cases that one can be certain of having identified a picture; it means that the painter depicting the story was familiar with all the refinements of the texts. In so far as he had not acquired his knowledge by study, he had to rely on the very precise instructions of an expert. The majority of paintings can therefore only have emerged through close co-operation between painter and expert—apart, of course, from the stereotyped forms of the decorative or instructive paintings with their repetitive and cliché-like pictures of people and biographies. This is true also of the unchanging series of godheads, which turn up again and again in groups, and have definite characteristics which make them familiar to everybody.

Series of paintings

One of the greatest problems posed by the identification of a certain painting on the basis of the available texts is whether the painting concerned is to be considered as complete in itself or as one item in a series. Sometimes a large part of a painting can be followed with almost complete precision by reference to a certain text; then we encounter other figures which are not mentioned directly in the text. This can often be explained by the fact that the picture once belonged to a series, and a certain group of gods has been distributed over the whole picture series in a very precise manner without it being necessary for the figures to have direct reference to the painting before us. This applies, for example, to the series of portraits of the Tashi Lama. They are sometimes inhabited by diabolic figures based on visions seen by the personages concerned; but in other cases they can only be explained by reference to the system in which a group of figures is distributed over a number of paintings.

Another difficulty in identification must be overcome. It often happens, for example, that the painter — probably on the instructions of the expert — has been allowed no freedom in the disposition and representation of a group of figures in the centre of the painting. He has, however, filled with other personages the upper and side edges of the picture surrounding the central figure and

PLATE 13 – The Bodhisattva Padmapāni; fragment of a radiant garland of gold bronze which belongs to a large Buddha statue originating in the dPal-k'or c'os-de monastery of Gyantse. 16th century.
The figure of the Bodhisattva, clad in princely clothing and inlaid with stones, is in the so-called *tribhanga* position — i.e., an S-shaped, bent posture characteristic of the Indian ideal of beauty of the Palā Dynasty and particularly popular in Nepal. Next to the Bodhisattva the elephant, lion and winged tiger *(vyālaka)* stand out against a background intertwined with lotus-shoots. The right side is bounded by a magnificently worked lotus-shoot growing from a *kumbha* (a pot-shaped vessel) and is enlivened with all sorts of small figures. This shoot is surrounded by a string of pearls and a line of *vajras;* the outer side is formed of a flame. *Rijksmuseum voor Volkenkunde, Leyden*

203

his subordinate figures (his *parivāra*). This applies particularly to the four corners. These additional figures are often extremely difficult to interpret. Generally speaking, a painting of this type can be compared with the arrangement of a mandala painting; here also, not only was the central portion the most important but its details were laid down precisely as well. The upper portion contained a series of figures which included the central figure of the system of the sect concerned, who was joined by a series of 'transmitters of the doctrine and the method'. It is precisely in this category that there are sometimes differences between individual monasteries which can only be resolved if the lists of abbots who have governed the monastery are available. On the lower border there appear the different demoniac 'protectors of the sacred doctrine' who basically belong to that group of godheads from which the mystic has chosen his special *Yidam*, his leader, known only to him and his instructor. It is for this reason that the central segment of a picture can sometimes be completely explained with the help of the available texts, whereas the 'filling-in figures' continue to remain a mystery. A fine example of this is the picture of the four-armed Mahākāla, 'Ye shes mGon po phyag bzhi pa rGva lo'i lugs': the four-armed wise prince in the manner of the rGva lotsāva, i.e., the four-armed figure of Mahākāla as seen by a certain saint. The latter is shown in the top left-hand corner of the painting together with his spiritual fathers, amongst whom some siddhas are to be found. They are naked ascetics who have rubbed their bodies with ashes. They also include the great Nāgārjuna, the philosopher of Mahāyāna, with his radiant crown encircled by snakes. The figure of the six-armed white Mahākāla to the right above the central figure does not belong to the latter's *parivāra* but must be brought into rapport with the predecessor of rGva lotsāva above, for he had depicted precisely this form of the Mahākāla as particularly important. Thus the upper part of the picture can be explained; but the three figures of the lower portion pose greater difficulties. Here we encounter the strange and unappealing figure of the demon Rahu, who in the course of time consumes the sun; he is joined by Simhavaktrā, the demon goddess with the lion's head, and the god of war Begtse. Between Rahu and Simhavaktrā a threefold *balin* sacrifice is spread out, that sacrifice offered to the terrifying ones and which consists of the five parts of a demon placed in a skull cup on the sacrificial fire — the gouged eyes, the cut-off ears and nose, the wrenched-out tongue and heart. At first sight this sacrifice seems most cruel, but on reflection the signs of the five senses may be recognized.

PLATE P. 219

PLATE 14 – A combined mandala picture showing stylistic influences from Kashmir, Guge and Nepal. Southern Tibet, possibly 17th century.
This artistic mandala was prepared on behalf of a monk or layman for the monastery of Nor, a daughter-monastery of the monastery of Sa-skya in Tibet, which was founded in the 15th century. The great fame of its founder attracted numerous monks and artists from Kashmir, Guge and Nepal. In order to acquire religious merit the latter enriched the monastery with their works, as is evident from the writing beneath the mandala. The work is a fine example of the possibilities inherent in the mixture of artistic styles, as must have taken place in southern Tibet particularly; but the iconography is based on precise rules. From G. Tucci, *Tibetan Painted Scrolls*, Plate Z

I have intentionally mentioned this last detail for it repeatedly appears in pictures of demoniac beings where, in fact, it must always be present. It is the demoniac counterpart to the sacrifice found at the foot of peace-loving gods, known as the *sarva-manggalam* sacrifice. It also consists of five symbols gathered in a cup — a mirror, a fruit, a musical instrument (a guitar or a conch-shell trumpet), a censer and a wrap — in which it is again not difficult to recognize the symbols of the five senses. Occasionally these symbols are not gathered together in a cup but are borne by five small dancing figures who also represent the five senses; all five are to be used in conjunction when the method of attaining supreme insight is employed.

A number of other small details could be adduced which would be of significance to the initiated but to the layman appear purely as adornment. The best known are those series representing the seven and eight treasures. The seven treasures *(sapta-ratna)* are the symbols of the mighty ruler, *cakravartin;* this series consists of the wheel (the doctrine), the jewel which grants all wishes, the woman who lovingly cares for her husband, the minister who conscientiously carries out the business of state, the white elephant, the symbol of absolute power, the horse as proof of this power, and the general who overcomes all his enemies. The series of eight treasures, the *asta-manggala*, bears the emblems of the spiritual ruler, *tathāgata*, and consists of the wheel (the doctrine), the conch-shell trumpet, the parasol, the banner of victory, the two golden fishes, the diagram of good fortune, the lotus, and the jug with the elixir of life. Again and again these two series re-appear in every conceivable arrangement: sometimes ranged side by side, often formed into a composite symbol, or else proffered by individual figures. These symbols are also regularly encountered as decorative motifs on the altars of Lamaist temples. If a painting contains any of these symbols of good fortune, then the others in the series concerned are at once identifiable, for they all belong together. Besides these, there are other series of 'treasures', although they are much less frequently used: for example, the seven signs of royal dignity, the seven world-conquering jewels and the seven personal jewels. These also are frequently made into a composite whole and put in the foreground of the work as, so to speak, a sacrificial gift.

Portrayal of the Buddha In paintings Buddha and the majority of the princes of the church are often shown seated on a throne. In Tibetan art this is usually formed of two parts, a pedestal and a back. These do not seem to be in contact with each other, all the less so as the great halo of rays surrounding the figures conceals the larger part of the back of the throne. Behind the heads of the personages a dark-green

PLATE 15 – Eleven-headed, thousand-armed Avalokiteśvara from a painting in the southern Tibetan style of the beginning of the 19th century.
The drawing and painting of the uncommonly complicated figure of this many-armed and many-headed Bodhisattva follows precisely the iconographic rules. The design of the peony-like lotus-blossoms and the side figures shows that it is a work originating from a monastery of the Red Hat Sect in Sikkim. *Rijksmuseum voor Volkenkunde, Leyden*

nimbus forms an arc which sometimes has a lilac-coloured edge; a much broader dark blue border runs round the halo of rays or aura surrounding the whole personage. This border is pierced by golden rays. A stylistic characteristic stemming from Sikkim is a circlet of heavy, peony-like flowers enclosing the aura. This is sometimes emphasized to such an extent that it attracts more attention than the halo itself. In actual fact, however, the back of the throne is formed of a cross-piece which must be at shoulder-height, but is usually somewhat higher, and rests on two beams which are formed of three animals placed one on top of the other: an elephant, a lion and a *vyālaka*, a type of winged tiger on which a small figure is sometimes to be seen sitting. This ornament is also undoubtedly symbolic and probably has some connection with the elements. This decoration is not only found in paintings but occasionally also in the ornamentation of the thrones of the more than life-size statues. Above the figure, as a sign of dignity, a parasol is suspended in mid-air; it seems to be an independent element.

A small low table often stands before the throne of the saints and princes of the church and sometimes directly in front of Buddha's throne also; it is a table used in Tibet when one is crouching cross-legged on a carpet. This small table supports a number of objects of ritual use, including the familiar instruments for the practice of the cult — the jug of consecrated water, the mirror, the prayer-bell, the *vajra* and the small double drum. At times they are replaced by symbols such as the *sapta-ratna*, the *asta-manggala* or the *sarva-manggalam*, whereby these objects may acquire a special significance.

Even if, however, all this still has reference to the central figure and its immediate surroundings, the background of the paintings also displays typical features. One of the most remarkable phenomena appears in those paintings which were produced after the middle of the eighteenth century; with very few exceptions, practically all the works known in the West belong to this period. Their background has nothing at all Tibetan about it but is formed of an Indian landscape suffused with sunshine and showing Chinese mountains and temples of a very Chinese appearance. Other details such as the pairs of birds and animals (e.g., deer) which appear here and there in the background are also clear evidence of Chinese influence. Even if the action depicted takes place in India, the architecture of the buildings is often altogether Chinese. If the action, however, takes

PLATE 16 – Portrait of a *yogin* (mystic) who has acquired supernatural gifts through treading the 'left path' and has thereby earned the right to wear a white linen garment *(ras-pa)*.
Mi-la (Milaraspa) belongs to this group and is often shown with the right hand cupped to his ear in order to hear the voices of the Dakinīs and other strange beings. They are indeed horrifying in appearance but are able to contribute to the attainment of the highest stages of initiation. It is expected of these ascetics that they practise the so-called *gtum-mo*, during which they are able to develop such inner warmth *(tejas)* that they become insensitive to the lowest temperature ever encountered in Tibet. This is probably a genuine portrait that does not show Milaraspa himself but one of his later followers. The background suggests that the work originated towards the beginning of the 18th century. From G. Tucci, *Tibetan Painted Scrolls*, Plate N

place partly in Tibet — if, for example, the visit of a saint to a certain monastery or palace is shown — then the building concerned has a typically Tibetan form. The outer wall is high, closed-in and whitewashed and along its top runs a sort of timber balcony containing windows; it has a flat roof displaying several lucky charms. On the roof of the Chinese-style temples the symbol of the Wheel of Doctrine is often to be found: two deer, which in Tibet sometimes take on the appearance of unicorn, lie at its side. They symbolize the Gazelle Park at Benares where Buddha proclaimed his doctrine for the first time. They are intended to indicate the area over which Buddha's teaching has spread. This symbol, cast in bronze and richly gilded, is also found as an altar decoration.

PAINTED SCROLLS (thang-kas)

Tibetan painting is generally known in the West only through scroll-paintings or *thang-kas*. These are paintings on lengthy pieces of rough canvas trimmed with Chinese silk; they hang from a thin pole and are firmly held in position by means of a round heavy stick which is attached to the lower hem. Bronze knobs often adorn the ends of the pole. If the painting is not being used then it is rolled up over the lower pole. We will now consider the different components more closely.

Technique

The painting is usually done on a somewhat rough piece of canvas which is covered with a mixture of chalk and size. If the canvas is not broad enough for the painting then additional strips are sewn on and covered with the same mixture. The whole surface is then rubbed down with a stone or shell. This produces a completely flat surface which does not betray the slightest trace of a stitch. As soon as the canvas has dried it is stretched on a simple wooden frame, usually consisting of four poles firmly bound together. It is tied fast and stretched with a cord wound round the frame and threaded through holes in the canvas. Care must naturally be taken so that the linen is not stretched out of shape and remains perfectly flat. The artist can then set to work. If he is to apply the drawing himself, then he must first compose a network of lines which determine the outline of the most important features of the central figure, as described earlier. He will, however, often use a tracing cloth or stencils (*ts'ags-par*), a sort of pounce pattern which is laid on the canvas, perforated and then dusted over with a fine black powder. The lines thereby produced are then carefully gone over with red or black ink and this provides the master-pattern.

PLATE 17 – Paradise of Padmasambhava on the holy mountain of Zangs-mdong dpal-ri, the 'copper coloured'.
An example of a carefully executed painting whose underlying text is known. The *gSol-'debs-leu-bdun-ma* gives a careful description of the mountain, the foot of which lies in the realm of the king of the Nāga and the summit reaches into Brahmā's heaven. The palace in which Padmasambhava resides is described in detail; according to the text it can all be seen both from the inside and the outside and is surrounded by enclosures sheltering all sorts of strange creatures. The text also mentions many types of heavenly beings who reside around the mountain and make music or offer different sacrifices. There are also several demoniac figures guarding the access to this paradise. It is, however, not the intention of the work to depict this paradise only, but rather to show the (mystical) path leading to it. This is proved, *inter alia*, by the lower portion of the picture. The life story of the third Dalai Lama refers to this difficult path, in the course of which many dangers must be overcome before the sacred mountain can be reached. *Rijksmuseum voor Volkenkunde, Leyden*

It is really nothing more than this, for when the painting is finished nothing more is to be seen of these lines.

In the case of very stereotyped pictures a sort of transfer can even be used; the master-pattern is imposed on the canvas with a woodcut. Blocks of this type are known to have been used in the great monastery of Tashi Lumpo. As soon as the master-pattern is imposed on the canvas, the painter's work begins, his duty being to fill in the spaces between the lines. Printer and painter do not need to be identical, for their crafts are quite separate. Above all, the painter must be able to prepare his colours skilfully. He uses in the main minerals and plants which he grounds to a fine powder in a small mortar with a wooden pestle. These colours are soluble in water and are mixed with size. As soon as they are applied to the canvas they unite with the base, which is covered with a layer of the same material. As both are easily soluble in water it is obvious that damp easily causes irreplaceable damage to such paintings. A drop of water running over the front or rear of the painting is sufficient to ruin it altogether. It will not only rob the work of its beauty but may make it invalid for ritual purposes. The Tibetan artist loves bright garish colours like those of the landscape in which he lives. Recently he has for this reason sometimes been attracted by the use of aniline dyes which he can prepare without overmuch difficulty. They fascinate him at first glance with their brilliance and spare him the onerous quest for the ingredients needed in the preparation of his own colours. In our view, however, the individual works lose a great deal of their beauty in this way; it was precisely the colouring-stuffs drawn from minerals and plants which, with their warm deep colours, gave these works their special value. These colouring-stuffs were by no means easy to prepare. Again and again the texts point out that the person commissioning the artist had to provide the latter with the requisite valuable raw materials in order that the work might be fittingly executed. This applied particularly to the use of gold as a colouring-matter. The base was formed of real gold, which had to be treated in a special way if it

PLATE 18 – 'Portrait' of a Dalai Lama, probably the third: bSod-nams rgya-mts'o. Tashi Lumpo school, beginning of 19th century.
This beautiful painting belongs to a series of 'portraits' of the Dalai Lama. The practice of preparing such 'portraits' can probably be attributed to the monastery of Tashi Lumpo; the first series is that of the Tashi Lamas or, more correctly, of the Pan-chen Rin-po-ce. As a consequence 'portraits' of the Dalai Lamas were created, probably also in Tashi Lumpo. Both series only go back to the middle of the 18th century. There is therefore no question of their being genuine portraits. There are different Dalai Lama series known but they all have the peculiarity of showing imprints of hands and feet in which the wheel symbol can still be clearly recognized. As is known, this is one of the characteristics of a reincarnation of the Dalai Lama. In the inscription beneath the figure there is usually a short tribute which contains the name of the relevant Dalai Lama. Here it has been damaged, but this figure probably represents the third of the line and is therefore the first to bear the title of Dalai Lama. Above the central figure the saintly Atīśa is shown, the pandit who went to Tibet after the death of the evil king Glang-dar-ma (841 A.D.) in order to lay a basis for the rapid development of Tantric Buddhism. Right at the foot are two demoniac 'protectors of the doctrine', the so-called black and red drag-po (= krodha = the wrathful one). Musée Guimet, Paris

was to be effective. The gold is first molten and beaten in an earthenware dish into thin leaves. About twenty of these gold leaves, sometimes mixed with a little earth, are then gripped with tongs and heated over a fire of yak dung. They are then washed, laid in the sun, cut up into small strips and finally rubbed down to a powder in a mortar. This takes about a week. The fine particles are now washed in water again, mixed with urine, and dissolved in it. This produces a paste-like substance which is then spread with a spoon over a bronze plate. Only now is it ready to be made into a colouring-matter. This whole process, which forms part of the esoteric specialist knowledge of the artist, made known to us by the diary of one of them, is of course extremely costly. In this case the man who commissions the work will have to provide the necessary material. In the older works it is possible to observe a difference between the gold colouring with which, for example, the golden skin colour of the Buddha is produced and the gold used to gild ornaments and objects. The object is to convey the impression that the latter are made of this precious material. Whereas the colouring-matter has a somewhat dull sheen — it is also mixed with size — in the case of genuine gilding the technique is to apply an extremely thin layer of gold-leaf. This has been cut to the desired shape and is reminiscent of the Japanese method of producing *kirikane* works.

When the painter has finished his work it is again the turn of the draughtsman. With a very thin brush he draws in the outlines of the different figures in black ink and also the fine details of the landscape. In the final phase of his work he fills in face and hands, paying greatest attention to the eye as the most important element. This indicates whether the artist is a true master and also explains the differences which are evident even if a picture has been begun by means of a transfer or a pounce pattern. These are purely auxiliary means to aid the artist in the execution of his work. At the same time he has sufficient freedom to shape his work as he wishes; it is rare, however, to be able to compare different works produced with the aid of the same transfer but painted in by different artists. This was once possible in the Verbert Collection, which consisted in the main of recent material.

Mounting   When the painting is finished it must be mounted, and this also is carried out in accordance with certain rules. The picture must be enclosed within a so-called red and yellow rainbow border symbolizing the power radiating from it. This border consists of two bands. The inner one is yellow and the outer one red; both are of silk and of equal width, as thick as a finger or a thumb. This rainbow border is surrounded by the actual frame, which consists of multi-coloured Chinese silk embroidered with various patterns. This silk frame is narrow at the two vertical sides of the painting, broadens out at the top, and is at its broadest at the foot, this gives it a somewhat trapezoid shape. The rear of the frame is usually covered with a lining of less precious material — often red linen — and the reverse of the picture is left blank. The frame has at the top a narrow hem in which a flat wooden or bamboo stick is inserted and made firm. About one-third in, calculated from the two sides, a fine cord is drawn through the frame and wound round the supporting pole on which the painting

PLATE 19 – The Tantrist Mañjuśrīmitra, a follower of the great magician Padmasambhava. Painted gold bronze from western Tibet, possibly 16th century.

This disciple of the founder of the Tibetan Red Hat Sect wears traditional clothing. With his raised right hand he grasps the *vajra*, the 'thunderbolt', symbol of the method, and with his left hand the *p'ur-bu*, the magic dagger with whose help he can subdue the demons once they are in his power. This work probably belongs to a series of figures arranged around a larger statue of Padmasambhava, as is clear from the treatment of the lotus-cushion, which has on its reverse an inscription giving the name of the figure. *Rijksmuseum voor Volkenkunde, Leyden*

can be hung. The ends of the hem are simply sewn together or bound with a narrow strip of leather. The lower portion of the frame has a double hem in which the heavy round pole, used to roll down the painting when it is to be displayed, is carefully inserted. This is a troublesome process; the painting can be pulled out of shape if insufficient care is taken. The lower border is now adorned with the so-called door *(thang-sgo)*. This consists of a piece of gold brocade or embroidered silk worked with motifs drawn from the symbolism of the primaeval waters, e.g., dragons, serpents, lotus-blossoms or waves. Where the more valuable thang-kas are concerned, portions of embroidered mandarins' clothing are used which have similar dragon, cloud and water motifs. The meaning of the symbolism of this so-called 'door' is not quite clear; it is also known as *rtsa-ba*, i.e., *bīja* or root. It is probably intended to signify the origin of all being.

Finally, a gossamer-thin veil, usually spun from very fine green silk, is affixed to the top of the border; sometimes it covers the whole thang-ka. The silk used for the more precious thang-kas is not of conventional quality but a specially prepared material, with embroidered signs of good fortune or even figures of the Buddha; in one case there are mystical letters such as the 'sign of the ten mighty ones'. The scroll-painting is always rolled together from the bottom upwards, that is, over the heavy hanging pole. By means of small leather straps affixed to the rear of the topmost supporting pole the rolled-up picture can now be fastened up into a scroll. Beneath the pole on the reverse of the border or on its lining there is often a short description of the painting as well as an indication of the position in which the painting is to be hung in relation to a central panel, as already mentioned.

Consecration   When the artist has finished his work and the painting has been furnished with an appropriate border the work must then be consecrated, to fit it for its ritual purpose. A very detailed ceremonial prepares the work of art as a temporary dwelling for the relevant god and his accompanying figures *(parivāra)*. This ceremonial is known in Tibet by the name *sgrub-byed*, meaning approximately 'putting in order' and corresponds to the ceremony known in India as *prāna-pratishthā*. This means, freely translated, 'blowing in the breath of life'.

When the officiating priest has purified himself, in accordance with the rules for this rite, he prepares the holy water to be used in the ceremony. He employs two vessels, one of which has the shape of a bowl, the other the shape of a pot *(kumbha)*. The ritual texts give precise indications of the requirements which these vessels must satisfy. The Śrīchakrasambhāra Tantra contains a description of the ceremonial which makes it clear that both vessels together form a world-picture, a mandala, and that divine power is now conferred on the water they contain. This is brought about when the officiating priest, by using the chosen breathing technique *(prānayama)*, leads the special protective deity (Yidam) from the heart-lotus in which he is waiting through a system of internal channels to his right nostril and from there, on a flower, to the two vessels used in the sacrifice. That this is a special ritual, most intimately connected with the view, already mentioned, which asserts that the heart is the

PLATE 20 – Painted wooden sculpture inlaid with stones representing the demoniac form of the Bodhisattva Vajrapāni. Southern Tibet, 19th century.
The demons can immediately be recognized by their heavy build and rigid bearing: the right arm and left leg are stretched out to the side and form a straight line. The right leg and the left arm are bent so as to emphasize the rigidity of the body. The faces also have a demoniac appearance: round eyes, bushy eyebrows, thick nose, gaping jaws with curled-up tongue, flowing hair and thick facial bristles. Behind the figure stands the flaming halo symbolizing the figure's magical glow. Figures of this type are almost always naked, with an animal's skin slung round their loins. On the pedestal the lotus-leaves are turned downwards. *Rijksmuseum voor Volkenkunde, Leyden*

seat of the self and must unite with the highest godhead, is evident from the fact that during the ceremonial the bowl is set on a prescribed figure representing the eight-leaved heart-lotus. While the protective god of the officiating priest (Yidam; Sanskrit: Ishtadevatā) is dipped in accordance with precise rules into the prepared water, the divine power is transmitted to the water so that it can be used for the ceremony of consecration. The water cannot, of course, be sprinkled directly over the painting, for this would spoil it completely. Instead, a mirror is used and this is sprinkled with the water. If a ritual work of art is to be repaired then the same method is used. The god is requested to leave his dwelling for a time and to enter the mirror, which is then carefully wrapped in a cloth. When the painting has been made good, the mirror is again set before it, unwrapped and the god requested to resume its former habitation.

The rear of the painting is now furnished with the *mantras*, the life-awakening formulae. These formulae are short, often consisting of single syllables only, which are written on the reverse of the relevant figures, reaching from the head to the buttocks. Originally each figure had its own special *bīja-mantra*. Nowadays, however, the stereotyped formula, *ōm āh hūm*, is met with on almost all the figures of the pantheon; only in exceptional cases is there a genuine consecration formula of detailed content. The reverse of the painting often reveals a lengthy incantation in which the man who has commissioned the painting implores the god depicted for a special blessing to achieve some specific end. The latter need by no means always be a spiritual objective. The incantation is often only a request for protection in this earthly existence, for prosperity and a long life for himself and his descendants.

Now and again the paintings also bear the imprint in red of the hands of the lama who consecrated the work. These examples are held in particularly high honour. Finally, it is to be noted that the reverse of the picture sometimes bears the seals and marks of ownership of certain monasteries or high dignitaries; but this only applies to the older works. Very rarely there will also be found a short note giving the date and creator of the work.

WALL-PAINTINGS   Hitherto we have discussed in the main the technique of scroll-paintings; it is these that we in fact know best because a number are to be found in western collections. But in many monasteries there are also wall-paintings, the oldest specimens of which were probably executed by means of a fresco technique. This subsequently dropped out of use. In the later murals the wall to be painted is treated precisely as though it were a scroll. It first has canvas glued on to it

PLATE 21 – Mandala of the four-armed Mahākāla, from the vision of the monk rGva lotsāva. Coloured painting on black background. Southern Tibet, end of the 18th century.
The technique of using bold colours on a black background makes the central figure stand out clearly. It is surrounded by all sorts of strange creatures, such as the eight demoniac goddesses with animals' heads and some terrifying figures. Above the figure stand the 'transmitters of the doctrine', i.e., the spiritual teachers of the monk rGva lotsāva who is himself shown to the left above the central figure. *Rijksmuseum voor Volkenkunde, Leyden. Cf. p. 204*

and this base is then coated with size. It is now ready for the colour to be laid on. Paintings of this type, which often include the 'Wheel of Transmigration' and the pictures of the protectors of the world, often decorate the entrance portals of monasteries. Those examples in the frontier area of Tibet, which is very much damper than the Tibetan plateau, have all too often been severely damaged and have had to be repeatedly restored.

In the interior of the temple there was sometimes painting on wood. Such paintings have frequently been more elaborately worked and better preserved on the rear walls of altars and on the ceilings, which are often decorated with great skill and artistry. However, as the light in most temples is very dim, the walls especially often being sunk in a mysterious gloom, these works can only be examined in favourable circumstances, which no longer exist today. This not only applies to the murals but equally to the larger sculptures, whether they are of metal, wood or stucco. Our knowledge of Tibetan plastic art rests almost exclusively on those items in western collections. These are for all practical purposes the smaller pieces and not even the best.

SCULPTURE So far as the representation is concerned, we may content ourselves with saying that what applies to painting applies also to plastic art. The art of casting bronze, however, demands a greater degree of technical skill and for this reason Tibetan works rarely attain the same visionary content as is to be found in first-class paintings. The production of great works depended primarily on the skill of the bronze-founder and not on the vision of the mystic, who was able to give shape directly to his experiences. The profession of bronze-founder was exercised mainly by Nepalese. Nepalese artists are mentioned in the earliest descriptions of this profession. It was through them that the art of the Pāla Dynasty of Bengal reached Tibet and until the collapse of Lamaism in China they were amongst the best practitioners in this special field to be found in Peking.

Cire-perdue The overwhelming majority of small bronzes were produced by the *cire-perdue* technique method. A clay core is covered with a layer of wax, carefully shaped in every detail so that the whole figure which is to be cast already exists as a wax model. Now a layer of clay is carefully spread over the wax figure; it is left to dry undisturbed after the outer envelope and the core have been joined together by a sheet of clay in which a number of holes have been pierced. The whole is now carefully heated and baked; the clay becomes hard and the molten wax runs off through the open holes. This creates a cavity between the clay core and the clay outer envelope which is now filled with molten bronze, carefully poured through one of the vents. Great care has to be taken to see that the air in the cavity is completely expelled by the liquid bronze and that enough bronze is available to fill up the mould completely. After it has all cooled down and the bronze has solidified the clay envelope is broken. The bronze is then removed. This means of course that a new mould is required for every individual bronze statue and that every work must be modelled in wax. In the case of very complicated bronzes, such as the multi-armed figures, the whole statue is cast in individual parts which are then joined together with pegs. Sculptures and (lotus-shaped) pedestals are also often cast separately and joined together with pegs or pins.

PLATE 22 – The mystical and demoniac god Hevajra, united with a Śakti. Lamaist bronze from the school of Peking, beginning of the 19th century.

The eight-headed and sixteen-armed Hevajra is a characteristic example of a composite figure formed by the concentration into one figure of what was originally a group of eight different figures. The skull cups in the eight right hands contain the steeds of the eight divinities whose unwarlike figures are shown in the skull cups in his eight left hands. The mystic Hevajra played an important part in the Tantric initiation of the Chinese Emperor Kublai Khan by Saskya-pandita. It was undoubtedly designed to reinforce his imperial power.

The head and hands of larger statues are modelled and cast separately; the remainder is formed from bronze sheets which are hammered into the right shape by the repoussé or embossing method. Where very large figures are concerned the bronze plates themselves must be fastened together by a type of dovetail join. Little is known with certainty of the bronze alloys used and the bronze colour itself varies from light chocolate brown to an almost black colour. The older bronzes have occasionally acquired in the course of time a magnificent natural patina which ranges from dark brown to bluish-green; this gives them a distinguished appearance.

Gilding   Most bronzes are then gilded; for this there were different methods, but they cannot always be determined with certainty. It is therefore not possible to give an accurate account of the process whereby the older bronzes were gilded, although it can be established that very thin sheets of gold-leaf were used which were applied to a red lacquer background with which the bronze was first covered. This gilding has a magnificent warm glow which can be immediately distinguished from the modern gilt bronzes whose colour has been produced by an amalgamation process. After the bronze has first been purified in a bath of nitric acid it is warmed and rubbed over with mercury, which produces the amalgam. The gold-leaf is now applied and the whole heated to a high temperature. In this way the layer of gold sticks to the prepared surface and the mercury dissolves. The layer of gold is indissolubly part of the bronze and the statue can be carefully polished. The sculptures now have a somewhat cold gleam as though of freshly polished brass.

The rather rare wooden statues are also frequently gilded and for this purpose are also covered with a red lacquer base. The gold is applied in powder form mixed with some honey and then rubbed on carefully. It does not stick so fast and the layer of gilt remains exceedingly thin, so that the red base sometimes shines through and in some places is fully visible.

Painting   Gilt bronzes and wooden statues are then painted: primarily the face — and in any case the eyes — the palms of the hands, soles of the feet, the hair of the head and, in the case of animals, the tail. The painter likes to use bright colours which are at first glance somewhat disturbing. Thus the hair of the Buddha will often be blue-black, the tail of a lion occasionally bright green, etc. The figures of the Bodhisattvas and Tārās which are shown in princely Indian dress are inlaid with small coloured stones, especially the turquoises or red corals which are so well known in Tibet. In the later works, however, coloured glass is often used.

PLATE 23 – Projection-mandala of the god of the dead, Yama. Coloured painting on black background. Eastern Tibet, 19th century.
Projection-mandalas of this type serve as a preparation for meditation on the occasion of the supreme rites of consecration. The complete armour, all the items of adornment, the weapons and the steed of the godhead concerned, are depicted in an appropriate context. The representation of the god himself takes place in the course of meditation through the evocative intellectual power of the practitioner, who projects him into the picture. Fine example of a contemplative painting. *Rijksmuseum voor Volkenkunde, Leyden*

The large stucco figures of saints, princes of the church and secular rulers which are often met with in many Tibetan monasteries are also brightly painted like the pictures. Here also the figure is generally covered with a layer of canvas, which is coated with size and water colours then applied. Statues of this type are almost entirely absent from western collections because their dimensions make it difficult to transport them.

In the final phases of Lamaism bronze figures as well as bronze tablets with representations of the gods were cast in moulds. The centre of this technique was the Chinese capital, Peking. These figures were produced in such a way that they could 'free themselves' from their mould. The best known are the figures of the 'Buddha of long life', Amitāyus, who can be recognized by the crown which he wears despite his monk's cowl, and by the jug with the water of life which he holds in his hands. The latter lie in his lap in a meditative position like those of Amitābha. This jug, as well as the aura behind the figure, are also cast separately in moulds and then affixed to the statues. Sculptures of this type are so similar to each other that they immediately suggest casting from a common mould.

Clay tablets　On the other hand, the use of moulds to produce clay tablets with images of gods must be much older. Sometimes such tablets are only a few inches across and are used as small amulet-boxes or travelling altars. But they may be much larger and be about one foot high. These tablets are also painted in the prescribed colours and sometimes arranged in groups on a wooden board enclosed with a sliding lid or small door and carried about, so to speak, as a mobile altar by a family on the move. Furthermore, there is also the custom whereby the ashes remaining over from the cremation of an abbot or very meritorious monk are mixed with clay from which tablets or statuettes are produced representing this person; or they are shaped into miniature *stūpas* which are sometimes met with in long rows before the altar of the monasteries and serve as mementos for lay visitors.

Sculptures, like paintings, must also be made ritually serviceable. They also receive a life-awakening formula *(mantra)*. A narrow roll of paper is inserted in

PLATE 24 – Cemetery mandala for the demoniac goddess Kālī (Lha-mo). Coloured painting on a black background. Southern Tibet, 19th century.
Paintings of this type belong to the 'secret' paintings which are only intended for the practice of the supreme rites of initiation. The outline figure of the demoniac goddess stands out in the centre against the background of the cemetery, which is shown with skulls and the skins of men and beasts, all sorts of diabolical animals and the so-called red sea of blood running along the lower border. The goddess' steed, all her armour, her clothing and adornments are shown; during the meditation her own picture has to be projected into the painting by the power of thought. The fact, however, that the cemetery is also to be regarded as a scene of salvation is proved by the symbols of benediction, such as the different flags (left, above the figure) and the group of the *sapta ratna*, the seven treasures (below, right). The background is strewn with treasures and sacrificial gifts, both of a peaceful and a demoniac origin. They include also the so-called *sarva-manggalam* sacrifice (centre, beneath the principal figure, on either sides of the sacrifice which represents the World Mountain). *Rijksmuseum voor Volkenkunde, Leyden*

the statue on which the *mantra* is printed or written. For this purpose use is often made of the lotus-shaped pedestal on which the figure sits or stands.

Standing statues also contain a hollowed-out portion which was later carefully closed up. Often some grains of corn and small stones were deposited; the pedestal was then closed up with a panel and secured so that everything would remain in place. The closure panel also bore the image of a double *vajra*, in the centre of which stood a circle. This circle enclosed a further figure which is of help in identifying the origin of the work. The more recent products of Lamaist-Chinese manufacture have a symbol here which is unknown in Tibet: it is the

FIG. 8 yang-yin symbol of the coiled S, which divides the small circle into two comma-like figures. On the other hand, the older Tibetan bronzes frequently have two smaller circles, slightly eccentric, engraved within the larger ones. There is no point in removing the closure panel from a bronze, where it is still intact; there are no treasures inside but only the *mantra* and a few trifles; moreover, the work of art would lose its ritual value if the panel were opened. Wooden sculptures intentionally contain a cavity hollowed out of the figure or pedestal which is also destined to preserve a roll of paper with the consecration formula. The opening is then carefully closed and, as soon as the objects to be preserved have been inserted in the pedestal, sealed by an imprint of the double *vajra* in gold ink. In the case of the larger bronzes and stucco pieces there is often a so-called 'tree of life' in the interior of the statue, i.e., a wooden stick, carved, and shaped like a much elongated *stūpa*; it is wound round with rolls of paper sometimes covered with consecration *mantras* and written or printed magic formulae.

We have already pointed out that a discussion of Tibetan art is tantamount to a

DECORATIVE ART discussion of the art of Lamaist Buddhism. It would not be justifiable, however, to dismiss without a single word the decorative art of certain favourite objects of daily use. The first of these must be the amulet which every Tibetan always carries with him as a protection against evil. The amulet usually consists of a small figure of a god in the form of a small clay tablet, a tiny figure cast in metal, or a picture of a god painted on paper which is wrapped up in several rolls of paper containing certain written or printed formulae. There may also be some loose leaves from any desired religious work.

Amulets The amulet is preserved in a small box of metal or wood which has several

PLATE 25 – Complete scroll-painting *(thang-ka)* in its silk frame, showing the group of the five Herukas (blood-swallowers) who incorporate the demoniac figures of the five Dhyāni-Buddhas from the five winds. Southern Tibet, 18th century.

Fine example of a thang-ka. The painting itself is bordered by the red and yellow rainbow and enclosed in a frame of brocade silk. The inset piece of silk with the lotus motif on the lower edge of the frame represents the primaeval waters from which all creation emerges. The eight signs of good fortune *(asta-manggala)* are worked into this lotus motif. This is known as the *bīja* (root) or as the 'door' of the thang-ka, which must always be present.

The Herukas belong to those demons encountered by the spirit of the dead as soon as it enters the intermediate world *(Bardo)* between death and reincarnation. *Rijksmuseum voor Volkenkunde, Leyden*

FIG. 8 – *Double or cruciform 'vajra' as is to be found on the closure panel of the pedestal supporting bronze figures. Right: Chinese-Lamaist form (showing yang-yin symbol); left: Tibetan form*

FIG. 9 – *Mystical letter 'ōm' worked into a decorative ornament on an amulet*

carrying-rings forming a sort of hinge. Through these rings a hollow bamboo stick is inserted, as the pivot of the hinge, and through the stick a supporting cord is drawn. Amulet-containers of this type are often elaborately worked and occasionally inlaid with numerous coloured stones; sometimes they bear an engraved figure representing a mystical sign or a combination of mystical signs. In this respect the sign *ōm* plays a particular part. It is the object of much mystic contemplation and is apparently composed of three letters: A, U and M, each of which has a mystical value. The first letter is masculine, the second feminine and the third the result of their union. At the same time they are also connected with the *triratna* (the three jewels) of the Buddha, the *dharma* (the doctrine) and the *sanggha* (the order), so that a whole philosophy is concealed behind this simple sign; but it is of course unknown to the overwhelming majority of those who carry small amulet-boxes with such signs. Another much more complicated sign, and one that is based on a highly complex philosophy concerning the systematic construction of the Creation, is the 'sign of the ten mighty ones' *(rnam-bcu-dbang-ldan)*. This consists of a series of seven intertwined letters, as though of a monogram, crowned by symbols of the moon (crescent), the sun (orb) and flame. Here again there is a cosmic figure which is the *point de départ* for meditative practices and forms a source from which the whole universe is constructed in the mind. It belongs to those mystic signs that are of central importance; it is known that in the tenth century the sage Cilu affixed it over the entrance to the great monastery of Nālandā with the inscription: 'He who does not know the Ādi-Buddha knows nothing of the cycle of time *(kāla-cakra)*'. This suggests that the figure occupies a central place in the *kālacakra* system, which is one of the best known schools of Tantric Buddhism. In this case again, a particularly important mystical sign has transformed itself into a symbol of good fortune, or at least of protection, although the wearer himself will hardly suspect its deeper significance. In only one case do we encounter the figure of the ten mighty ones on representations: they are shown standing on a lotus pedestal or on a lotus flower emerging from the primaeval waters. An artist such as Paul Klee was inspired by this figure to create a singular work of

FIG. 9

FIG. 10

PLATE 26 – Priest's helmet of gilt bronze showing the Buddhas of the different compass-points and their Tārās. Nepal, 17th century.
The officiating priest *(vajrāchārya)* wears a helmet of this type while he is preparing the holy water. The helmet is crowned by *vajra*-shaped knob. It symbolizes the sphere of *sambhogakāya*, i.e., of bliss, in which the Dhyāni-Buddhas and their Tārās reside. *Rijksmuseum voor Volkenkunde, Leyden*

FIG. 10 – *So-called 'Symbol of the Ten Mighty Ones' (rnam-bcu-dbang-ldan): combination of seven letters and symbols of the moon, sun and flame*

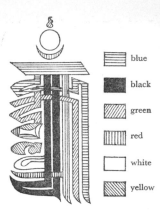

▦	blue
■	black
▨	green
▥	red
☐	white
▧	yellow

art. He entitled it 'The Dissolution of a Phenomenon', from which it may be concluded that he had some inkling of the deeper meaning of this symbol which is, in addition, so interesting from an ornamental point of view.

Apart from these small amulet-boxes, which are mostly of simple and dignified design and made of solid bronze, there are also still more elaborately worked amulet-caskets. Almost always these latter have the form of a rectangle of which the longer sides are vertical; it has on its upper side a projection terminating in a pointed arch. Whereas the actual holder containing the amulet is of sheet bronze the front, which resembles a lid, is often of silver and bears the eight auspicious signs — *asta-manggala* — embossed on it. As already mentioned, these signs belong to the spiritual ruler — the *tathāgata* — but they can obviously also stand for the eight great Bodhisattvas. Here again the ornamentation clearly conceals a whole symbolism. This also applies to the background or foreground against which these figures stand out; this usually consists of a rich lotus vegetation. The tip is often worked into the strange head of a monster. Both elements repeatedly appear on paintings and in the framing of statues. They must be looked on as symbols of the opposed elements water (the lotus vegetation) and fire (the head of the demon), which are harmoniously united in the central figure standing between them. An amulet-casket of this type may also have a sort of window opening, sometimes covered by a small piece of glass. Behind it stands the small amulet figure in the form of a statuette, a tablet, or a painting of the protective deity of the owner of the casket.

Vajra and prayer-bell

Of the other objects in daily use which are artistically decorated, the first are the religious attributes of the lama, especially the *vajra* and the prayer-bell. These have a ritual use and symbolize the method and the doctrine. The *vajra* is the strange short sceptre which originally represented Indra's weapon with which he clove through the clouds and freed the waters; it has here become the weapon of the priest with which he splits the clouds of darkness and ignorance and releases the higher knowledge. This object has the appearance of two claws placed opposite one another on a short rod. They have five and sometimes nine nails, of which one is straight and stands in the middle, always surrounded by

PLATE 27 – Reliquary casket of gilt bronze from the monastery of dPal-l'or c'os-de in Gyantse, southern Tibet, 16th century.

A precious casket of this type was used in the monastery to hold the clothing and the writings of the founder or his immediate successors. The work consists of gilt bronze plates decorated with all sorts of ornaments, some of which are bronze figures cast individually, some rosettes formed of small stones, and larger stones carved like cameos; these depict Ganeśa, the 'destroyer of obstacles'. On all four sides and on the lid stand out in high relief the multi-armed forms of Avalokiteśvara who is accompanied by two worshippers, shown as monks with a fly-whisk. This is the characteristic symbol of the worshipper or servant. *Rijksmuseum voor Volkenkunde, Leyden*

four (or eight) others which are bent and almost touch the tip of the centre nail. The priest's bell *(ghantā)* has a similar point. Under it there is often the head of a god with a friendly aspect which, together with the *vajra* claw, forms the handle. It is cast separately from the bell itself and affixed to it with a pin. The bell is cast from a metal alloy which can best be compared with our pinchbeck: it is a bronze alloy to which a certain quantity of silver is added, giving the bell its fine tone. The bell has the actual shape of a stupa, and it is not by chance that it is often decorated with the garlands with which these monuments were adorned in former days. *Vajra* and prayer-bell form to such a degree an indissoluble whole that they are often kept in the same case. The latter follows their outline precisely and has on its outside a most colourful pattern in lacquer.

P'ur-bu A very typical ritual attribute is the *p'ur-bu* or magic dagger, which always has a clover-leaf blade and is crowned by the threefold head of a monster in whose mane there is either a *vajra* or a horse's head. This is of course one of the shapes assumed by the demon Hayagrīva, the 'horse-headed one' or 'god with the horse's head' as he is usually known. He belongs to the series of the eight fearful ones *(drag-gsed)*. This magic dagger should really be made of *khadira* wood but it is usually made of bronze. Sometimes, however, specimens made of wood are met with, and also specimens in precious metal. During the Tantric ceremonial it was their function to cast a spell on the devils that had been summoned up — i.e., to hold them fast. An inexpert use of this attribute could cause great harm, as we know from many popular Tibetan tales; these tales are reminiscent in a high degree of the Sorcerer's Apprentice. But this object, too, has already degenerated into a mere article of decoration; at the end of the nineteenth century specimens up to a yard long were manufactured by Nepalese bronze-founders in Peking.

Ritual objects For certain ceremonies in Tantric practices of the left path, all the attributes of the demoniac godheads had to be available. Solemn actions of this type demanded, to some extent, an identification of the officiating priest with the godheads. Thus all the fearful attributes of these demons are also familiar to us as objects of ritual use: e.g., loin-coverings made of human bones, often beautifully carved, double drums made of human skulls, skull cups, sacrificial knives, ritual swords, and trumpets made of human thigh-bones. These objects have given rise to all sorts of gruesome stories, invented by an unbridled western fantasy. In reality these objects were used for specific rites which there was neither the ability nor the desire to explain to outsiders or the non-initiated. These objects are often carved and inlaid with small stones. One group has become rather famous: it includes the wonderfully worked skull cup mounted in metal (mostly gilt bronze), with a magnificent lid, shaped like half a skull, and a *vajra* handle. It is heavily embossed; the skull itself rests on a triangular pedestal in the form of a sacrificial fire with skulls. It was all in gilt bronze. However fascinating these objects may be, they are no longer used for ritual purposes but were manufactured in Peking for tourists at the end of the nineteenth and beginning of the twentieth century.

The prayer-wheels and the enormous telescope-shaped temple trumpets are amongst those objects of ritual use which are indissolubly connected with the idea of Tibet. They do not actually belong within the framework of Tibetan art, despite the skill with which they have been manufactured and the taste with which they have been decorated. But as they are most intimately related to certain themes of Lamaist Buddhism we would like to mention them briefly here.

In its simplest form the prayer-wheel consists of a hollow bronze cylinder. On the outside it usually has, in a simple decorative form, embossed mystical syllables; inside there is a roll of paper which is as broad as the cylinder is high and bears the ever-repeated prayer formula, usually *ōm māni padme hūm*. The bronze cylinder is sometimes enclosed on both sides with a round lid. The lower lid is decorated with a figure of a double *vajra* (cross) and the upper one has a many-leaved lotus-blossom. In the middle of this round lid there is an opening through which an iron pivot can be inserted. Its lower side has a wooden handle; its upper end projects some distance beyond the top lid of the cylinder, on which there is a locking knob in the form of a jewel cast in bronze; this holds the cylinder fast to its metal axis. In the middle of the side of the cylinder there is a metal eye to which a small chain is fastened; at its end hangs a heavy piece of metal, usually in the form of a cube with trimmed corners. When the prayer-wheel is set in gentle circular motion centrifugal force causes this heavy mass to describe a circle behind the cylinder and its contents. Every turn corresponds to as many prayers as there are paper rolls inside the cylinder; it is for this reason that contemptuous reference is often made to 'automatic praying'. But this view needs correction. It is by no means a question of 'prayer' in the Protestant Christian sense of the word. The origin of the prayer-wheels has quite a different source, lying in the realm of mysticism. It is supposed that when the formula *ōm māni padme hūm* is uttered in a particular way during mystical practices and in a mood of intensive theoretical contemplation, it has a clear symbolic meaning; the words *māni padme* mean the jewel in the lotus — the jewel being the traditional symbol of the masculine and the lotus of the feminine principle — and thus salvation is induced compulsorily, so to speak. Two factors must be borne in mind: correct inner concentration and correct technique. For those who cannot be taught the correct technique, as the utterance of the formula demands, the written word can be a substitute, provided that it is endlessly repeated. The same result will be achieved. Of course this writing must be combined with true fervour and reverence. Those who cannot write may use the printed word but, because of its lesser effect, this means must be repeated much more often and so the next step is the prayer-

Prayer-wheels

PLATE 28 – Leaves from illustrated manuscripts.
The upper leaf with its magnificent calligraphy in *umed* script shows the four guardians of the world recognizable by their armour and attributes. There are also inscriptions which mention them by name. From left to right: Dhrtarāshtra (East, with the mandoline), Virūdhaka (South, with the sword), Virūpāksha (West, with the snake) and Vaiśravana (North, with the banner of victory).
The two other leaves are taken from a written work dealing with magical practices, especially with warding off diseases and protection against snakes. *Rijksmuseum voor Volkenkunde, Leyden*

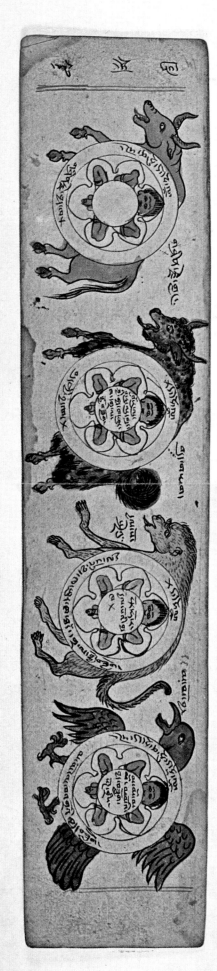

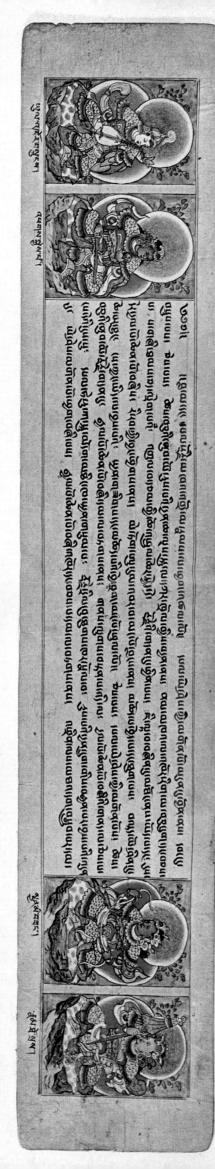

wheel. It may not be set in motion thoughtlessly and automatically, but must be used in a spirit of complete concentration if it is to lead to any positive result. Theory and practice diverge, of course; nor do the external decorations in any way enhance the ritual value of the prayer-wheel.

The prayer-wheels do, however, include some magnificent works. Some are even manufactured of semi-precious stones and decorated with gold and inlaid with small precious stones. They reveal a disposition to colourful adornment and an almost overpowering love of magnificence. This is also evident in the richly decorated clothing of Central Asia and gives a gay appearance to a dress that is otherwise somewhat monotonous, perhaps as a result of climatic and living conditions.

Musical instruments   Although the great temple trumpets have a most picturesque appearance, they are by no means the only, and still less the most important, musical instruments used in the cult. It must of course be admitted that their meaning does not emerge particularly clearly from the descriptions of those travellers who have seen them being blown. This is not surprising, for they play a part in certain rites to which no outsiders are ever admitted.

To understand them better we must first distinguish those musical instruments which have a ritual use from the others. In addition to the long temple trumpets already mentioned, there are clarinets which also have a ritual purpose, as well as horizontal and vertical cymbals, and vertical flat drums with a wooden handle which are struck with a drumstick that has the form of a question mark.

FIG. 12   These instruments have a part to play in the devil-dances or mystery plays whose climaxes are heralded by the prayer-bell. This music, which is accompanied by recitations, is based on a written notation but it has hitherto been insufficiently studied by western musicologists for it to be completely understood. The great difficulty inherent in this music when it is used to accompany a dance, and also its peculiar power of attraction, is based on the varying initial tempo of the instruments and dance movements which do, however, eventually unite in a common rhythm. This takes place during an hour-long action which is accompanied by a strange chanting recitation. It never fails to make its impact on the public although the words cannot always be followed. This is a spectacle that must be experienced in its own environment for its true beauty to be recognized. The great temple trumpets are only blown once at the beginning of the dance; but they have a part to play in certain nocturnal

PLATE 29 – The Buddha with his hands outspread as though to touch the earth (*bhūmisparśamudrā*) surrounded by godlings and saints. Gold painting technique, *gser-thang*. Southern Tibet, second half of the 18th century.

In using this technique either red and black lines are drawn on a gold background or gold and black lines on a dark red background. Draughtsmanship is of the greatest importance; enormous technical mastery is required as no corrections can be made. The figure of the Buddha drawn with the utmost precision stands out against the background of a richly decorated throne. The figures surrounding him are also drawn with graceful strokes and their names are given. The beautifully painted background with rocks and waterfalls reveals Chinese influence. *Museum van Aziatische Kunst, Amsterdam*

237

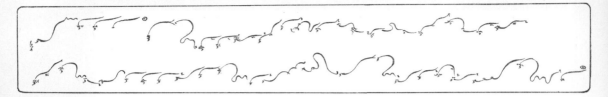

FIG. 12 – *Sample of Tibetan notation used for ritual music and recitation*

ceremonies, in which five of these trumpets of somewhat different timbre are skilfully blown. This evokes the impressive atmosphere of a mighty whirlwind in which the most important demoniac beings seem to manifest themselves. I myself was once able to participate from a distance in this experience, and I still have a lively memory of the enormous impact made by this strange music. CONCLUSIONS And so we finally reach a conclusion which must of necessity be unsatisfying, for we can never grasp the deeper values of true Tibetan art without making ourselves familiar with its background. Those examples known in the West are in fact no more than disconnected objects, torn from their surroundings. They may indeed captivate us with their incomparably accomplished technical mastery or their mysterious aura. But they can only partially reveal to us their hidden values, for they are to a high degree interwoven with a culture which is essentially alien to us and must remain so. It is, moreover, a culture which, if the auspices do not err, is fated to collapse. And in this case much of the legacy of a uniquely beautiful culture will pass into oblivion. It was a culture that once blossomed in the Indian province of Bengal, whence it spread over the whole of South-east Asia as far as the Indonesian archipelago. Tibet, screened by its mighty chains of mountains, was for a long time the secure repository of this culture, for these mountains prevented other forms of culture from intruding. But in our epoch of almost unlimited technical possibilities man has succeeded in overcoming these natural obstacles — man who has no longer any reverence for the deeper humane and religious values and whose destructive technical omnipotence is annihilating a culture which for many centuries gave colour to the life of the simple man, despite the burdens it imposed. Moreover, it has cast a spell over the minds of great learned men, emboldening them to penetrate into the secrets of the human spirit until they were able to embody their ideas in an incomparably beautiful symbolism.

This symbolism gave to every man his own, in accordance with his capacity for comprehension; it was a symbolism whose highly skilled and specialized technique created for itself its own form. This has fascinated outsiders and inspired and challenged us to understand it. It is the tragedy of this epoch that when we began to have some inkling of the values embodied in this art, the culture suddenly met its end, through means that the East acquired by virtue of western scientific research. The Tibetan would say: 'we are all bound to the wheel of life and we must follow our fate whether we wish to or not.' Western

FIG. 13

FIG. 13 – *Modern caricature showing Chinese oppression of the Tibetan people, in which the old draughtsmanship survives*

man can adjust himself less easily. But even in remote Tibet there seem to be changes stemming from a formal language which is beginning to replace the language of religious art. In satirical caricature the oppressed mind seeks an outlet. An unmistakable western origin is evident, and yet, strangely enough, it links up with the traces of an ancient, deeply rooted tradition of draughtsmanship.

It is impossible to foresee how Tibet's future will develop; but it may definitely be affirmed that it will soon lose its character as the 'land of miracles' and of mysterious insight. But the works of art which the West has assembled retain some trace of the past. In the future also they will yield testimony to the strange but fascinating culture which found its expression in these beautiful forms. Thus our interest in this evidence of a cultural epoch that is perhaps no more is fully justified.

PLATE 30 – The terrifying goddesses with beasts' heads of the thirteenth day of Bardo, that inter- ▶ mediate world between death and reincarnation. Detail of a Bardo-mandala.
In the second stage of Bardo, whither the spirit of the dead arrives, if it has not been able to profit from the first stage, the spirit encounters manifold strange figures who become ever more terrifying. Finally the forty 'goddesses of terror' *(mC'ams-men-ma)* appear. They belong to the last phase of this kingdom of the intermediate world and make it clear that the deceased must bear in full the consequences of the laws of his karma. The artist has kept strictly to the text and executed the small figures in a masterly fashion. Here and there a word taken from the text is inserted to give an occasional explanation. Such paintings have a wholly visionary character; the painter is attempting to prepare himself for the events which await him after his death. These works belong to the most beautiful products of Tibetan painting. *Museum van Aziatische Kunst, Amsterdam. Cf. p. 181*

APPENDICES

CHRONOLOGICAL TABLE

B.C.	JAPAN	KOREA	CHINA
200	200: Beginning of Yayoi period		206: Han Dynasty established
100		108: Kingdom of Chosŏn overcome by Han armies; Han establishes Lo-lang and three other Chinese provinces 57: Silla established (traditional date) 37: Koguryŏ established (traditional date) 18: Paekche established (traditional date)	
0 A.D.			8: Uprising of Wang Mang; end of Early Han 25: Late Han established
200			222: Dissolution of Late Han; beginning of Three Kingdoms
	250: Beginning of Tumulus period		265–589: Six Dynasties in south; nomad dynasties in north (Northern Wei, 386–535)
300		313: Fall of Lo-lang to Koguryŏ 372: Introduction of Buddhism to Koguryŏ 384: Adoption of Buddhism by Paekche	
500		524: Buddhism officially adopted by Silla court	
	552: Beginning of Asuka period		581: Sui established
600			618: T'ang established
		663: Paekche defeated by Silla	
	645: Beginning of Early Nara or Hakuho period	668: Koguryŏ defeated by Silla; Great Silla period begins	
700	710: Beginning of Late Nara or Tempyo period		
800	794: Beginning of Early Heian period		

CHRONOLOGICAL TABLE

BURMA	TIBET	INDIA	B.C.
Spread of Buddhism		264–226: King Aśoka	200
		176–164: Śunga Dynasty	100
			0 A.D.
		Kushān Dynasty	
		Decline of Kushān; Gandhāra art	200
		375: Establishment of Gupta Empire by Chandragupta II	300
Mòn period Dvāravatī Kingdom Influence of Gupta from India Śrīksetra Kingdom		Chalukya	500
	650: King Srong-btsan-sgam-po, first king of all Tibet	Pallava	600
Nan-chao Kingdom		Rashtrakuta	700
	750: King K'ri-srong-lde-btsan summons Buddhist monks from India to his court; introduction of Buddhism into Tibet 770: Foundation of Buddhist monastery of Sam-yas by Padmasambhava	Pāla	
800: Flowering period of Pyu in Central and Upper Burma 832: Nan-chao attacks Pyo, the capital	817: Buddhism attacked by the 'evil king' Glang-dar-ma King Ral-pa-can, brother and successor of the 'evil king', promotes Buddhism by founding numerous monasteries Impoverishment of population; enrichment of nobles and abbots	Pratihara	800

243

A.D.	JAPAN	KOREA	CHINA
	898: Beginning of Late Heian or Fujiwara period		
900		918: Koryŏ founded by Wang Kon 935: End of Great Silla	906: Dissolution of T'ang 960: Sung established
1000			
1100			1126: End of Sung; Chin active in North China (1113–1234)
	1185: Beginning of Early Kamakura period		
1200		1206–36: First Mongol invasion; beginning of Mongol domination 1236–70: Court takes refuge on Kanghwa Island	1206–36: Mongols supersede Chin in North China 1271: Yüan established
	1249: Beginning of Late Kamakura period		

BURMA	TIBET	INDIA	A.D.
Immigration of Burmese into Upper Burma from east and north-east, who win control of Kyauksè and Pagán; beginning of Pagán period	835: King Ral-pa-can murdered by rebels; seizure of power by his elder brother Glang-dar-ma; further persecutions of Buddhists 836: Glang-dar-ma murdered by Buddhist monk; end of royal dynasty; kingdom breaks up into small independent principalities; monasteries regain power	Chola	900
1000: Building of Ordination Hall of Pagán 1044–77: King Aniruddha ruler of Pagán; spread of power into Mòn areas; library built to house Buddhist scriptures from Thaton 'National style' 1084–1112: King Kyanzittha ruler of Pagán. Period of great temples Influence of Mòn culture Nat-hlaung-kyaung (Visnu temple) erected for Brahmaist advisers of king in Pagán Ananda temple 1112–67: King Alaung Sithu ruler of Pagán Development of independent Burmese style of temple 1160: Erection of Dhammayangyi, largest temple of Pagán, in Mòn style 1173–1210: King Narapati Sithu ruler of Pagán; links with Ceylon Foundation of Sinhalese sects Introduction of Tantric Buddhism Mahābodhi temple erected in Pagán on model of temple in Bodhgayā; Tantric frescoes with erotic scenes 1254–87: Narasīhapati, last sovereign of Pagán		985–1014: Rājarāja 998–1030: Mahmud of Ghazni 1100: Vikramāditya Sena and Hoysala 1186: Mahmud of Ghor 1202: Fall of Benares 1206: Mamelukes	1000 1100 1200
	1270: Establishment of theocracy by abbot of monastery of Sa-skya; golden age of Buddhist monasteries		

CHRONOLOGICAL TABLE

A.D.	JAPAN	KOREA	CHINA
1300			
	1336: Beginning of Ashikaga or Muromachi period		
			1368: Ming established
1400		1392: Yi Dynasty established	
1500			
	1568: Beginning of Momoyama period		
		1592–8: Hideyoshi invasions	
1600			
	1615: Beginning of Tokugawa period		
			1644: End of Ming; Ch'ing established
1700			
1800			
			1839–44, 1856–60: Wars and treaties with Western Powers
	1868–1912: Meiji period	1868: Modern period begins	
	1894: Sino-Japanese War		
1900			

246

BURMA	TIBET	INDIA	A.D.
1287: Pagán attacked and conquered by Mongols		1300: Moslems in Deccan; Sultanate of Delhi	1300
1320: Fall of Pagán; end of Pagán period; artistic decline	1345: Theocracy of Sa-skya ruler destroyed by King Chang-chub Gyal-tsen; foundation of second monarchy; restriction of monastic power		
1347: Toungoo Kingdom			
1368: Thai Kingdom of Ava		1351–88: Firoz Shah	
	1358: Birth of Tsong-k'a-pa, Buddhist reformer and founder of dGe-lugs-pa (Yellow Hat) sect, founder of monasteries of Ganden and Sera		
Artistic renaissance under Mòn Dynasty in Pegu	1391–1478: dGe-'dun-grub, first Dalai Lama	1398: Timur	1400
1520: First Burmese chronicle		1510: Portuguese in Goa	1500
		1560–1605: Sultan Akbar	
1628: Pegu Kingdom		1605–27: Sultan Jahangir	1600
	1635: A prince of Tsang (Central Tibet) rebels against the monarchy and obtains power for a few years		
1658: Chinese invasions	1642: Gushi Khan, prince of Oelöt Mongols, conquers Tibet		
	1682: Death of 'Great Fifth' Dalai Lama, venerated as reincarnation of Bodhisattva Avalokiteśvara: ruler becomes a god		
	1702: Sangs-rgyas-rgya-mts'o, his successor, renounces power		1700
	1705–50: Tibet gradually falls under Chinese rule		
1720: U Kalā Chronicle	1729–47: P'o-lha-nas rules as vice-regent, later as independent prince	1741: Dupleix	
1753: King Alaungpaya establishes Burmese Empire			
	1747–50: Rule of 'Gyur-med-rnam-rgyal (murdered 1750); China restores order in Tibet; government by council of ministers, Dalai Lama nominal ruler	1780: British in Ceylon	
1770: Manchu invasions		1803: Conquest by East India Company	1800
1784: Conquest of Arakan			
1824–6: Anglo-Burmese War		1832–7: British expansion in India; Christian influence	
1829: Glass Palace Chronicle		1857–8: Revolt against British power	
1852: Lower Burma incorporated into Indian Empire by Britain		1869–1948: Mahatma Gandhi	1900

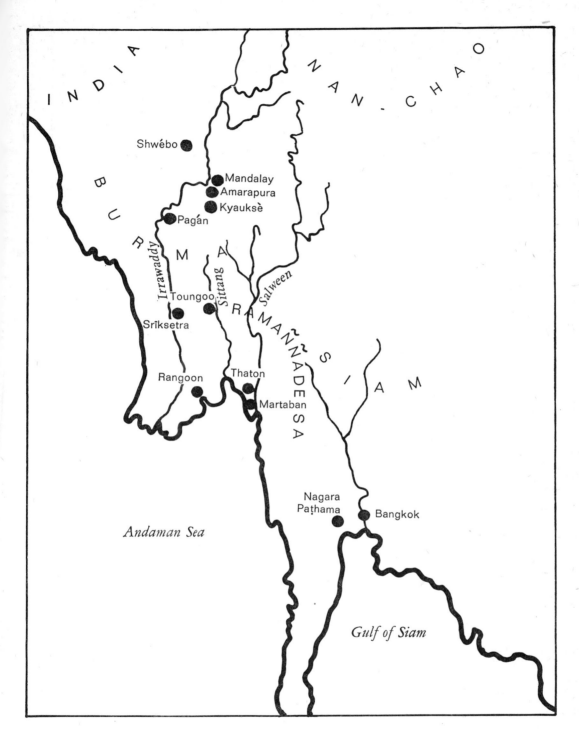

BURMA

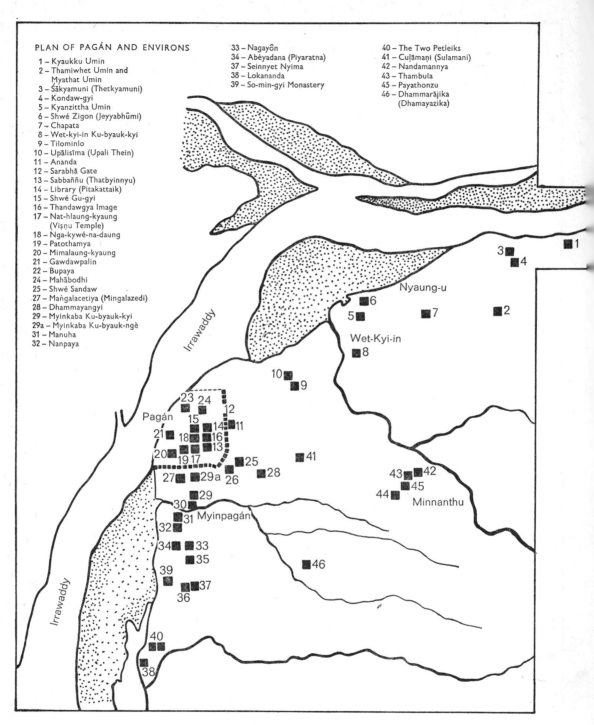

PLAN OF PAGÁN AND ENVIRONS

1 – Kyaukku Umin
2 – Thamiwhet Umin and Myathat Umin
3 – Sākyamuni (Thetkyamuni)
4 – Kondaw-gyi
5 – Kyanzittha Umin
6 – Shwé Zigon (Jeyyabhūmi)
7 – Chapata
8 – Wet-kyi-in Ku-byauk-kyi
9 – Tilominlo
10 – Upālisīma (Upali Thein)
11 – Ananda
12 – Sarabhā Gate
13 – Sabbaññu (Thatbyinnyu)
14 – Library (Pitakattaik)
15 – Shwé Gu-gyi
16 – Thandawgya Image
17 – Nat-hlaung-kyaung (Viṣṇu Temple)
18 – Nga-kywé-na-daung
19 – Patothamya
20 – Mimalaung-kyaung
21 – Gawdawpalin
22 – Bupaya
24 – Mahābodhi
25 – Shwé Sandaw
27 – Maṅgalacetiya (Mingalazedi)
28 – Dhammayangyi
29 – Myinkaba Ku-byauk-kyi
29a – Myinkaba Ku-byauk-ngè
31 – Manuha
32 – Nanpaya

33 – Nagayôn
34 – Abèyadana (Piyaratna)
37 – Seinnyet Nyima
38 – Lokananda
39 – So-min-gyi Monastery

40 – The Two Petleiks
41 – Culāmaṇi (Sulamani)
42 – Nandamannya
43 – Thambula
45 – Payathonzu
46 – Dhammarājika (Dhamayazika)

PLAN OF PAGÁN AND ENVIRONS

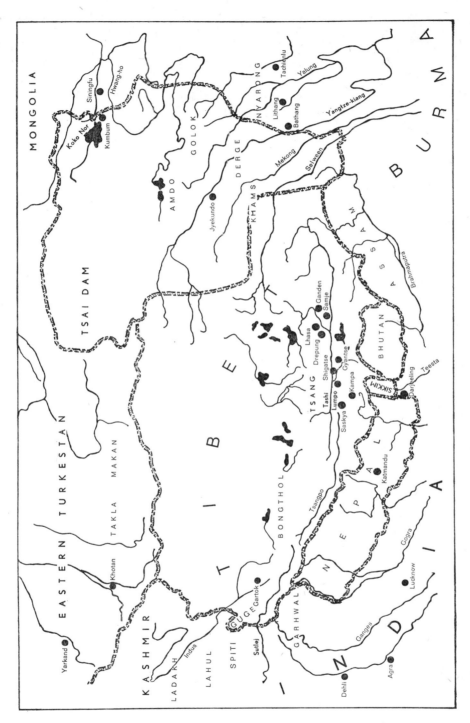

TIBET AND NEIGHBOURING LANDS

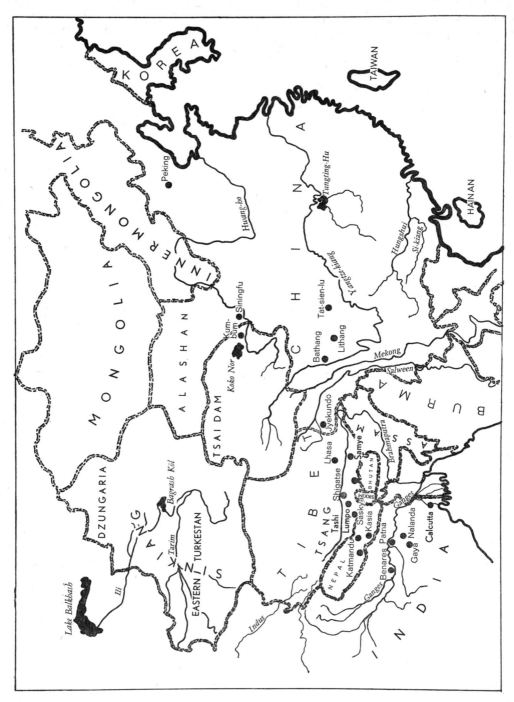

AREAS UNDER LAMAIST INFLUENCE
(after Schulemann)

CHINA

Tumen

T'ung-kou

KOGURYŎ

Yalu

P'yŏng-yang

SEA OF JAPAN

Kaesŏng

Seoul

Han

PAEKCHE

Puyŏ

SILLA

YELLOW SEA

Puan

Kyŏngju

Pusan

JAPAN

KOREA

BIBLIOGRAPHY

BURMA

Aung, U Htin, Burmese Alchemic Beliefs, in: JBRS, XXVI/2.

Aung, U Htin, Folk Elements in Burmese Buddhism, London, 1962.

Aung, Htin, The Lord of the Great Mountain, in: JBRS, XXXVIII/1.

Aung, U Htin, The Nine Gods, in: JBRS, XXXVII/2.

Aung, U Htin, The Thirty-Seven Lords, in: JBRS, XXXIX/1.

Bigandet, P., The Life or Legend of Gaudama, the Buddha of the Burmese, London, 1880.

Bode, M., The Pali Literature of Burma, London, 1909.

Cunningham, A., Mahābodhi, London, 1892.

De Beylié, L., L'architecture hindoue en Extrême-Orient, Paris, 1907.

De Beylié, L., Prome et Samara, Paris, 1907.

Duroiselle, C., The Ananda Temple at Pagan, in: Mem. ASI, no. 56, Delhi, 1937.

Duroiselle, C., The Apocryphal Geography of Burma, in: ASIAR, 1923–4.

Duroiselle, C., The Art of Burma and Tantric Buddhism, in: ASIAR, 1915–6.

Duroiselle, C., Excavations at Halin, Hmawza, and Pagan, in: ASIAR, 1926–7, 1927–8, 1928–9, 1929–30.

Duroiselle, C., Excavations in Pegu District, in: ASIAR, 1913–4, 1914–5.

Duroiselle, C., Exploration in Burma, in: ASIAR, 1935–6, 1936–7.

Duroiselle, C., Pageant of King Mindon, in: Mem. ASI, no. 27, Calcutta, 1925.

Duroiselle, C., Upagutta et Māra, in: BEFEO, IV.

Duroiselle, C., Blagden, C. O., Mya, Taw Sein Ko, etc., Epigraphia Birmanica, 4 vols., Rangoon, 1919–36.

Fielding-Hall, H., The Soul of a People, London, 1907.

Griswold, A. B., The Holy Land Transported, in: S. Paranavitana Felicitation Volume (to appear in 1964).

Griswold, A. B., Some Iconographical Peculiarities in Siam and Burma, in: R. C. Majumdar Felicitation Volume (to appear in 1964).

Grünwedel, A., Buddhistische Studien (Glasuren von Pagan; Pasten aus Pagan; Skulpturen aus Pagan). Museum für Völkerkunde, Berlin, 1897.

Hall, D. G. E., Burma, London, 1950.

Harvey, G. E., History of Burma, London, 1925.

Hla, Nai Pan, Mon Literature and Culture, in: JBRS, XLI.

Huber, E., La fin de la dynastie de Pagan, in: BEFEO, IX.

Huber, E., Les bas-reliefs du temple d'Ananda à Pagan, in: BEFEO, XI.

Ko, Taw Sein, Excavations at Hmawza, Pagan, Peikthano, Prome and Halin, in: ASIAR, 1905–6, 1909–10, 1911–2, 1929–30.

Ko, Taw Sein, The Kalyāṇī Inscriptions, Rangoon, 1892.

Le May, R., The Culture of South-East Asia, London, 1954.

Luce, G. H., A Century of Progress in Burmese History and Archaeology, in: JBRS, XXXII/1.

Luce, G. H., An Old Temple at Lawksawk, in: JBRS, XVIII.

Luce, G.H., Burma's Debt to Pagan, in: JBRS, XXII.

Luce. G. H., Chinese Invasions of Burma in the Eighteenth Century, in: JBRS, XV.

Luce, G. H., Draft Scheme for the Burma Museum, in: JBRS, XXXIII/2.

Luce, G. H., The 550 Jātakas in Old Burma, in: Artibus Asiae, XIX/3–4.

Luce, G. H., Geography of Burma under the Pagan Dynasty; Note on the Peoples of Burma in the 12th–13th Century A.D.; Old Kyaukse and the Coming of the Burmans, in: JBRS, XLII/1.

Luce, G. H., The Greater Temples of Pagan; The Smaller Temples of Pagan; Fu-kan-tu-lu; The Tan and the Ngai; Countries Neighbouring Burma; The Ancient Pyu; Economic Life of the Early Burman, in: Burma Research Society, Fiftieth Anniversary Publications, no. 2, Rangoon, 1960.

Luce, G. H., Mons of the Pagan Dynasty, in: JBRS, XXXVI/1.

Luce, G. H. and Shin, Ba, A Chieng Mai Mahāthera Visits Pagan (1393 A.D.), in: Artibus Asiae, XXIV/3–4.

Luce, G. H. and Tin, Pe Maung, Shwegugyi Pagoda Inscription; Burma down to the Fall of Pagan, in: Burma Research Society, Fiftieth Anniversary Publications, no. 2, Rangoon, 1960.

Mahler, J. G., The Art of Medieval Burma in Pagán, in: Archives of the Chinese Art Society of America, XII (1958).

Marchal, H., L'architecture comparée dans l'Inde et en Extrême-Orient, Paris, 1944.

Mitra, R. L., Buddhagayā. Calcutta, 1878.

Mya, U Exploration in Burma, in: ASIAR, 1930–4, 1934–5.

Mya, U Note on the Buddha's Foot-prints in Burma, in: ASIAR, 1930–4.

Mya, U Note on the Nanpaya Temple, in: ASIAR, 1934–5.

O'Connor, V. C. Scott, Mandalay and other Cities of the Past in Burma, London, 1907.

O'Connor, V. C. Scott, The Silken East, London, 1904.

Parmentier, H., L'art architectural hindou dans l'Inde et en Extrême-Orient, Paris, 1948.

Phayre, A. P., History of Burma, London, 1883.

Ray, N.-R., Brahmanical Gods in Burma, Calcutta, 1932.

Ray, N.-R., Introduction to the Study of Theravāda Buddhism in Burma, Calcutta, 1946.

Ray, N.-R., Sanskrit Buddhism in Burma, Calcutta, 1936.

Report of the Director, Archaeological Survey of Burma, 1959.

Report of the Superintendent, Archaeological Survey of Burma, 1901–27.

Sangermano, V., The Burmese Empire a Hundred Years ago, Westminster, 1893.

Sinclair, W. B., Monasteries of Pagan, in: Burma Research Society, Fiftieth Anniversary Publications, no. 2, Rangoon, 1960.

Slater, R. L., Paradox and Nirvāna, Chicago, 1951.

Symes, M., An Account of an Embassy to the Kingdom of Ava, London, 1800.

Temple, Sir R. C., Notes on Antiquities in Rāmaññadesa, Bombay, 1892.

Temple, Sir R. C., The Thirty-Seven Nats, London, 1906.

Thaung, U, Burmese Kingship in Theory and Practice under the Reign of King Mindon, in: JBRS, XLII/2.

Thaw, U Aung, Preliminary Report on the Excavations at Peikthanomyo, Rangoon, 1959.

Thaw, U Tin Hla, History of Burma, A.D. 1400–1500, in: JBRS, XLII/2.

Tin, U Pe Maung, Women in the Inscriptions of Pagan; Buddhism in the Inscriptions of Pagan, in: Burma Research Society, Fiftieth Anniversary Publications, no. 2, Rangoon, 1960.

Tin, U Pe Maung and Luce, G. H., The Glass Palace Chronicle, London, 1923.

Tun, U Than, Religion in Burma, A.D. 1000–1300; Religious Buildings of Burma, A.D. 1000–1300; Mahākassapa and his Tradition; History of Burma, A.D. 1300–1400, in: JBRS, XLII/2.

Tun, U Than, Social Life in Burma, A.D. 1044–1287, in: JBRS, XLI.

Win, U Lu Pe, Pictorial Guide to Pagan, Rangoon, 1955.

Win, U Lu Pe, Some Aspects of Burmese Culture, in: JBRS, XLI.

Yi, Daw Yi, Life at the Burmese Court under the Konbaung Kings, in: JBRS, XLIV/I.

Yi, Daw Yi, The Thrones of the Burmese Kings, in: JBRS, XLIII/2.

Yule, Sir H., Narrative of the Mission to the Court of Ava in 1855, London, 1858.

Abbreviations used for works frequently cited above:

ASIAR	Archaeological Survey of India, Annual Report.
BEFEO	Bulletin de l'École Française d'Extrême-Orient.
JBRS	Journal of the Burma Research Society.
Mem. ASI	Memoirs of the Archaeological Survey of India.

KOREA

Chin Tan Hakhoe (ed.), Hankuk Sa (Korean History), Vols. I–VII, Seoul, 1959–62.

Chosen Sotokufu (The Government General of Korea) (ed.), Chosen Koseki Zufu (Album of Korean Antiquities), I–XV.

Chosen Sotokufu (ed.), Bukkoku-ji to Sekkutsu-an (Pulguksa and Sokkulam Cave), Seoul, 1938.

Chosen Sotokufu (ed.), A Royal Tomb 'Kinkan-Tsuka' or The Gold Crown Tomb at Keishu and its Treasures. (Special Report of the Service of Antiquities, III), Seoul, 1924–7.

Eckhardt, P. A., Geschichte der koreanischen Kunst, Leipzig, 1929.

Fujishima, G., Chosen Kenchiku Shiron (History of Korean Architecture), Tokyo, 1930.

Fujita, R., Chosen Kokogaku Kenkyu (Archaeological Studies on Korea), Kyoto, 1948.

Heine-Geldern, R., Weltbild und Bauform in Südostasien, in: Wiener Beiträge zur Kunst und Kulturgeschichte Asiens, Vol. IV (1930), p. 28.

Honey, W. B., Corean Pottery, London, 1947.

Honey, W. B., The Ceramic Art of China and other Countries of the Far East, London, 1944.

Hubert, H. B., The History of Korea, Seoul, 1905.

Ikeuchi, H., T'ung-Kou, I. The Ancient Site of Kao-Kou-Li in Chi-An District, T'ung-Hua Province, Manchoukuo, Tokyo/Hsin-Ching, 1938.

Ikeuchi, H. and Umehara, S., T'ung-Kou, II. Kao-Kou-Lian Tomb with Wall Paintings in Chi-An District, T'ung-Hua Province, Manchoukuo, Tokyo/Hsin-Ching, 1940.

Kim, Ch., The Stone Pagoda of Koo Huang Li in South Korea, in: Artibus Asiae, XIII/1-2 (1950).

Kim, Ch., Two Old Silla Tombs, in: Artibus Asiae, X/3 (1947).

Kim, Ch., Two Old Silla Tombs: Ho-U Tomb and Silver Bell Tomb, Seoul, 1947.

Kim, Ch., Masterpieces of Korean Art in America, in: Artibus Asiae, XX/4 (1957).

Kim, Ch., Treasures from the Songyimsa Temple in Southern Korea, in: Artibus Asiae, XXII/1-2 (1959).

Kim, Ch., Han Dynasty Mythology and the Korean Legend of Tangun. (Archives of the Chinese Art Society of America, III), New York, 1948-9.

Kim, Ch. and Youn, M., Kam Eun Sa: a Temple Site of the Silla Dynasty, Seoul, 1961.

Kim, Ch. and Gompertz, St. G. M., The Ceramic Art of Korea, London, 1961.

Kim, Won-yong, Early Movable Type in Korea, Seoul, 1954.

Kim, Yong-up, Hankuk Sohwa Inmyong Saso (Dictionary of the Names of Painters and Calligraphers in Korea), Seoul, 1959.

Ko, Yu-sop, Hankuk T'appa ue Yonku (Study of Korean Pagodas), Seoul, 1948.

Koizumi, A., Rakuro Saikyo Tsuka (The Painted Basket Tomb of Lo-lang), Seoul, 1934.

Korean Studies Guide, Berkeley – Los Angeles, 1954.

Masterpieces of Korean Art, Boston, 1957.

McCune, E., The Arts of Korea: an Illustrated History, Rutland, Vt. – Tokyo, 1962.

Ministry of Education, Republic of Korea (ed.), Kukbo Torok (Korea's Treasures – Registered National Treasures of Korea), 1–5, Seoul, 1959–61. (1: Bells and Buddhistic Instruments, Ceramics, and Archaeological Materials; 2: Books and Calligraphy; 3: Buddhistic Images; 4. Monuments in Stone; 5. Stone Pagodas.)

Musée Cernuschi (ed.), Trésor d'Art Coréen, Paris, 1961-2.

National Museum of Korea (ed.), Misul Kokohak Yong-o-chip, Konchukpyon (Korean Vocabularies in the Field of Art and Archaeology, Architecture), Seoul, 1955.

Nomori, K., Korai Toji no Kenkyu (Studies on Koryo Potteries and Porcelains), Kyoto, 1944.

Oba, T. and Kayamoto, K., Rakuro Oko Bo (The Tomb of Wang Kuan of Lo-lang), Seoul, 1935.

Osgood, C., The Koreans and their Culture, New York, 1951.

O Sechang, Kun Yok So Hwa Ching (Sourcebook of Painters and Calligraphers of Korea), Seoul, 1928.

Reischauer, E. O. and Fairbank, J. K., East Asia: the Great Tradition, Boston, 1960.

Rioke Hakubutsukan Shojohin Shashincho (Album of the Yi Household Museum Collection): Butsujo no bu (Buddhist Sculpture), Kyoto, 1929; Tojiki no bu (Pottery and Porcelain), Kyoto, 1932; Kaiga no bu (Paintings), Kyoto, 1933.

Rioshoku (Yi Household), Chosen Kohun Hekigashu (Collection of Mural Paintings of Korea), Seoul, 1916.

Rowland, B., Jr., A Study of Style and Iconography in Oriental Art, in: Art in America, XXIX/3 (July 1941), p. 115.

Sekino, T., Chosen Bijutsu Shi (History of Korean Art), Kyoto, 1932.

Sekino, T., Yatsui, S., Kuriyama, S., Oba, T., Ogawa, K. and Nomori, T., Rakurokun jitai no Iseki (Archaeological Researches on the Ancient Lo-lang District), Seoul, 1925-7.

Sekino, T., Yatsui, S., Kuriyama, S., Oba, T., Ogawa, K. and Nomori, T., Kokuri jitai no Iseki (Archaeological Researches on the Ancient Kokuri District), Seoul, 1929-30.

Sekai Toji Zenshu (Ceramics of the World), XIV: Richohen (Yi Dynasty Wares), Tokyo, 1956.

Sekai Toji Zenshu, XIII: Chosen Kodai Korai-
hen (Korea: Early Period and Koryo
Period), Tokyo, 1955.
Sickman, L. and Soper, A., The Art and Archi-
tecture of China, London–Baltimore, 1956.
Sugiyama, S., Chosen Kenchikushi Kenkyu
Hokoku (Research Report on Korean Archi-
tecture), Kyoto, 1949.
Toh, Yu-ho, Anak Sambobun Balkul Boko
(Report on the Excavation of Tomb No. 3 in
Anak), Pyongyang, 1958.
Umehara, S., Chosen Kodai no Bosei (Tomb
Structure of Ancient Korea), Kyoto, 1947.

Umehara, S., Newly Discovered Tomb with
Wall Paintings of Kao-Ku-Li Dynasty
(Archives of the Chinese Art Society of
America, VI, 1952).
Umehara, S., Kankoku Keishu Kofukuji to
hakken no Shari Yoki (The Reliquary Dis-
covered in the Pagoda of the Kufuku-ji
Temple, Keishu, Korea), in: The Bijutsu
Kenkyu, no. CLVI/1, Tokyo, 1950.
Umehara, S. and Fujita, R., Chosen Kobunka
Sokan (Selected Specimens of Ancient Cul-
ture of Korea), I–III et seq., Kyoto, 1947.
Warner, L., Korean Grave Pottery of the Korai
Dynasty, in: Bulletin of the Cleveland Mu-
seum of Art, VI/5 (April 1919).

TIBET

The literature on Tibet is so vast that it is scarcely possible to provide a survey of it here. For general guidance, see *H. Cordier*, Bibliotheca Sinica, IV (with addendum), which contains practically all the literature published before 1920. An extensive bibliography has been compiled by *Robert Fazy*, Essai d'une bibliographie raisonnée de l'exploration tibétaine, in: Bulletin de la Société Suisse des Amis de l'Extrême-Orient, II (1940), pp. 3–22. Most of the works mentioned are, however, travellers' accounts. The works listed below are the most important ones for the study of Tibetan art. This bibliography is divided into four sections, only the third of which (Tibetan Art and Lamaism) is intended to be comprehensive.

I. GENERAL

Bell, Ch., The People of Tibet, Oxford, 1928.
Bell, Ch., Tibet, Past and Present, Oxford, 1924.
Bell, Ch., Portrait of the Dalai Lama, London,
1946.
Candler, E., The Unveiling of Lhasa, London,
1905.
Chapman, F. S., Lhasa, the Holy City, London,
1940.
Csoma de Körös, A., Tibetan Studies, Calcutta,
1912.
Das, S. Ch., Journey to Lhasa and Central
Tibet, London, 1902.
David Neel, A., Mystiques et magiciens du Thi-
bet, Paris, 1929.
David Neel, A., Initiations lamaïques: des théo-
ries, des pratiques, des hommes, Paris, 1930.
David Neel, A., Meister und Schüler; die Ge-
heimnisse der lamaistischen Weihen auf
Grund eigener Erfahrungen dargestellt,
Leipzig, 1934.
Desgodins, A., Notes ethnographiques sur le
Thibet, in: Mém. Soc. Acad. Indochin., I
(1879), pp. 289–293.
Filchner, W., Wissenschaftliche Ergebnisse der
Expedition Filchner nach China und Tibet
1903–5, 13 vols., Berlin, 1910–3.

Filippi, F. de, An Account of Tibet: the Travels
of Ippolito Desideri of Pistoia, S.J., 1712–
1727, London, 1937.
Francke, A. H., A History of Western Tibet, one
of the Unknown Empires, London, 1907.
Francke, A. H., Antiquities of Indian Tibet,
2 vols., Calcutta, 1914–26 (Archaeological
Survey of India, New Imperial Series,
XXXVIII and L).
Kozlow, W. P. K. and Filchner, W., Mongolei,
Amdo und die tote Stadt Chara-Choto: die
Expedition der Russischen Geographischen
Gesellschaft 1907–1909, Berlin, 1925.
Landon, P., Lhasa: an Account of the Country
and People of Central Tibet, and of the
Progress of the Mission sent there by the
English Government in the Year 1903–4,
2 vols., London, 1905.
Maraini, F., Segreto Tibet, Bari, 1951 (Paris–
Grenoble, 1952; London, 1952).
Olschak, B. Ch., Tibet; Erde der Götter; Ver-
gessene Geschichte; Mythos und Saga,
Zurich–Stuttgart, 1960.
Pallis, M., Peaks and Lamas, London 1939;
4th ed., 1946.

Rockhill, W. W., The Land of the Lamas: Journey through Mongolia and Tibet, London, 1891.

Rockhill, W. W., Notes on the Ethnology of Tibet, based on the Collections in the United States National Museum, Washington, 1895.

Sis, V. and Vanis, J., Der Weg nach Lhasa: Bilder aus Tibet, Prague, 1956.

Tafel, A., Meine Tibetreise, 2 vols., Stuttgart–Berlin–Leipzig, 1914.

Tucci, G. and Ghersi, E., Cronaca della Missione scientifica Tucci nel Tibet occidentale (1933), Rome, 1934.

Tucci, G. and Ghersi, E., Secrets of Tibet, London, 1936.

Waddell, L. A., Lhasa and its Mysteries; with a Record of the Expedition of 1903–4, London, 1905.

II. DEVELOPMENT OF LAMAISM

Bell, Ch., The Religion of Tibet, Oxford, 1931.

Bleichsteiner, R., Die gelbe Kirche, Vienna, 1937.

Chatterji, B. R., Tholing Monastery in Western Tibet: a Cultural Link between Greater India, Pāla Bengal and Tibet, in: Journal of the United Provinces Historical Society, XIII (1940), pp. 30–4.

Das, S. Ch.: Contributions on the Religion, History and Culture of Tibet, in: Journal of the Asiatic Society of Bengal, 50/1 (1881), pp. 187–251; 51/1 (1882), pp. 1–75.

Das, S. Ch., The Hierarchy of the Dalai Lama, 1406–1745, in: Journal of the Asiatic Society of Bengal, 73 (1904), pp. 80–93.

Das, S. Ch., On the Kala Chakra System of Buddhism which Originated in Orissa, in: Journal of the Asiatic Society of Bengal, New Series, 3 (1907), pp. 225–7.

Filchner, W., Kumbum Dschamba Ling, Leipzig, 1933.

Filchner, W., Kumbum: Lamaismus in Lehre und Leben, Zurich, 1954.

Francke, H., Ein Besuch im buddhistischen Kloster Hemis (Ladāk), in: Globus, LXXIII (1898), pp. 1–8.

Georgi, A. A., Alphabetum Tibetanum Missionum Apostolicarum Commodo editum, Rome, 1762.

Glasenapp, H. von, Der Buddhismus in Indien und im Fernen Osten: Schicksale und Lebensformen einer Erlösungsreligion, Berlin–Zurich, 1936.

Glasenapp, H. von, Buddhistische Mysterien: die geheimen Lehren und Riten des Diamantfahrzeugs, Stuttgart, 1940.

Godwin–Austen, H. H., Description of a Mystic Play as Performed in Ladak, Zaskar, etc., in: Journal of the Asiatic Society of Bengal, 34/1 (1865), pp. 71–9.

Hodgson, B. H., Essays on the Languages, Literature and Religion of Nepal and Tibet, London, 1874.

Hoffman, H., Die Religionen Tibets: Bon und Lamaismus in ihrer geschichtlichen Entwicklung, Freiburg–Munich, 1956.

Koeppen, C. F., Die Religion des Buddha und ihre Entstehung; Die lamaistische Hierarchie und Kirche, 2 vols., Berlin, 1857–9.

Laufer, B., Der Roman einer tibetischen Königin, Leipzig, 1911.

Laufer, B., Milaraspa: tibetische Texte in Auswahl übertragen, Hagen–Darmstadt, 1922.

Pozdnejev, A. M., Dhyāna und Samādhi im mongolischen Lamaismus, in: Zeitschrift für Buddhismus, VII (1926), pp. 378–421.

Rock, J. F., Life among the Lamas of Choni, describing the Mystery Plays and Butter Festival in the Monastery of an almost unknown Tibetan Principality in Kansu Province, China, in: National Geographical Magazine, Nov. 1928, pp. 569–619.

Schlagintweit, E. de, Buddhism in Tibet, London, 1868 (Lyon, 1881).

Schulemann, G., Geschichte der Dalai-Lamas, 2nd ed., Leipzig, 1958.

Waddell, L. A., The Buddhism of Tibet or Lamaism, with its Mystic Cults, Symbolism and Mythology, and in its relation to Indian Buddhism, London, 1895; 3rd ed., Cambridge, 1939.

Wentz, W. Y. Evans, The Tibetan Book of the Dead, of the After-Death Experiences on the Bardoplane, according to Lama Kazi Dawa Samdup's English Rendering, London, 1927.

Wentz, W. Y. Evans (ed.), Das tibetanische Totenbuch, aus der englischen Fassung des Kazi Dawa Samdup. Übersetzt und eingeleitet von Louise Göpfert–March. Mit einem psychologischen Kommentar von C. G. Jung, Zurich, 1948.

Young, G. M., A Journey to Toling and Tsaparang in Western Tibet, in: Journal of the Panjab Historical Society, VII (1919), pp. 177–198.

III. TIBETAN ART AND LAMAISM

Adam, L., Hochasiatische Kunst, Stuttgart, 1923.

Bacot, J., L'art tibétain, in: Annales du Musée Guimet, Bibl. de Vulgarisation, 28 (1908), pp. 35–71.

Bacot, J., Kunstgewerbe in Tibet/Décoration tibétaine, Berlin–Paris, 1924.

Bosch, F. D. K., Eenige opmerkingen over Tibetaanse kunst, in: Phoenix, IV/I (1949), pp. 23–8.

Bryner, E., Thirteen Tibetan Tankas, Colorado, 1956.

Cammann, Sch., Tibetan Painting, Freer Gallery, in: Gazette des Beaux Arts, VI, xxv, 1944.

Deniker, J. and Deshayes, E., Catalogue de la première partie des œuvres d'art et de haute curiosité du Tibet, Paris, 1904.

Foucher, A., Catalogue des peintures népalaises et tibétaines de la collection B. H. Hodgson à la Bibliothèque de l'Institut de France (Mémoires presentées par divers savants à l'Académie des Inscr. et Belles-Lettres, 1e série, XI, Paris, 1897).

Francke, A. H., Notes on Rock Carvings from Lower Ladakh, in: Indian Antiquary, XXXI (1902), pp. 398 ff.; XXXII (1903), pp. 398 ff.

French, J. C., Tibetan Art, in: Indian Art and Letters, XVII (1943), pp. 92–6.

Galestin, Th. P., Iets over Tibetaansche schilderkunst, naar aanleiding der expositie van Tibetaansche religieuze kunst uit de collectie Leon Verbert in het Koloniaal Instituut, in: Cultureel Indië, 1 (1939), pp. 193–208.

Gangoly, O. C., On some Nepalese Incense Burners, in: Rūpam, 7 (1921), pp. 13–5.

Gangoly, O. C. and Van Manen, J., A Tibeto-Nepalese Image of Maitreya, in: Rūpam, 11 (1922), pp. 1 ff.

Ghose, A., Tibetan Paintings, in: Rūpam, 27 (1926), pp. 83–6.

Ghosh, M., A Study of Tibetan Paintings of the Patna Museum (Transactions and Proceedings, 7th Oriental Conference, pp. 785–90).

Godwin–Austen, H. H., On the System employed in Outlining the Figures of Deities and other Religious Drawings, as practised in Ladak, Zaskar, etc., in: Journal of the Asiatic Society of Bengal, 33/1 (1864), pp. 151–4.

Gordon, A. K., Tibetan Religious Art, New York, 1952.

Gordon, G. B., Some Art Objects from Tibet, in: Philadelphia Museum Journal, V (1914), pp. 10–14.

Gordon, G. B., The Alexander Scott Collection of Art Objects from Tibet and Nepal, in: Philadelphia Museum Journal, V (1914), pp. 55–7.

Grünwedel, A., Buddhistische Kunst in Indien, Berlin, 1900; 2nd ed., 1919.

Grünwedel, A., Buddhist Art in India, London, 1901.

Grünwedel, A., Die Tempel von Lhasa; Gedicht des ersten Dalai Lama für Pilger bestimmt, Heidelberg, 1919 (Sitzungsberichte der Heidelberger Akademie der Wissenschaften, Phil.-Hist. Klasse, 14. Abhandlung).

Hackin, J., Sur les illustrations tibétaines d'une légende du Divyāvadāna, in: Annales du Musée Guimet, Bibl. du Vulgarisation, 40 (1913), pp. 145–57.

Hackin, J., Les scènes figurées de la vie du Bouddha dans l'iconographie tibétaine, in: Mémoires concernant l'Asie Centrale, II (1916), pp. 1–116.

Hackin, J., Some Notes on Tibetan Paintings, in: Rūpam, 7 (1921), pp. 11–13.

Hackin, J., Guide-Catalogue du Musée Guimet: Les collections Bouddhiques; Exposé historique et iconographique: Inde centrale et Gandhâra, Turkestan, Chine septentrionale, Tibet, Paris, 1923.

Hackin, J., Indian Art in Tibet and Central Asia, in: The Influences of Indian Art, London, 1925, pp. 129–43.

Hackin, J., La sculpture indienne et tibétaine au Musée Guimet, Paris, 1931.

Hummel, S., Geheimnisse tibetischer Malereien, Leipzig, 1949.

Hummel, S., Elemente der tibetischen Kunst, Leipzig, 1949.

Hummel, S., Lamaistische Studien, Leipzig, 1950.

Hummel, S., Die lamaistischen Tempelfahnen und ihre Beziehung zum Yoga, in: Jahrbuch des Lindenmuseums, Stuttgart, 1953, pp. 239–53.

Hummel, S., Geschichte der tibetischen Kunst, Leipzig, 1953.

Hummel, S., Die lamaistische Kunst in der Umwelt von Tibet, Leipzig, 1955.

Hummel, S., Tibetisches Kunsthandwerk in Metall, Leipzig, 1954.

Hummel, S., Grundzüge einer Urgeschichte der tibetischen Kultur, in: Jahrbuch des Museums für Völkerkunde, Leipzig, 1955, pp. 73–134.

Jísl, L., Tibetan Art, London, 1958.

Joyce, T. A., Objects from Lhasa, Tibet, collected by General Sir James Macdonald, in: British Museum Quarterly, VII (1932), pp. 54 f.

Juynboll, H. H., Mitteilungen aus der Tibetanischen Abteilung des Ethnographischen Reichsmuseums in Leiden, in: Ostasiatische Zeitschrift, Berlin, III (1914), pp. 243–52.

Le Mesurier, Tibetan Art, in: The Studio (1904), pp. 294–301.

Linossier, R., Les peintures tibétaines de la collection Loo, in: Études d'orientalisme publiées par le Musée Guimet à la mémoire de R. Linossier, Paris, 1932, vol. I, pp. 1–97.

Lucas, H., Lamaistische Masken: der Tanz der Schreckensgötter, Cassel, 1962.

Manen, J. van, On making Earthen Images, repairing old Images, and drawing Scroll Pictures in Tibet, in: Journal of the Indian School of Oriental Art, I (1933), pp. 105–11.

Manen, J. van and Gangoly, O. C., A Tibeto-Nepalese Image of Maitreya, in: Rūpam, II (1922), pp. 1 f.

Meurs, W. J. G. van, Tibetan Temple Paintings, 2nd ed., with an introduction by P. H. Pott, Leyden, 1953.

Monod-Bruel, O., Peintures tibétaines, Paris, 1954–5.

Olson, E., Catalogue of the Tibetan Collection and other Lamaist Articles in the Newark Museum, 4 vols., Newark, 1950–3.

Pascalis, C., La collection tibétaine du Musée Louis Finot, Hanoi, 1935.

Pott, P. H., De 'Ars moriendi' van Tibet; eenige beschouwingen naar aanleiding van een fraaie Tibetaanse schildering met voorstellingen uit de wereld na den dood, in: Phoenix, I (1946), no. 9, pp. 1–12.

Pott, P. H., A Tibetan Painting from Tun-Huang, in: Orientalia Neerlandica, 1948, pp. 303–11.

Pott, P. H., Introduction to the Tibetan Collection of the National Museum of Ethnology, Leyden, Leyden, 1951.

Pott, P. H., The Tibetan and Nepalese Collections of the Baroda Museum, in: Bulletin of the Baroda Museum and Picture Gallery, IX (1953), pp. 1–7.

Pott, P. H., De Tibetanica in de Collectie Bierens de Haan, in: Bull. Museum Boymans, Rotterdam, IX (1958), pp. 3–14.

Pott, P. H., Schilderkunst van Tibet, in: Kroniek van Kunst en Kultuur, X (1949), no. 1, pp. 6–8.

Roerich, G., Tibetan Paintings, Paris, 1925.

Roerich, G., Le Bouddha et seize Arhats; suite de sept bannières de la province de Khams au Tibet, in: Revue des arts asiatiques, VI, (1930), pp. 94–100.

Rousseau, P., L'art du Tibet: I. Les peintures; II: L'architecture, in: Revue des arts asiatiques, IV (1927), pp. 21–39, 83–97.

Shuttleworth, H. Lee, Lhalung Temple, Spyti-ti, Calcutta, 1929 (Memoirs of the Archaeological Survey of India, vol. XXXIX).

Smith, A. D. Howell, Tibet: its religion and its art, in: Indian Art and Letters, XII (1938), pp. 14–25.

Stael–Holstein, A. von, On two Tibetan Pictures representing Some of the Spiritual Ancestors of the Dalai Lama and the Panchen Lama, in: Bulletin of the National Library of Peiping, 1932.

Stael–Holstein, A. von, On the Sexagenary Cycle of the Tibetans, in: Monumenta Serica, I/2 (1935).

Stein, R., Trente-trois fiches de divination tibétaines, in: Harvard Journal of Asiatic Studies, IV (1939), pp. 296–371.

Tucci, G., Indo-Tibetica, vols. I–IV, Rome, 1932–41.

Tucci, G., On some Bronze Objects discovered in Western Tibet, in: Artibus Asiae, V (1935), pp. 105–116.

Tucci, G., Indian Paintings in Western Tibetan Temples, in: Artibus Asiae, VII (1937), pp. 191–204.

Tucci, G., Tibetan Painted Scrolls: an Artistic and Symbolic Illustration of 172 Tibetan Paintings, preceded by a Survey of the Historical, Artistic, Literary and Religious Development of Tibetan Culture, 2 vols. and vol. of plates, Rome, 1949.

Vidyābhūsana, S. Ch., On certain Tibetan Scrolls and Images lately brought from Gyantse, Calcutta, 1905 (Memoirs of the Asiatic Society of Bengal, I/I).

Walsh, E. H. C., The Image of Buddha in the Jo-wo-khang Temple at Lhasa, in: Journal of the Royal Asiatic Society, 1938, pp. 535–540.

Whitney, W. B., Tibetan Collection, in: Natural History, XXXVIII (1936), pp. 397–402.

IV. ICONOGRAPHY OF LAMAISM

Bernet Kempers, A. J., Nepaleesche en Tibetaansche plastiek in de collectie Bianchi te Amsterdam, in: Maandblad voor Beeldende Kunsten, X (1933), pp. 128, 291–300, 361–71.

Bhattacharyya, B., The Indian Buddhist Iconography, mainly based on the Sādhanamālā and other cognate Tāntric texts of rituals, London, etc., 1924.

Bhattacharyya, B., Sādhanamālā, 2 vols., Baroda, 1925–8 (Gaekwad's Oriental Series, vols. XXVI, XLI).

Bosch, F. D. K., De God met den paardekop, in: Tijdschrift van het Bataviaasch Genootschap van Kunsten en Wetenschappen, LXVII (1927), pp. 123–53.

Bose, P. N., Pratimā – Māna – Laksanam, Lahore, 1929 (Greater India Society Publications, no. 4).

Cammann, Sch., Suggested Origin of the Tibetan Mandala Paintings, in: Art Quarterly, XIII (1950), pp. 106–117.

Clark, W. E., Two Lamaistic Pantheons, Cambridge, Mass., 1937 (Harvard Yenching Monograph Series, nos. 3, 4).

Dokumente der indischen Kunst. 1. Malerei: Das Citralakshana nach dem tibetischen Tanjur. Übersetzt und herausgegeben von B. Laufer, Leipzig, 1913.

Foucher, A., Étude sur l'iconographie bouddhique de l'Inde d'après des documents nouveaux, Paris, 1900.

Foucher, A., Étude sur l'iconographie bouddhique de l'Inde d'après des textes inédits, Paris, 1905.

Getty, A., The Gods of Northern Buddhism: their History, Iconography, and Progressive Evolution through the Northern Buddhist Countries, 2nd ed., Oxford, 1928.

Gordon, A. K., The Iconography of Tibetan Lamaism, New York, 1939.

Grünwedel, A., Mythologie des Buddhismus in Tibet und der Mongolei, Leipzig, 1900 (French translation: Paris–Leipzig, 1900).

Grünwedel, A., Padmasambhava und Verwandtes, in: Baessler Archiv, III (1913), pp. 1–37.

Grünwedel, A., Die Geschichten der vierundachtzig Zauberer (Mahāsiddhas), aus dem Tibetischen übersetzt, in: Baessler Archiv, V (1916), pp. 137–228.

Grünwedel, A., Der Weg nach Sambhala (Sambalai lam yig) des dritten Gross-Lama von bKra śis lhun po bLo bzang ldan Ye śes, Munich, 1915 (Abhandlungen der Königlichen Bayerischen Akademie der Wissenschaften, Phil.-philos. und hist. Klasse, XXIX, Abh. 3).

Grünwedel, A., Die Teufel der Avesta und ihre Beziehungen zur Ikonographie des Buddhismus Zentralasiens, Berlin, 1924.

Grünwedel, A., Die Legenden des Nā-ro-pa, Leipzig, 1933.

Gulik, R. H. van, Hayagrīva: the Mantrayanic Aspect of Horse-cult in China and Japan, Leyden, 1935.

Hackin, J., Notes d'iconographie tibétaine, in: Mélanges d'Indianisme Lévi, 1911, pp. 313–28.

Hackin, J., Mythologie du lamaïsme, in: Mythologie Asiatique Illustrée, Paris, 1928, pp. 121–62.

Kramrisch, St., The Vishnudharmottara III: a Treatise on Indian Painting and Image-making, 2nd ed., Calcutta, 1928.

Kühn, A., Zwei Darstellungen des Padmasambhava, in: Artibus Asiae, V (1935), pp. 117–26.

Lalou, M., Iconographie des étoffes peintes (pata) dans le Mañjuśrīmūlakalpa, Paris, 1930.

Lessing, F. D., Yung-jo-kung: an Iconography of the Lamaist Cathedral in Peking, with notes on Lamaist Mythology and Cult, Stockholm, 1942 (Reports from the Scientific Expedition to the North-western Provinces of China under the Leadership of Dr. Sven Hedin, vols. XVIII, VIII, Ethnography 1).

Manen, J. van, Concerning a Bon Image, in: Journal of the Asiatic Society of Bengal, New Series, XVIII (1922), pp. 195–211.

Nebesky-Wojkowitz, R., Ein Beitrag zur tibetischen Ikonographie, in: Archiv für Völkerkunde, Vienna, V (1950), pp. 138–58.

Nebesky-Wojkowitz, R., Oracles and Demons of Tibet: the Cult and Iconography of the Tibetan Protective Deities, The Hague, 1956.

Oldenburg, S. F., Sbornik izobrazheniy 300 Burkhanov po albomu Aziatskogo Muzeya, St. Petersburg, 1903.

Pander, E., Das lamaistische Pantheon, in: Zeitschrift für Ethnologie, XI (1889), pp. 44–78.

Pander, E., Das Pantheon des Tschangtscha Hutuktu, Berlin, 1890 (Veröffentlichungen des Königlichen Museums für Völkerkunde, I/2–3).

Pander, E., Iconographie du Bouddhisme, Peking, 1933.

Peter, F. A., The 'Rin-Hbyun': Introduction to an unpublished Tibetan Iconographical Work, in: Journal of the Asiatic Society of Bengal, Letters, IX (1943), pp. 1–27.

Pott, P. H., A Remarkable Piece of Tibetan Ritual Painting and Its Meaning, in: Internat. Archiv für Ethnographie, XLIII (1943), pp. 215–41.

Pott, *P. H.*, Yoga en Yantra in hunne beteekenis voor de Indische archaeologie, Leyden, 1946.

Pott, *P. H.*, Plural Forms of Buddhist Iconography, in: India Antiqua, Leyden, 1947, pp. 284–90.

Pott, *P. H.*, Een 'Duivels-dans' in Tibet's grensgebied, in: Bijdragen tot de Taal-, Land- en Volkenkunde, vol. 114, The Hague, 1958, pp. 197–209.

Ribbach, *S. H.*, Vier Bilder des Padmasambhava und seiner Gefolgschaft, Hamburg, 1917 (Mitteilungen des Museums für Völkerkunde, Hamburg, v).

Tucci, *G.*, The Theory and Practice of the Mandala, London, 1961.

Zimmer, *H.*, Kunstform und Yoga im indischen Kultbild. Berlin, 1926.

INDEX

The numerals in italics refer to the plates and figures.